Community Policing

Community Policing

Misnomer or Fact?

VEERENDRA MISHRA

SAGE   www.sagepublications.com
Los Angeles • London • New Delhi • Singapore • Washington DC

First published in 2011 by

SAGE Publications India Pvt Ltd
B1/I-1 Mohan Cooperative Industrial Area
Mathura Road, New Delhi 110 044, India
www.sagepub.in

SAGE Publications Inc
2455 Teller Road
Thousand Oaks, California 91320, USA

SAGE Publications Ltd
1 Oliver's Yard, 55 City Road
London EC1Y 1SP, United Kingdom

SAGE Publications Asia-Pacific Pte Ltd
33 Pekin Street
#02-01 Far East Square
Singapore 048763

Published by Vivek Mehra for SAGE Publications India Pvt Ltd, typeset in 10/12 Aldine 401 BT by Star Compugraphics Private Limited, Delhi and printed at Chaman Enterprises, New Delhi.

Library of Congress Cataloging-in-Publication Data Available

ISBN: 978-81-321-0727-9 (HB)

The SAGE Team: Rekha Natarajan, Swati Sengupta, Anju Saxena and Rajinder Kaur

Contents

List of Figures

List of Abbreviations

ACP	Assistant Commissioner of Police
ADGP	Additional Director General of Police
AJK	Azad State of Jammu and Kashmir
ASI	Assistant Sub-inspector
ASP	Assistant Superintendent of Police
BLOC	Business Leaders against Organized Crime
CBI	Central Bureau of Investigation
CEO	Chief Executive Officer
CID	Criminal Investigation Department
CIVPOL	Civilian Police
CL	Conceptual Literacy
CRM	Customer Relations Management
COPS	Community Oriented Policing Services
CP	Community Policing
CPOP	Community Patrol Officer Program
CPO	Community Policing Officer
CPU	Community Policing Unit
CSE	Commercial Sexual Exploitation
CTO	Compulsory Time Off
DCP	Deputy Commissioner of Police
DGP	Director General of Police
DIG	Deputy Inspector General
DSP	Deputy Superintendent of Police
DVRF	Domestic Violence Redressal Forum
EIS	Energy Investment Strategy
EOE	External Objective Evaluation
FALINTIL	Forças Armadas para a Liberação Nacional do Timor-Leste
FCC	Family Counseling Center
FD	Field Duty
FIR	First Information Report
FOP	Friends of Police

FRETILIN	Revolutionary Front for an Independent East Timor
FTD	Faith–Trust Deficit
GOP	Gazette Order Permanent
HC	Head Constable
HR	Human Resource
ICPS	International Community Policing Stations
ICRW	International Center for Research on Women
ID	Image Dating
IDP	Internally Displaced Persons
IGP	Inspector General of Police
IIPS	International Institute for Population Sciences
IM	Image Mapping
IO	Investigating Officer
IPC	Indian Penal Code
IPS	Indian Police Service
KBE	Knowledge-based Expectation
NAB	Need Analysis Based
NCPHU	National Community Policing and Humani- tarian Unit
NFHS	National Family Health Survey
NGO	Non-governmental Organization
PAS	Performance Appraisal System
PIP	Partners in Policing
PME	Performance Matching Expectation
PNTL	Policia Nationale de Timor-Leste (National Police of East Timor)
PP	Participative Policing
PPT	Precision Policing Technique
PR	Public Relations
PSI	Person Steered Initiative
PSS	Predecessor and Successor Syndrome
RAF	Rapid Action Force
RDTL	Republica Democratica de Timor-Leste
RSS	Rashtriya Swayamsewak Sangh
SAF	Special Armed Force
SARA	Scanning, Analysis, Response and Assessment
SC	Scheduled Caste
SDOP	Subdivision Officer of Police
SES	Socioeconomic Status

SI	Sub-inspector
SIMI	Student Islamic Movement of India
SP	Superintendent of Police
ST	Scheduled Tribe
TL	Timor-Leste
TLTV	Timor-Leste Television
TISS	Tata Institute of Social Sciences
TPF	Tracking Participation Footprint
TRP	Target Rating Point
TV	Television
UDC	Urban Defense Council
UDT	Timorese Democratic Union
UN	United Nations
UN CIVPOL	United Nations Civilian Police
UNICEF	United Nations Children's Fund
UNMIBH	United Nations Mission in Bosnia Herzegovnia
UNMIK	United Nations Mission in Kosovo
UNMISET	United Nations Mission of Support in East Timor
UNMIT	United Nations Integrated Mission in Timor-Leste
UNOTIL	United Nations Office in Timor-Leste
UNPOL	United Nations Police
UNTAET	United Nations Transitional Administration in East Timor
UXO	Unexploded Ordinance
VAW	Violence against Women
VDC	Village Defense Councils
VIP	Very Important Person

Acknowledgments

This book began life as a chapter in my PhD thesis, "Changing Image of Police: An Empirical Study." It brought me closer to the realm of community policing, as conceived by many protagonists. Then my stint in United Nations Mission in Kosovo (UNMIK) as Regional Chief of Community Policing provided me with the opportunity to implement my thoughts into action, in an attempt to reassure and integrate the minorities into the mainstream. My following tenure as Assistant Nodal Officer, Community Policing Branch, Police Headquarters, Bhopal, gave me ample scope and privilege to study community policing from close quarters. Taking it as a challenge to prove my belief in community policing, I put into effect all my ideas and thoughts about the actual content of community policing in field during my posting as SDOP, Narsinghgarh, District Rajgarh, Madhya Pradesh. The overwhelming response, support, and understanding accrued were incredibly amazing. The people of Narsinghgarh whole-heartedly accepted and utilized the new mode of communication to their benefit, endorsing that I was on the right path. They definitely reaffirmed my faith in the strategies of community policing and concretized my convictions.

I firmly believe that my three UN Mission area experiences added a lot of value to my knowledge and intellect. I happened to assimilate and reflect a lot what I experienced during mission exposure in Bosnia-Herzegovina, Kosovo, and East Timor. These seven years of continuous submergence in community policing paved the path for writing my experience. But, to convert it into book was no cakewalk.

The book took shape after sincere, serious, and thought-provoking deliberations with many colleagues. Some hailed from different disciplines and a few were police officers like me. One of the most important persons who pepped me into writing on community policing was my colleague, batch-mate, and better half—my wife Priyanka Mishra. Whenever I passionately discussed community policing, she would vehemently insist on reducing my thoughts in black-and-white, which

I finally did. I heartily thank her for being my spirit. My elder brothers Rajesh Mishra (IPS) who is currently IGP in Chhattisgarh and Sanjeev Mishra (serving in IB) were great motivators. They diligently backed me to write, appreciating my academic fervor, and chipped in valuable professional inputs. Dr Suresh Mishra, Retired Professor of History, S. N. College, Khandwa, Madhya Pradesh, and an academician to the core, nagged me intermittently whenever I dropped my pen. He averred on the import-ance of sharing and saving experiences for generations to read (a purely historians purview).

My friend Trupti Jhaveri Panchal from Tata Institute of Social Sciences, Mumbai, was of enormous help. She gave her critical views and generously gathered materials for me to read. An expert in running Special Cells for Women in more than six states of India, she collaborated with me in writing Chapter 13 of this book, a case study titled "Coordinated Response to Combat Violence against Women: A Participative Policing Initiative of Madhya Pradesh Police, India." Besides, I owe my intellectual debt to many more friends like Dr Tara Singh (Professor of Psychology at Banaras Hindu University, Varanasi, and my Phd guide), Shabnam Siddiqui (a social activist based in Mumbai), Aferdita Bytyqi (my language assistant in Kosovo), and seniors like Keshav Kumar (IPS–IG, CBI, Delhi), P.M. Mohan (IPS–CVO Ports, Visakhapatnam), and many others, who directly or indirectly ignited in me the desire to study the subject, helped me execute my belief, and in many ways prompted me to pen down.

Last but not the least, I owe this book to my two sweet children, Anhad and Aarav, who have some way or other suffered due to my indulgence in this book during the time which was meant for them.

It is not possible for me to name everyone, but through this I wish to express my deepest gratitude to all who have been part of my journey in the police organization and others who have impressed me in my thoughts and actions.

1

Points to Ponder
An Introductory Note

The movement toward community policing has gained impetus in recent years as the police and the community leaders seek more effective ways to promote public safety and to boost the quality of life in their neighborhoods. Community policing encompasses a variety of philosophical and practical approaches and it is still evolving. Community policing strategies differ depending upon the requirements and responses of the communities involved; however, certain basic principles and considerations are common to all community policing efforts, which are discussed in this book.

Equity is embedded firmly in the Constitution of India, which all police officers are under an oath to uphold. A foremost precept of community policing is equity, i.e., all citizens should have a say in identifying and addressing their problems. Community policing can, thus, become a force for enhancing democratic principles. All citizens, regardless of their caste, class, religion, region, personal characteristics, or group affiliation, must have equal access to police services for a full and productive partnership with the community, abiding by the principle of inclusiveness and involvement.

But the partnership, which is innate, over a period has reformed into a selective companionship, with lack of willingness on either part to participate. Over the years, the natural partners have drifted away, thereby widening the gap. It is in the best interest of both to join hands and bridge the increasing chasm. The mindset of alienation has to be changed. Development of mindset means that the new experience becomes very real, very important, and almost vital. Altered mindset in favor of partnership and participation has to be ascertained. The interest behind putting this book together has been to agitate the mind of both, the community and the police, about the need to rejuvenate the lost fervor of their partnership, to synergize their actions, and plan and work together for a common goal. Unless this realization does not seep in—becomes the mindset—no honest attempt in the desired area can be made.

For the concept of partnership to become a mindset, it is necessary to have Conceptual Literacy (CL). It indicates that the knowledge of the concept should precede action. CL increases adaptability to changes. With more situational changes on a daily basis, technological changes knocking at the doorstep, and more opportunities and challenges being thrown open, only CL comes to the rescue. It prepares to adapt to changes. It also helps in strategizing the energy investment. Energy Investment Strategy (EIS) is a method to optimize the outcome from investment of energy. Energy, here, includes the efforts put in for planning, developing, implementation, collaboration, evaluation, and refurbishing. CL and EIS are complementary to each other.

Community policing alters the modern-day functions of supervisors and managers. Under community policing, management serves to guide and motivate rather than dominate the actions of the subordinate field officers and to ensure that the police officers have the necessary resources to solve the problems in their area. Creativity and innovation must be fostered if satisfactory solutions to the community problems are to be found. This book discusses how transition to community policing requires recognition of the new responsibilities and decision-making power of the field officers which must be supported, guided, and encouraged by the entire organization. In addition, it requires establishing clearly stated ethics that provide both the police organization and the public with a clear sense of the police's expanded focus and direction.

The reason for attitudinal hassles has been the "intuitive approach" in policy decisions adopted by seniors.[1] They think that they are the best judge to decide upon the operational intricacies at the ground level without bothering to collect data from the field. Even their hierarchical rigidity and attitudinal stubbornness (as described by theory X by Douglas McGregor) gives rise to communication gap.[2]

---

[1] Prasad, B.V.S. and Kalai Selvan. 2007. *Customer-Centric Business Mode: An Introduction.* The Icfai University Press, Tripura: Icfai Books.
[2] McGregor, Douglas. 1960. *The Human Side of Enterprise.* New York: McGraw-Hill Companies.

Time has come when Precision Policing Techniques (PPTs) must be used. The approach toward policing has to be more decentralized and localized. This will help in the conceptualization of literacy of the implementers and service receivers. Quite naturally then, the policing activities will fall under the "zone of acceptance," which has been a far cry for police actions in the past. The involvement of the community in policing activities will enhance once they start identifying their presence in the approach. The current shift to community policing reflects the conscious effort of a profession to reexamine its policies and procedures.

In this book, an attempt has been made to understand the cause and effect of community policing. Various variables, which are deterrent to an effective participation of the community in policing activities, have been explored. There has been a conscious effort in this book to deliberate on the relationship between various sections of the community with the police, the perspective angle, and the organizational police and personnel issues.

In the book, the term "public" has been used as a synonym to the community. When we talk about "public–police" partnership, it connotes "community–police" partnership. This has been deliberately done because, in layman language, the public always denotes the community. The intention here is to speak in the layman language rather than as a specialist. The idea is that when we speak as a public servant, our voice should be different from that of a government servant. Let the public servant be construed as one providing services to the community than to the powerful government body headed by politicians.

The book does not lay a blueprint for community policing but can act as a signpost. The purpose of this book is to examine recent and less recent developments in major policing innovations/experiments dubbed as community policing. It is an effort to make a dent in the mindsets of both the police and the community, so that they partner and participate for each others' benefit.

2

The Philosophy and Concept of Community Policing

In general parlance, the term "policing" is ascribed to the role performed by law enforcement agencies. This has become synonymous with the duties and responsibilities of the *khakhi* uniformed services in India and other specifically designated uniformed personnel in other countries. Is policing really restricted only to the law enforcement functions performed by the police personnel? Is the definition of this term so narrow? Are the laws regulating the acts of citizens, enacted only by the state government, the only ones that come under the purview of policing?

Barack Obama, the President of the United States, while replying to the students' questions at St Xaviers College in Mumbai, on November 7, 2010, at some point said, "we have to police each other." Of course, it had nothing to do with the police in uniform. What would we call the norms, which should be followed by all members of a family? Isn't there any authority within the family structure that can ensure the adherence to family norms? The conventional head of a family unit in the Indian family is that authority and is referred to by the sociologists as the *karta*. The parents closely monitor what the *karta* decides upon. They supervise the overall abidance of law in the family. Similarly, in schools, the teachers; in offices, the supervisors; in field, the coaches; in companies, the board members and the stakeholders, and so on, try to ensure obedience to the accepted rules and regulations. The norms sanctified by the society, therefore, become the societal norms.

Every citizen, individually and collectively, acts as a law enforcer in the society, by criticizing the avoidance and developing a mechanism of pressure for observance. Can we then acknowledge that enforcement of law at any level, in any institution is policing? I think there is no doubt about it. Policing, in the broader spectrum, constitutes enforcement of laws, in any form, in any institution which is approved and endorsed by consensus.

So, what is the difference between the policing that we are going to talk about in this book and law enforcement policing in social life? The simple difference is that here the lawmakers are the legislators or House of Representatives of citizens of the State. The State has set up an executive hand in the name of police to enforce the sanctioned laws and a particular uniform has been allocated to give them an independent identity. They are recruited from the same community that we are part of. They are public servants—as any employee of any government department is—and are paid from public exchequer.

There are still many self-policing societies. They do not rely much on the formal police structure set up by the State. They are the societies where the traditional societal policing structure is still prevalent. In India, especially in the rural areas, caste panchayats or tribal heads have enough influence on their people and they decide upon many issues, even issues of heinous nature without referring to the formal institution of the state police.

During my visit to East Timor (Timor-Leste) in 2009, I found that the prevailing criminal justice system of Timor-Leste, the youngest democracy of the world, was quite similar to the traditional policing system. In that country, the *suco* chiefs and the community leaders have important roles to play. Seventy-five percent of the general public in Timor-Leste primarily relied on traditional justice mechanisms (i.e., elders, *suco* chiefs, and community leaders in general) for maintaining security.[1]

The Need for Community Policing in India

The evolution of modern policing in India can be traced back to 1861 when the Police Act was codified. It was promulgated with the intention to subserve the colonial interests. The Police Commission of 1860

---

[1] The Asia Foundation. 2009. *A Survey of Community Police Perceptions: Timor Leste (TL) in 2008*. Report published in The Asia Foundation, Dili, Timor-Leste (East Timor).

recommended the abolition of the military police as a separate organization and the constitution of a single homogeneous force of civil constabulary for the performance of all duties. In 1902, this police system was reviewed by the Fraser Commission. The report of this commission incorporated a chapter on "popular opinion" regarding the police. This chapter very openly narrated the corrupt and oppressive character of the police of that time. Throughout the country, the police was in a most unsatisfactory state and had seriously injured the feelings of the populace and also disgraced and discredited the government by their depraved activities. In those days, it was based on the setup thought over by the British during their rule in India which was mainly meant to oppress the people. Prevention and detection of crime was only an ancillary function in those days. The current police are accused of having picked up the existing attitude and behavior from there. Because of this legacy, the present police administration is under criticism as never before.

The Government of India document of the year 2002 stated:

> … there are innumerable complaints of misuse of powers by the police including arbitrary arrests and unnecessarily long detention in custody, not to mention the large-scale violations of human rights. The Criminal Justice System does not seem to operate evenly, as the rich and the powerful hardly get implicated, much less convicted, even in case of serious crimes. The growing nexus between crime and politics has added a new dimension to the crime scenario. Victims feel ignored and are crying for attention and justice. In sum, not only is the system slow, inefficient, ineffective, but also costly and corrupt. People, by and large, have lost confidence in the Criminal Justice System and fear that the country is dangerously racing towards anarchy.[2]

What does this indicate? Does this mean what the Police Commission opined in 1902 was seconded exactly a century later by the Government of India document in 2002? So, does this imply that the police have not changed over all these years? The British legacy, as expressed by the 1902 Police Commission, still exists in the current police organization in our country.

The police underwent a radical change with respect to their role and function when India became independent. From an instrument of coercion used by a foreign government, they became an important

---

[2] Rizvi, S.K. 2002. "Delivery of Service by Police: Quality and Cost," *The Indian Police Journal*, IL(3), July–September: 96.

administrative wing of a democratic government requiring distinctly different policing patterns and attitudes.

> In a welfare state, the police role is not only one of protection and social defense, but of social welfare as well. They have to function as a social service organization and deal with crime and public order in a manner so as to gain the goodwill and cooperation of the public.[3]

Gone are the days when police banked on psychological fear for its success. Staying in isolation and interacting by choice is no more a privilege. The existing chasm between the police and the community—developed due to the police subculture—is no more affordable. Now the scenario has changed; the citizens are better educated and more aware of their rights. The pressure of the community's expectations from the police has left no scope for them to keep at bay.

There has been a tenable shift in the role of police everywhere in the world. No longer is it considered to be an executive tool in the hands of the governing body, simply structured to put into effect the stakes of the powerful. To be specific, its role has transformed from being a mere "force to an agent of social change." There have been focused attempts to bring about changes in the attitude of the police which make them more sensitive toward the community. Participative policing has replaced the traditional policing concept.

Furthermore, community policing is a philosophy that promotes organizational strategies which support the systematic use of partnerships and problem-solving techniques to proactively address the immediate conditions that give rise to public safety issues such as crime, social disorder, and fear of crime.[4]

Community policing concentrates on proactively preventing crime and eliminating the atmosphere of fear that it creates rather than simply responding to crimes once they have been committed. Earning the confidence of the community and making those individuals stakeholders or partners in their own safety enables the police to better understand the community and address both the needs of the community and the factors that contribute to crime.

---

[3] Singh, N.K. 1985. "Police Accountability to the Law and the People," In *Essays on Police Community Relations*, pp. 37–47. Hyderabad: S.V.P.N. Academy.
[4] Community Oriented Policing Services (the COPS Office) is the component of the US Department of Justice. United States Department of Justice. "Community Policing Defined," http://www.cops.usdoj.gov/default.asp?item=36 as visited on February 3, 2010.

Moreover, community policing is a concept which advocates involvement of people in policing activities. Community-oriented participatory policing calls for better understanding and sharing between the community and police, so that their energy is synergized in tackling the problems of the society. It is a philosophy of policing based on the concept that the police officers and private citizens should work together in creative ways which will subsequently help solve contemporary community problems related to crime, social and physical disorder, and neighborhood decay.[5]

Community policing is becoming the order of the day as more and more countries are bringing it on its official agenda, introducing it as a leading workable model. One of the most challenging and difficult aims of this concept is to build meaningful understanding and partnership between the police and the community for enhancing public safety. Conventionally, the police department has a dubious distinction of having proclivity toward working autonomously. It is their inner desire to keep themselves detached from societal dynamics. They have a tendency to dictate, under the garb of professionalism, on issues of crime control and security, in the process alienating the community. However, community policing urges the police departments to renounce their autonomy and collaborate practically with everyone: civil society/community groups and institutions, social service providers, government institutions including panchayats, other police and security forces, elected representatives, businesses communities and houses, and so on. This interpretation of community policing has implications for police practices, roles, and requires change/reform in the value system of the police.

The close association forged with the community should not be limited to an isolated incident or series of incidents, nor should it be confined to a specific time frame. Community policing not only comes handy during tensions or for disaster management but also has relevance in day-to-day activities of the police. The partnership between the police and the community must be long-term and balanced, which includes a police officer assigned to an area, and meeting and working with the residents and business people who live and work in his area of operation. The citizens and police work together in identifying the problems faced in the area and collaboratively plan workable solutions

---

[5] Definitions Associated with Prevention Tasks. 2003. www1.cj.msu.edu/~outreach/wmd/odppreventiondefinitions.doc as visited on December 24, 2009.

for those problems. The police act as a catalyst, mobilize neighborhoods and communities toward solving their own problems, and encourage people to help and look out for each other. Thus, the hallmark of the whole effort of community policing is the collaboration between the citizens and the police toward solving problems emanating at the local level. This endeavor satisfies the pressing needs of citizens leading to improvement in the people's quality of life. The community policing strategy encourages assisting the citizens by contacting them on one-to-one basis and in groups. The goal is to establish communication leading to some common understanding of accepted action and implementation by the residents. The involvement of the community would basically be at three stages:

- identification of problems by the community requiring attention;
- taking inputs from the community, involving them in the planning process, and implementation stage for addressing the problems; and
- feedback from the community about the participative involvement and the results achieved.

These initiatives are not a packet of tactical plans but involve reforming decision-making processes, redefining the goals of policing, and creating new work cultures within the police system. It is an organizational strategy of looking at policing through the community lens, which leaves the means of achieving the goals to the practitioner in the field. Thus, it is a process-oriented phenomenon rather than a result-oriented one. To accomplish these goals, the police department must work hand-in-hand with the community's influential people, religious groups, social services organizations, youth clubs, and other governmental agencies within the community. Pressing concerns must be defined, and problem-solving strategies should then be designed to address these concerns. And most importantly, these plans for improvement must be evaluated frequently to weigh their effectiveness.

Community policing is a response to the changing needs of the society. The idea is to prevent and detect crime, maintain order and ensure safety and security of the community in partnership with the people and provide the community with efficient, transparent, and responsive law enforcement machinery, which perpetuates the rule of law. It must replace the traditional concepts of professional versus civilian, powerful versus weak, expert versus beginner, and authority figure versus subordinate. The police and the community must be collaborators in the pursuit to promote and preserve peace and prosperity.

Thus, the essence of community policing is a matter of giving people what they deserve. The innocents have the right to be protected and the police should honor their right. Their safety and security should be the police's top priority. The persons in conflict with law must carry that deterrent feeling that they will not be spared; they will be brought to the book for their illegal acts and produced before the court of law for prosecution. They must feel that the police are keeping a tab on their movements and actions at all times.

Roles are the bundles of socially defined attributes and expectations associated with social positions. The police, as an organization, have to carry out certain expected behaviors irrespective of their personal feelings at a given place or time and, therefore, it is possible to generalize about their behavior based on the professional role regardless of their individual characteristics.

This belief is reflected in the constitution of the new police act drafting committee set up by the Government of India which has been entrusted to redeem the archaic law. Here too the committee members have realized the importance of community policing and are planning to add a chapter on the same. Community policing is looked upon as a panacea to most of the inborn ills of policing. Community policing is a subject discussed worldwide and India is no exception.

The community, which has to participate with the police and reap the benefit of the services, has been distancing itself over the years. They have little confidence in the police as the protector, and the disenchantment has widened with the belief that the police has failed in its role of controlling and detecting crime. On the contrary, the police are suffering from alienation and they perceive that the public approach is totally ambivalent. Their contact is opportunistic where every member of the community, in the law enforcement process, wants to benefit but at the same time detests being a victim. The new concept of participative policing advocates that, both, the police and the community have equal stake on the subject of crime control, protection, safety, social stability, and progress. The most striking element of the community policing paradigm is that it enables the legitimization of the police's enforcement action by the community.

One aspect which is strongly recommended by community policing is proactive policing. Traditionally, the police are expected to react to a call of the need, an incident of crime and provide services. The reactive role is unavoidable as usually, these incidents are of an emergent nature and action must be rapid and not well considered in advance. But the concept of proactive policing seeks to recognize the areas of concern and work accordingly for the decline in the occurrence and seriousness of the incidents.

Different approaches have emerged in the last century, appreciating the "proactive techniques" in policing. In many countries, approaches based on application of scientific management, emphasis on human relations, systems approach, and behavioral concerns have dominated. But in our country, there is a lot more to be done. We still bank upon the traditional centralized administrative ranked structure with little feedback mechanism, thwarting proper two-way communication, which practically cannot be ignored anymore. The latest approach has been a "community policing approach," leading to a "proactive participative policing approach." The proactive policing approach not only aims at the prevention of crime but also equips the prospective victim of the crime to fight back by adopting a consultative approach both within the rank and file and with the public. It is an approach seeking togetherness where the public is associated with both planning and working of the police. The priorities are set with taking community into confidence rather than solely being decided by the police managers. However, the traditional adverse image of the police, however, prevents the common man from coming forward to share the information. If conscious efforts are made to befriend the citizens through community policing, they cannot only become the eyes and ears of the police but can also actively supplement the latter's role in preventing crime. Good public relations also save the police from undue criticism and make the working more transparent.

All police–community relation programmers, in any society, revolve around the basic concept of the "community" and the "police". The inbuilt societal danger in the application of community policing, particularly in a developing country like India, is due to the heterogeneity of classes, groups, and organizations which shape the behavior of their respective members, making them work at cross-purposes. Riggs, an administrative thinker, has delineated the characteristics of his "prismatic" social order. The main characteristics are the heterogeneous nature of organization (society), overlapping in functions, formalism, and polynormativism in behavior. This would result into widespread nepotism, favoritism, and official corruption.[6] The conflict of interests emanating from this situation makes the society oppose the idea of togetherness. A natural consequence is uncontrolled administration which works in an antidemocratic manner.

Schools of Thought

In view of its different perceptions and applications, there have been varied responses to the concept of community policing. Here, we would try to understand the different perspectives. To comprehend their approach, we will categorize them as schools of thought.

FIRST SCHOOL OF THOUGHT: PARALLEL INSTITUTIONS

The followers of this school of thought consider community policing as a different self-regulating unit in police setup. They envisage a community policing unit (CPU) independent of executive field force. Their claim is to institutionalize community policing. CPUs are established as a parallel structure inside or outside the traditional police stations with sole responsibility of decreasing the existing chasm between the community and the police.

The officers posted in such units are merely given the duty of putting into effect the community policing agenda which incorporates meeting people, selecting target group, and area of operation; establishing rapport with the concerned group to be attended and help them with their problems. This is based on the premise that due to the negative image of the police, community is wary of interaction. Traditional policing work too is time consuming hence both the problems of image and time constraint can be solved by assigning special officers to break the ice and communicate with community and redress the problems.

---

[6] Riggs, F.W. 1964. *Administration in Developing Countries: The Theory of Prismatic Society.* Boston: Houghton Mifflin Company.

CASE STUDY

The United Nations (UN) works on these principles. I witnessed a similar condition in UN Mission in Kosovo or UNMIK (2004–2005) and UN Integrated Mission in Timor-Leste or UNMIT (2009) and was told that a similar setup existed in Bosnia Herzegovnia (UN-MIBH) after my departure in 1998. International CPUs were established independently in the headquarters to monitor and coordinate community policing work in various police stations. Separate CPUs were setup in each local police station and local officers along with international officers were deputed as community policing officers (CPOs). Their job was to meet the people of majority and minority community, hear their grievance, and bring it to fore. In UNMIK, distinct international community policing stations (ICPS) were established and were exclusively operated by international police officers (Civilian Police or CIVPOL). The CPOs were totally kept away from the traditional policing job and in case of any criminal case, they had to report it to the normal police stations to come into action. CPOs used to patrol and meet the people and analyze the situation, try to find solution, and work as a bridge between the community and the police.

Strengths
- The existing lack of trust in the local police, because of ethnic problem in war torn areas, was taken care of by CPOs' intervention.
- The people started recognizing the patrol vehicles and CPOs of ICPS and started sharing their problems with them.
- The CPOs started acting as a conduit for communication between the locally operating agencies and minorities.
- The very existence of police and their sensitivity which was questioned and debated was put to rest.
- These CPOs were able to take heed to the problems of the community as that was the only job they were assigned. The problem of time constraint was taken care of. They even proved to be effective as far as following up of the case was concerned.

Weaknesses
- The trust in the local police was never established and the minorities always looked for the CPOs to come to their rescue.
- The local police never attempted to reach out and understand the problems of minorities and always expected the CPOs to furnish

them with necessary details. The gap, in actuality, between the field officers and the community widened.

- The CPO had to rely on field police for action due to their limited operating power and responsibilities. Field officers always looked upon them with despise for intruding into their domain. Eventually, the grievances remained unattended and the communication chasm widened than narrowing.
- It is a piecemeal approach and not a permanent solution.
- In fact, in all practicality, there is an overlapping of functions and an air of distrust and lack of coordination within the police.

Figure 2.1 marks that the field duty officers and the CPOs are different parallel institutions.

FIGURE 2.1
Community Policing (CP) and Field Duty (FD) as
Parallel Institutions

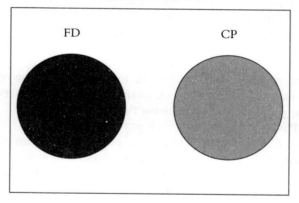

SECOND SCHOOL OF THOUGHT: PROJECT-ORIENTED

The supporters of this school of thought implement their community policing initiatives in the form of pilot projects entrusted to the field-duty personnel for its execution. Projects are conceptualized and planned at the center level and the implementation is decentralized to field officers. Parting little from the former school of thought, this group is not averse in involving field officers; though they stick to the belief that community policing is different from normal policing. Community policing is restricted to community-based programs and project initiatives which are pruned according to the need of police and community.

CASE STUDY

In the state of Madhya Pradesh, various initiatives like Family Counseling Centers, Nagar/Gram Raksha Samiti, and so on, have been conceived at the police headquarter level and implemented at the police station level across the state. These defense councils (Raksha Samities) were set up to draw community participation in policing. There are 47,061 village defense councils with 514,445 members. There are 5,447 urban defense councils with 72,777 members. Similarly, there are 212 family counseling centers in 48 districts of Madhya Pradesh. Since its inception, around 85,000 cases have been delved within these centers from 1995–2006.[7]

"Project Prahari" of the Assam Police, "MAITHRI:" Community Policing in Andhra Pradesh, "Sahayata:" A Community Policing Initiative in West-Bengal, Nadia District, are some other examples of project-oriented community policing initiatives in other parts of our country.[8]

Strengths
- The community finds a way to interact with the police and participate in their projects.
- Police gets an extra hand by community participation and some degree of trust and faith is restored.
- Field officers being involved in community projects tend to come out of isolation.
- For implementation, taking community into confidence results in less degree of opposition.
- As the community comes closer to the police, it is able to comprehend the limitations of the police and an understanding develops between the two.

---

[7] Data collected from Community Policing Branch, Police Headquarters, Bhopal, Madhya Pradesh, 2006.
[8] Commonwealth Human Rights Initiative (Police Unit). "Community Policing Experiments/Outreach programmes in India." http://www.humanrightsinitiative.org/new/community_policing_experiments_in_india.pdf as visited on February 3, 2010.

Weaknesses

- When projects are being conceptualized by someone influential at the police headquarters or at the district level, it becomes a person-based approach and always becomes a victim of predecessor and successor syndrome.
- As indicated earlier, the projects last till the incumbent is in office. The project is wound up soon after his/her removal from the post.
- The projects or initiatives are imposed on the subordinates and lack the spirit of the planner (i.e., lack of conceptual literacy explained later in this book).
- As no effort is taken to make aware the cutting edge level, more often than not the projects are not uniformly comprehended and the tinge of police image is reflected in all projects.
- Community policing initiatives are looked upon as extra work or burden; and to satisfy seniors, more is done on paper than at ground level. Hence the very purpose of its conception fails.
- The projects are not need-based and suiting demand of the locality, hence participation is limited (i.e., intuitive approach, explained later in this book).
- The participating groups from the community who are handpicked and guided by the police personnel are more yes-mans than contributors. The pressure is on them to adapt to the established system and accept the existing norms and conditions.

Figure 2.2 represents that the CP is one of the jobs of the field officers in police stations.

FIGURE 2.2
Community Policing as per Part of Field Duty

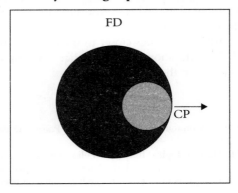

THIRD SCHOOL OF THOUGHT: INDIFFERENT

According to this school of thought, community policing in itself is nothing but a publicity gimmick. They do not believe the term community policing. They propound that community policing is a term coined by "politicians in police uniform" who have their own vested interests. They state that the police is already overburdened with its traditional policing work, and trying to interact with the community for no proper reason is nothing but sheer waste of time. They also argue that the police is paid from the community's pocket (via taxes) and, hence, it is illogical and criminal to ask the community to come forward to protect themselves. It is totally unjustifiable to expect the public to squeeze their time and do the work that is entrusted to the police, and who are solely responsible for its execution.

The believers of this school of thought vehemently criticize the community's policing efforts. They think that the police are the trained personnel to take care of the policing job. If there is any laxity or failure, it is because of unprofessional approach of the police. If the job of the police is handed over to laymen, then the results would be drastic. They do accept that the police is suffering from a resource crunch but that can be overcome by professionalism. Strict adherence to written legal books is the answer to all problems of the society. Figure 2.3 represents only the field duty officers in the police. There is neither any community policing setup nor duties assigned to field duty officers.

FIGURE 2.3
Field Duty Having No Community Policing Constituent

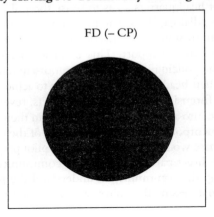

FD (– CP)

FOURTH SCHOOL OF THOUGHT: PROCEDURAL CONCEPTUALIZATION OF COMMUNITY POLICING— PHASED IMPLEMENTATION

I think community policing has been misconstrued by many. It will not be fair to discard any of the viewpoints mentioned above. It would be appropriate to describe the thoughts as phases of application of community policing.

Total negation of the concept of community policing (as done by the third school of thought) is a primitive and traditional approach. This is the approach of those who believe that policing is aggressiveness, tough-mindedness, decisiveness, and task-oriented. They consider policing to be a masculine job, to be thoroughly taken care by tough taskmasters, particularly males (they even detest the increasing participation of females in the job), and the traits of community policing involving emotionalism, warmth, nurturance, and so on, are feminine, which would affect the proper execution of work. When a feminist group found the characteristics assigned to the feminine a little derogatory and prejudiced, they ascribed a new term: "alternate masculinity." During this phase, the concern had been the end result and not the means adopted to achieve the result. They have been more "result-oriented" than "course-oriented." Hence, traditional policing always espoused easier way of resorting to excessive and unethical means of achieving results.

The second phase would be starting some selective activities by centralized power centers in the organization like the police headquarters and district headquarters so as to sense the pulse of the community and to start a dialogue between the community and the police. The initiative is taken by non-field officers on experimental basis to ensure acceptance and garner support. This is an ice-breaking mechanism realizing that the policing job requires multidisciplinary action. Many specialists put their heads and hands together to achieve the end result. In many cases, forensic experts, medical experts, revenue department, and so on, come into action to assist the police in their job. Similarly, it is desirable to incorporate the direct assistance of the community.

The third phase would be to initiate some pilot projects by the field officers so that direct participation of the community is encouraged. This would help the community to understand the police better and the hesitation in accessing the police would be done away with.

The following up of this phased implementation depends on which stage the organization is in. In places where the police is predominantly adopting traditional means of law enforcement, crime control, and maintenance of social order (as is in many countries affected by war and ethnic clashes), it will be necessary to first break the ice before expecting the community to develop trust and faith in the formerly aggressive institution. Otherwise, depending on where they stand, the organization can move into the other phase.

The final phase would be "participative policing." It requires imbibing the fact that community policing demands an attitudinal change in every police personnel and each of them has to view the community as a natural partner. Limited and conditional participation is always fraught with danger of falling into the trap of prevailing value systems in the police organization.

This would involve application of all the knowledge, skills, and available resources by the police working in partnership with the community to provide quality services, protect life and property, prevent crime, and resolve problems so that the people can live without fear in a safe environment. Community policing is not just a special program or one unit within the police department. It is a combination of traditional police work, prevention programs, and community partnerships.[9]

Perhaps, much of the misunderstanding about community policing stems from the misguided view that it is yet another community relations or "CR" effort, without real substance. The fact is that community policing does promote excellent police/community relations, but it is only a byproduct of this new philosophy of policing that stresses on community involvement in combating crime and disorder. However, at first, all too often the emphasis was on "public relations," and not in making a substantive philosophical change in the way police related to their constituents.[10]

---

[9] Palmer, Ron. 2007. *The Philosophy of Community Policing*. Report published by Tulsa World, Tulsa Police, USA. http://www.tulsapolice.org/media/world/documents/ PalmerPhiloCommPolicing.pdf as visited on September 11, 2009.
[10] Trojanowicz, Robert C. and David Carter. 1988. "The Philosophy and Role of Community Policing." National Center for Community Policing, School of Criminal Justice, East Lansing, MI: Michigan State University. http://www1.cj.msu.edu/~people/cp/ cpphil.html as visited on November 23, 2009.

Logical Explanation

Community policing, as the name denotes, involves the community and police in an inseparable mode. Community policing can be translated as:

- Policing for the community
- Policing with the community
- Policing by the community

This fundamental definition is derived from the basic tenet of community policing: "police is community and community is police."[11] If one tries to understand the basic traditional policing job, which is the spine of its existence, one will be able to comprehend the relevance of community policing more vividly. Traditional policing involves registration of cases, investigation, detection (apprehension of accused), and prosecution. The last term, prosecution is nothing but handing over of the conclusive report to the judiciary, therefore, the police's involvement is limited. The action of police and linkage of community can be explained by the following description:

- Registration of cases/receiving of complaints: by community members.
- Investigation/collection of evidence: as witnessed by the community, evidences provided by the community, and with the help of community members.
- Detection/apprehension of accused: from the community and assisted by the community.
- Prosecution is done for the community's peace.

Figure 2.4 represents that field duty and community policing are the same.

Community policing has been found to be the panacea to all the ills of the police system as well as means to fulfill the dearth of resources that the police is witnessing due to increased role and ever-increasing

---

[11] Larrabee, A.K. 2007. "Law Enforcement: Sir Robert Peel's Concept of Community Policing in Today's Society." http://www.associatedcontent.com/article/435980/ as visited on December 22, 2009.

FIGURE 2.4
Community Policing and Field Duty as Same

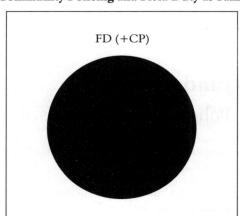

FD (+CP)

expectations of the public. In fact, community policing is a silent global policing revolution covering most forces of the US, Britain, Australia, Canada, South Africa, Israel, and even stretches across China, Singapore, Japan, and many other countries. The evolution and refinement of the community policing philosophy and practice have had an impact on the attitudes and behaviors of police officers at every level. There is a very unrealistic differentiation in the mindset of the doubters of this philosophy. They presume that the real cops are tough hard cops, and the police officer who believes in community policing and works as everyone's policeperson or the neighborhood police officer is a soft cop "wearing a velvet glove while tackling a crime" or a "social worker."

Emphasis on community policing should not be viewed as a de-emphasis on traditional policing. It is both complementary and supplementary. The paramount objective of community policing is to control crime and maintain peace and order. Community policing can be termed as progressive policing as it calls for policing with, for, and by the community.

In the following chapters, we will try to explore the reasons as to why participative policing with the community has not made the desirable inroads; the cause and effect of various factors acting as deterrents, and how meaningful collaboration can be established.

3

Active Quadruple
Four P's—Police, Politician, Press, and Public

This chapter will discuss the four P's (police, politician, press, and public), their interaction and influence on the police's working, and how distortion in the desired relationship between them is transformed into the police's digression. All the P's mentioned above are a part of the community. First, to save ourselves from confusion, let us make it very clear that in this book, public will be used as a synonym for community. Otherwise, normally in official usage, whenever public–private partnership is mentioned, it connotes the government–community partnership. The other three P's—police, politician, and press—are being dealt with as entities separate from the community (public) because these three P's have their own subculture, which is conspicuously different from the culture of the community from where they originate. This culture of the first three P's—police, politician, and press—has, over time, indigenously evolved due to a particular characteristic of the job, their distortion and selfish interpretation. They have invariably tried to isolate themselves and have a distinctive behavior. So, it becomes quite pertinent to take them as independent units other than the public in general.

Now, to understand the image of the police, it is necessary to comprehend the dynamics of interaction between the police and the other three P's of society. In fact, these three P's are the three important sections of society. They are recruited from the public and are supposed to serve them. It is from the public that they draw their power and authority. It is the public (ideally) which assigns the tasks they have to undertake and the roles they have to play. On the basis of the theory of accountability, it is the public who act as the controlling agency for their acts of omission and commission. Only if all the four P's act as desired and expected, a utopian society can be established. In reality, each P digresses from its assigned role, which has resulted in the prevailing discrepancy in the system. When we say each P, it includes public too.

Here, we would be interested in understanding the interaction and relationship between the police and the other three P's. That will give us a picture about how the role and duties of police are defined and the nature of diversion and distraction that comes into existence. In order to explain this interaction, a model has been proposed and presented in Figure 3.1.

FIGURE 3.1
The Relationship between the Four P's:
Diagrammatic Representation of Four P's Interaction

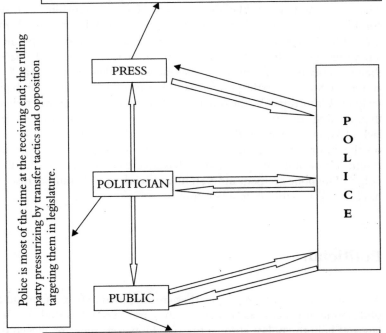

Relationship is lopsided. The press is dominant as they report what they perceive, unconcerned as to how damaging it may be. Police seldom take offense to negative reporting.

Police is most of the time at the receiving end; the ruling party pressurizing by transfer tactics and opposition targeting them in legislature.

PRESS

POLITICIAN

PUBLIC

P O L I C E

This bond is the strongest. Public do complain of being neglected by the police, however, they feel secure in their presence. Police is totally dependent on public for success.

The broad arrows depict the strong interaction between the P's. The direction of the arrows show who is dominating these interactions. The single line shows that the interaction is weak. For example, in case of the police and the press, the single arrow reflects that when the police are interacting with the press, it is always on defensive mode. At the same time, when the press interacts with the police (broad arrow), the press is dominating and aggressive. In case of other interactions—interaction between other P's and the police—the interaction is strong (marked by broad arrows) as the situation makes either one of them dominating. So, they have strong interactions with each other, and it is more or less situational.

Public

The police and the public share a very close relationship. Victim/complainant and accused are from the public. The police too are from the public. Police is from the public, by the public, and for the public. They draw power from the public and use it on them. The public have their own methods of expressing grievances: by rallies, protests, *bandh*s, and so on. Some go to the politicians and some to the press to vent their feelings. Unfortunately, the other two P's exploit this difference rather than making constructive criticism. Bitter experience from the police, lack of knowledge about the organization, and perception built based on the information gained from unreliable sources are, to a great, extent responsible for the growing chasm between the public and the police. The police remain indifferent and work in isolation because it has become a victim of its subculture.

Politician

As a representative of the people, they are supposed to be a guide and a philosopher for them. As lawmakers, they are expected to abide by the law and help the police enforce the law. However, they are alleged of violating the law, making nexus with criminals. They keep the police at ransom by threatening them of transfers and postings, and sometimes cornering them in legislative houses. Opposition finds the police as the best weapon available to embarrass the ruling party. The police is not allowed to function independently, freely, and impartially. For personal gain, the police play into the hands of politicians and illegally misuse their power to serve them.

Press

The relationship between the police and the press is very dicey. Formally, the press is meant to be a constructive critic of the police. They are supposed to point out the failures and highlight the good work done. Unfortunately, they are more interested in the former and sometimes the latter is also distorted to make it look like failure. They are the main opinion-building source for the public. Yellow journalism and tabloid journalism is in vogue; harming the police's image. In the present era of electronic media, the concern for Target Rating Point (TRPs) has further vitiated work ethics.

Police

The police, being a service-oriented organization, is supposed to work for the benefit of its customers, i.e., the community (public) at large. Its interaction with the other three P's has to be such, that it helps them in achieving the set goal of services. But in actuality, the police develop their own culture and alienate themselves from the rest of the society, effectively pushing themselves into isolation. An atmosphere of mistrust comes into existence blocking constructive, participative interaction. We will discuss the interaction of the police with each P separately in detail.

Police–Politician Interaction

In a democratic country, politicians are a vital part of the system. They are the representatives of the people vested with the role of putting forth the demands and aspirations of the people. They are empowered with the authority to legislate, regulate, and put into effect the purpose for which they are brought to power. "Power corrupts and absolute power corrupts absolutely." Although these so-called powerful people have been given the sanctified role, but to everybody's dismay, they have left no stone unturned to belie the expectations of their followers. The vista of these so-called public speakers has become so narrow that all their energy is channelized in making their short-term gains, which is deleterious and unhealthy. Politics is war without bloodshed and the police have always been bearing the brunt of the chagrin and hostile attitude adopted by the politicians. Being the easiest and the safest target, the police are always targeted by the party not in power to embarrass the one in power. The police are always at the receiving end; even its imperceptible flaws are blasted out of proportion resulting in a lot of humiliation to the force.

"That politician tops his part, who readily can lie with art." This art is so deftly displayed that despite the fact that the vile intention of the politician is known, still he/she manages to put through their obnoxious goals and take others for a ride. Everybody talks about the weather but nobody does anything about it. Though politicians are known for their foul play, no one bothers to salvage the image of the police; rather, the police are left with the burden of their own exculpation. The party in power shows indifference to the strides made by the force in its policing field and there is little appreciation and accolade for its success. Contrarily, now-a-days, political interference is at its peak. The force is not allowed to function independently. At the police station level, the local politician tries to influence the working and at the district level, the higher politicians try to dictate the terms. The postings of the officers are largely dependent on the whims and fancies of the powerful politicians.

The executive government for purely political expediency or convenience has subverted "rule of law." Implementation of unpopular policies of the government adds to the public's resentment against the police, who are the most visible representatives of the authority.[1]

The basic flaw of the police organization is that it is still guided by the antiquated legislation of 1861, which was enacted in the wake of the Revolt of 1857, essentially to subserve, uphold, and promote the

---

[1] Krishnamurthy, S. 1985. "State of Police–Community Relations in India Today: How to Improve It?," *Essays on Police–Community Relations*, pp. 98–113. Hyderabad: Sardar Vallabhbhai Patel National Police Academy.

interest of the *Raj*. The police, as a matter of policy, was placed under the executive. Immediately after independence, the quality of politics was good and lots of hopes were pinned on these visionary politicians. However, unfortunately with time, there has been a qualitative change in the style of politics. It has deteriorated from bad to worse. A symbiotic relationship has been developed with the intention to grab power. The normal interaction between the politicians and the police for the avowed objective of better administration with better awareness of public feelings and expectations soon degenerated into different forms of intercession, intervention, and interference with mala fide objectives unconnected with public interest.

POLITOXICATION

Politoxication is defined as getting overawed by and intoxicated to the political power. The "politoxication" of the police has resulted into a subservient attitude of the police. They are so awed by their political master's influencing power that what is right and what is wrong in accordance with the law is overlooked. Politicization of bureaucracy, weak leadership, and invasion of uncertainty in postings (tenures) are some causes and effects issues.

Different commissions and reports portray gloomily the relationship between politics and the police.

> The police was used and allowed themselves to be used for purposes some of which were, to say the least, questionable. Some police officers behaved as though they are not accountable at all to any public authority. The decision to arrest and release certain persons was entirely on political considerations which were intended to be favorable to the ruling party.[2]

> Excessive control of the political executive and its principal advisers over the police has the inherent danger of making the police a tool for subverting the process of law promoting the growth of authoritarianism and shaking the very foundations of democracy.[3]

---

[2] The Shah Commission interim report highlights disastrous consequences as seen duing the period of emergency in 1975–77.

[3] Prasad, K.N. 1979. *Political and Administrative Manipulation of the Police*, Research Paper by Bureau of Police Research and Development.

The nexus between the politicians, criminals, and the police is "virtually running a parallel government, pushing the State apparatus into irrelevance."[4] Members of political parties, particularly of the ruling party, whether in the legislature or outside, interfere considerably in the working of the police for unlawful ends.[5] The rule of law in modern India, the frame upon which justice hangs, has been undermined by the rule of politics.[6]

As observed, eventually, such culture has resulted in the declining standards of the police and its growing alienation from the people. Professionalism is at discount. M.N. Venkatachaliah, in his inaugural address to the Criminological Congress held at Bangalore in 1996 said, "Insulating it (the police) from unlawful political interferences" required serious and immediate attention. A.M. Ahmadi also said, "The investigating agency needs to be relieved of extraneous pressures" and that the time was ripe to "set up an independent agency which would be free of internal and external pressures."

A mechanism must be devised to safeguard the police from becoming a tool in the hands of unscrupulous politicians. They pull out all the stops to oblige them and go to any extent to protect criminals patronized by them. The police should statutorily be made accountable to the people of the country and the laws of the land. The police, by virtue of their background and because of their accountability to the executive, generally support the entrenched vested interests. They should actually be facilitating the forces of socioeconomic change and playing the role of protagonists rather than antagonists. Such a transformation is however possible only if its working philosophy is redefined.[7]

Talking on politician–policeman nexus, Vir Sanghvi writes "India's politicians are in bed with the police. They help each other subvert the law and persecute the citizenry."[8]

In the Indian context, today, the political process has turned malignant; distorting the society, its structure, social relations and

---

[4] Vohra, N.N. 1993. *Vohra (Committee) Report* submitted to Union Government, Ministry of Home Affairs, New Delhi.

[5] Punjab Police Commission. 1961–62. *Report of the Punjab Police Commission*. Chandigarh: Controller of Printing.

[6] Bayley, D.H. 1969. *The Police and Political Development in India*. Princeton: Princeton University Press.

[7] Singh, P.P. 2000. "Police Reforms—The Raison D'etre," *S.V.P. National Police Academy Journal*, January–June, 52(1): 25–33.

[8] Sanghvi, V. 2010. "Don't Let Ruchika's Death be in Vain," *Hindustan Times*, Bhopal, January 17.

values, and thus the process of development itself. The political process has ceased to respond to the issues of social change, making the average citizen wonder whether a military rule would be a better alternative. The professional ethos of the police are eroded not only by the politician outside, but equally so by the "politician" (partisan) within the police organizations. The outside politician erodes professionalism in collusion with the internal politician. If the top layers tend to develop equations with the political bosses in power, the middle level officers forge their own equations with the elected representatives and the lower level develops equations either with the local politician or the mafia as a "safety-valve." An important consequence is the process of "nexus," so vividly analyzed by Vohra Committee as a process which leads to social rejection and the very negation of police.[9]

Second, the West Bengal Police Commission found that generally, the political influence is exerted through distribution of favor and sometimes by the threat of deprivation. The threat of transfer to a less important job, the allurement of posting to a high profile job, or the temptation of the postretirement appointments are the most commonly used methods of making the higher officers pliable. Recently, the role of Gujarat Police was questioned and the blame lies on the ever-growing negative dangerous interpretation of Committed Bureaucracy. Similarly, in the high profile cases, the police have always been blamed of attempting to woo the powerful by giving a cold hand to the victims.

Two ex-Director Generals of Police (DGPs), J.F. Ribeiro and Arvind Inamdar, on the occasion of the release of the book, *Carnage by Angels*, by Y.B. Singh (IPS, Maharashtra Cadre), lambasted the political leadership in the state for putting police postings up for sale and for the "yes-man policy" adopted by some senior police officials.[10]

The party in power is accountable to the legislature for the happenings in their jurisdiction; so, they have legal base to question the functioning of the police and make the force accountable for omission and commission of its actions. They can call for transparency in the working of this executive agency. However, it must be ensured that in the name accountability, they do not hamper and impede the proper and

---

[9] Rao, U.N.B. and A. Khurana. 1999. "Proactive Policing Approach: What Is It?" *The Indian Police Journal*, XLVI–XLVII (4 and 1): 90–95.
[10] HT Correspondent. 2003. "Police Officers Book Rakes Up Controversy," PTI, *Hindustan Times*, Bhopal, May 21.

impartial functioning of the police. The police must be treated as an executive agent and not as a submissive agency. The police should not yield to mild pressures and resort to shirking its enshrined responsibilities. Otherwise, this will set a trend of partisan, sycophant organization supporting the non-committal powerful party.

Interaction between the Police and the Press

Here, the spectrum of press is deliberately widened and mass news and entertainment media are included in its ambit. These media can affect perceptions of and expectations for agents in the criminal justice system. As direct contact with an officer affects the citizens' perception of the police and influences their willingness, as victims or as witnesses, to support and report to the police, so does what people hear, read, or see about the police. "Mass news media" would include radio, television (TV), movies, newspapers, pamphlets, billboards, and mass demonstrations. The 24×7 news channels, social networking websites, news on websites, and other computer linkages like transistor radio, communication satellite, and combinations of these and other technologies has made access to news and information quick and beyond geographical bounds. Entertainment media would include films, TV serials, and others. For our convenience, we will use both as mass media.

The draconian image of the police, as perceived by most of the people, is more or less a result of information received from the secondary source. The secondary source of information purports to sharing of information from a party who had firsthand interaction rather than having a tryst by oneself. A study on the opinion and perception of students, a vulnerable section of society, was done in Bhopal. Normally, what students perceive at this tender age is hard to erase. It was a revelation to witness what conclusions were drawn from the study. The police was viewed as an agency which is neck-deep into corruption, undetachable from barbaric acts, and insensitive to any feelings. A sizeable chunk of the students opined that the police are corrupt and adopt brutal methods to get their work done. They had little knowledge about the multifarious role of the police but their viewpoint was crystal clear: the police were a dreaded organization, insensitive to the problems of the public. Surprisingly, around 85 percent students had never directly interacted with the police and whatever they had perceived was based on the information received through the mass media and through the grapevine.[11]

However, it is debatable that how perilous it is to the society when this image is held by most of the people cutting across caste, class, and creed. Is the image projected a reality or distorted? Is this perception built due to the lack of knowledge or little knowledge, which is dangerous or based on facts? The image portrayed by mass media has largely contributed in the formation of this indelible impression in the minds of the people. Mass media serve two purposes: the disclosure of information (the right to know) and entertainment. The disclosure of information is a part of the broad concept of freedom of expression, which includes freedom of speech and freedom of the press. Freedom of speech is such an enormous concept that even the court has been plagued with the problem of determining where to draw the line. Freedom of speech and freedom of the press are not absolute rights but more or less they are being used as such.

"Opinion Journalism" has the potential to break and make a person in public domain. It builds the image of a person in public and every word uttered, even in person, is taken as meaningful. The press exercises much influence on the mind of the public. By presenting news in a certain way and by giving it a particular slant, it can mould public opinion in any direction it wants.

Entertainment is the second primary function of mass media. The police department has been used as themes of entertainment by the media. Here, the relevant point is that whether the public can effectively distinguish between what is news information and what is entertainment. Sadly, not many people can distinguish real police work (which they have not seen) from the unreal police work (which they see through media all the time). The point is that media can shape public opinion even through entertainment. The shaping of public opinion by the media in terms of police activities may be misleading and may create problems for the police. A more realistic image of the police on TV could help the citizens understand the restraints placed on officers such as lack of equipment, shortage of personnel, and lack of legal jurisdiction.

---

[11] Mishra, V. 2004. "Changing Image of Police: An Empirical Study," PhD thesis, Department of Psychology, Bhopal: Barkatullah University.

It is paradoxical that public opinion about the police is largely build through minimum or lack of interaction with the police. The widespread belief is that the police are responsible for most of the existing vices of the society. People, at large, are kept in the dark about the functions performed or even the existence of other government departments. Surprisingly, many show ignorance about the fact that judiciary is not an extension of the police. Trials or court proceedings, acquittal and conviction, and bail and imprisonment are still not accepted as not being within the purview of the police and are domain of judiciary. Are the police to be blamed for this precarious situation? The police are, in fact, a negligible part of the system but most visible portion of the government. Every person believes to know most about it, though they are loaded with dangerous misconceptions. Interestingly, the mass media is frequently blamed for such misdemeanor of spreading it. They have been treading on this irresponsible path with impunity. It is necessary to realize that just as a hundred good works done by the police get eclipsed by only one folly, similarly, a hundred truths get overshadowed by one false reporting. Eventually, the harm done is unimaginably big because what is done is irretrievable with far-reaching impacts, extending to every household. Good work is taken for granted, as part of duty, and mistakes are blown out of proportion. Many a times it has been observed that important issues do not find second reference in news but trivial affairs attract disproportionate attention if it suits the reporter. The press rarely involves in advising the public to assist the police in the duties and join them to enforce law.

How can the media be tamed? Is there a need to formulate a law to punish for deeds such as misreporting, misleading, and tarnishing image? I do not think merely changing the laws would be a solution to all malaise. Both institutions, the police and the press, will have to appreciate their role and responsibilities. Primarily, the police will have to shed their obsolete ways of functioning which has been a tradition carried forward from the colonial days. At the same time, the role of the institutions which are responsible for showing the face to the public will have to play a more constructive role. Mass media, the fourth pillar of democracy, will have to be more responsible in its task of building the police's image. The mass media has the broadest base encompassing every geographic corner and human being. Hardly there is anyone to question regarding what is printed in the papers and most of the time whatever is appearing in black-and-white or on-screen is taken at its face value. There is hardly any method available and any inclination present in the common person to verify the veracity of news; hence, what is shown by mass media is ultimate.

The mass media has some positive and negative points. Positively, the mass media attracts most attention by reaching the broadest possible audience at one specific time; it is a very inexpensive means to reach the maximum number of people. With an attitude of societal improvement and fairness, the mass media reporting has brought about, either directly or indirectly, improved police-management techniques, improved manpower and salaries, better selection and training procedures, removal of corrupt administrators, more efficient court criminal systems and speeding justice, and a host of other benefits to the society at large. Courts, in their new role of judicial activism, are passing judgment on various issues of social importance instigated and influenced by the media trail. This indeed has brought a revolution and the power of media has increased by geometric proportion. Large-scale protests, criticism, and even appreciation have been created by media's over exposure of issues. This has certified its strength in swaying and persuading public opinion. Be it the case of S.P.S Rathode, an ex-DGP, in Haryana being dragged back into court for abetment of suicide, under media pressure, or garnering unprecedented support in the case of Bombay 26/11 terrorist attack, the media has manifested its reach. That strength of the media is so important that if it desires, it can topsy-turvy the whole system by proper usage of its pen and paper. The media trails have brought to the notice of the public many cases which otherwise would have gone unnoticed. Little vigilance, integrity, and honesty on the part of the press may bring to fore the irregularities and undoing of the organs of the system. A case in point is the "Best Bakery Case" of Vadodra in Gujarat, where the activism of the press resulted in a lot of criticism of the verdict of the lower court and the Supreme Court finally had to intervene and reopen the case for a proper trial. Similarly, in the case of killing of a gangster—Sohrabuddin's killing by Gujarat police—the media reports led to criticism and taking over of the case by the Central Bureau of Investigation (CBI). In the case of sedition slapped against the *Times of India*, Judge D.T. Soni of Supreme Court said: "Every newspaper has fundamental right under article 19 to publish the news with reasonable restrictions."[12]

---

[12] *Times of India*. 2010. "Gag Order Against TOI Dismissed," *Times of India*, Ahmedabad, February 7.

However, negatively, writers, editors, ultimately decide the substance of the message and the agency (police) being reported has little or no control. The image and basic message to be presented is ultimately determined by the media and not by the agency. The idea of the police agency about what is newsworthy may not converge with the media's notion of an interesting story. Besides, yellow press is harming the most by turning the public opinion against the police. National Police Commission has viewed that the extortion or blackmail by newspapers belonging to yellow press should be made, specifically, an offence.

With this backdrop, taking into consideration its reporting reach and mindset influencing capacity, it becomes very important that some mechanism is put in place to curb the spreading of wrong image of the police. Punitive action must be taken against the perpetrators; otherwise no effort will be made to put breaks on the whims and fancies which are jeopardizing the police–community relationship, threatening the peace of the society. If personal whims and fancies find place in sacrosanct medium, putting at stake the faith of millions, then such activities should be brought under the purview of heinous crimes. Others should check wisdom lost by one in the hierarchy to ensure that healthy message goes to the masses. The mass media collectively become the national "watchdog." Dedicated journalists can and do bring government inefficiency and corruption to the awareness of the public. The freedom of the press is so important that in order to flourish, it must do so without censorship. If, however, something reported is untrue, the respective organization stands to be sued.

The police–press relationship has never been steady. It fluctuates from good to hostile in no time. That can be more appropriately called as a love–hate relationship. The press assumes to have an edge over the police because the latter is an executive agency and the former is vested with responsibility of reporting after occurrence of the action. Fault-finding is always more easy and, at the same time, more appealing to the masses. It is seen that if the press feel that their feathers are brushed opposite, they do not miss the slightest opportunity to pin down the police personnel. Every opportunity is capitalized upon to corner the police and scandalize a non-issue. A policeman's failure to detect a crime is highlighted as they have acted hand in glove with the criminals after having their palms greased. These accusations, more often than not, are not supported by proper evidence but these publications are enough to create ripples and give a jolt to the normal functioning of the force and make detestable. Citations of corruption, dereliction of duty, high-handedness, violation of human rights, and lack of humaneness can be witnessed daily in the publications of the press but seldom one comes across any sort of encomium showered on the police for their work which is done putting at stake their family and social life. This negative attitude of the press has left deep wounds, which are bleeding the force white. An irresponsible stance can paint an irreversible, irretrievable, and a scornful picture of the police in the mind of the people negating all good done in the past. Hence, the press has a lot to do with enhancing or tarnishing the favorable perception of the police held by the public. The press should tread carefully looking at the way it can influence the whole gambit of law and order situation and the inter-relationship between the police and the public.

Only a marginal populace is aware of the scanty means at the disposal of the force and the pathetic plight they live in. Brought to notice of the man in the street are the atrocities and the devilish image. Scarcity of working sinews is no one's botheration but lack of promptness due to exiguous resources is upbraided. Lack of objectivity on behalf of the press is highly disgusting, disgraceful, and excruciating. The callousness of the press is at its peak while depicting the cases of deaths in the police custody, i.e., custodial deaths; without even getting into the depth of the fact, they are despised, all sorts of derogatory remarks squandered at them, and they made an object of hatred.

There is an increasing trend in the news media to concentrate their coverage on a few sensational cases in a tabloid style of journalism. The net impact of the tabloid-style coverage appears to be a decline in confidence in the police. Entertainment media present images of the police that distort the realities of everyday police work. According to the Police Committee report in Madhya Pradesh, the relation between the police and the media are important for three reasons: first, the media is an important intermediary between the police and the public.[13] Second, the media has a useful part to play in helping the police. Third, the police have a useful part to play in giving information to the media. The relations between the police and the media come under strain when one tries to be dishonest to the other; for example, when the police try to cover an incident and try to mislead the media by giving inadequate and incorrect information and accuse the media for not supporting them. On the other hand, the media blames the police

---

[13] Tirkha, M.C. 1997. *Report of Tirkha Committee*, draft submitted to the State Government of Madhya Pradesh, India.

and blows incidents out of proportion so that officers concerned are transferred or punished. Similarly, when the press intentionally publishes baseless information and places it in the hands of the opposition parties to the government, i.e., when they work as committed press than free press. In such situations, the police tries to ignore and avoid them.

The committee has recommended to improve the relations between the police and the public by establishing a full-fledged media section in the police department to publicize its achievements and share its genuine problems with the public so that it may appreciate its difficulties. There is a need to establish a publicity cell in every police district office to give prompt information to the press for unbiased publicity. Any incorrect news published should be promptly contradicted. A change from the present practice of withholding every piece of information to sharing as much information as possible is recommended. The negative reports of the press are more damaging to the police image than anything else.

The impact of media on the populace can be understood through this example. I witnessed an overwhelming reaction of the public while watching the movie *Gangajal* (directed by Prakash Jha) in Bhopal on August 30, 2003. The movie was a story of an honest Superintendent of Police (SP) who had to face all sorts of problems when he gets his first district posting. The story is based in some district of Bihar where hell breaks due to political and antisocial elements' complete grab over system. The movie was largely inspired by "Bhagalpur blinding" incident where hardcore criminals were blinded using acid by the police. As the movie progressed, people got so involved that for good actions of the SP, the audience shouted, clapped, and appreciated. This manifestation clearly depicts what a common person expects from the police. This gives rise to many other questions as well; whether they are happy on finding their dream police, which is otherwise missing outside the theater? Or, is it that they were trying to vent out their own helplessness, because they are themselves accepting that system? They have become mute spectators to the hijacking of the system by these antisocial elements. To one concluding dialog by the actor that, people get the police that they ask for, there was pin drop silence showing acceptance. I witnessed a similar reaction a few years back while watching the movie *Shool*. This again was an exclusive story about an honest police officer in Bihar. Again, the film was well dramatized and very much appreciated by the public. The million-dollar question is that why this spirit gets contained to merely theaters and seldom reflects in public's day-to-day behavior. Perhaps, it is due to the fact that the public do not come to know about the good deeds of the police because of the lack of proper media response or failure of the police institution to enlighten them due to poor public relation system.

Police and Public Interaction

A person goes to the police when he/she is in trouble. On that occasion, what he/she requires badly, besides their help, is sympathy and assurance. If the police are rude on such occasions, the impression carried by the complainant would be damaging to the image of the police, since this impression would be conveyed from person to person. The impression based on hearsay is more dangerous, dogmatic, and damaging than the one based on experience. Studies show that most of the people with a negative view of the police have had little contact with the police. Findings based on surveys[14] clearly indicate that large number of people who were critical of the police had either no contact or very less contact with the police. Another study points out, that those who have come in contact with the police, have a better understanding of their behavior than those who have had no come into contact with them.[15] This happens because the public judges the police by feelings and attainments of the individual policeman with whom it has had contact and its opinion is formed by its reactions to these personal and isolated experiences of the members of the public.[16] According to McNee, the "appropriate measure" of the police's efficiency as well as effectiveness is "public satisfaction with its police force."[17] However, it seems that the charges of rudeness against the police are based more on hearsay than on personal contact.[18]

---

[14] Bhambhri, C.P. and K. Mathur. 1972. *Students, Police and Campus Unrest: A Study of Images and Perceptions*. Jaipur: H.C. Mathur State Institute of Public Administration; Bayley, D.H. 1969. *The Police and Political Development in India*. Princeton: Princeton University Press.

[15] Srivastava, S. 1972. "Public Image of the Police," *Journal of the Society for Study of State Governments*, 3(4): 243–63.

[16] Ghosh, S.K. 1972. *Law and Order (From Police Point of View)*. Calcutta: Eastern LawHouse.

[17] McNee, D. 1983. *McNee's Law*. London: Collins Publishers.

[18] Colaso, F.T.R. and K.S. Shukla. 1973. *Reluctance of the Public to Aid the Police in the Detection of Crime and Crime Reporting at Police Stations*. New Delhi: Mimeo, BPR&D, Ministry of Home Affairs, Government of India.

Image of the police as perceived by the public and the policeman's opinion, especially in the Indian cultural context, depends on a number of factors such as structure and function of the police organization, historical and political context of police functioning, interaction of the police with the public and other agencies, working conditions of police, and the response of either side toward each other. The law-enforcing agency should upgrade itself, and the parallel counter-need is for the people to build up an attitude of respect and cooperation with the guardians of the law.[19]

Perception toward the police does not exist in isolation but is a part of much broader attitude complex. Those in particular who are most negative to the police often feel somewhat alienated from and powerless in relationship to the larger political system. People who are most involved in operation of the system often feel more powerful in relationship to it and consequently less negative toward the police. Unfortunately, a common man rarely gets an opportunity to have direct contact with the police, unless some untoward happens to them. The hidden services provided by the police through preventive actions, due to faulty approach of the police as they do not directly involve the public in their operations and keep toiling and planning in isolation, seldom provide chances of interaction. Hence, a major chunk of the society is oblivious of the operations of system and remains alienated from the police developing a negative attitude and consequently getting prejudiced.

Police–community relations are an art concerning with the ability of the police to understand and deal appropriately with the community's problems and the community's awareness of the role and difficulties faced by the police with conscientious effort for harmony and cooperation. Relations acts as a radar, identifying feeling, criticisms, and comments of the police about police work. Police–community relations turn out to be a fellowship, a fraternity, and a brotherhood, binding the people and the police for the realization of a common goal, namely, preservation of peace and order and vindication of social rights and civil liberties.[20]

Public opinion alone can keep a society pure and healthy. Their opinion depends on the perception they carry and their perception

[19] Bopp, W.J. 1972. *Police Community Relationships*. Springfield, Illinois: National Criminal Justice Reference Service.

[20] Krishnamurthy, S. 1985. "State of Police–Community Relations in India Today: How to Improve It?," *Essays on Police-Community Relations*, pp. 98–113. Hyderabad: Sardar Vallabhbhai Patel National Police Academy.

takes shape based on their experiences, on hearsay, and a number of times their expectation is fulfilled by the same. Learning without thought is labor lost, thought without learning is perilous. Opinion made by the public depends, to a great degree, on the information received from external sources. Majority are those who have never come in direct contact with the police. To admit candidly, they are oblivious of the style and mode of the police functioning. However, it is heartrending to know how querulous and pejorative an image the public holds of the police.

One cannot ignore the fact that the police are already being called upon to perform numerous duties for which they were never trained or equipped. Legislations aimed at curbing social and economic offences have added a new dimension to the role of the police. The spectrum of punitive, regulatory, and restrictive functions of the police is very wide today; and many of these have been thrust upon the police without realizing the damage caused to their image. While the functions of the police have to expand and become increasingly service oriented, care should be taken to ensure that these functions do not become a source of increasing annoyance and irritation to the people.

Who is to be blamed for this incongruity? Solely blaming the police for the same is not justified. It is the misunderstanding, misinterpretation, and misrepresentation which have led to conjuring up of this blotted image. The public is so cynical about the police that one untoward incident nullifies long time efforts of the police. The general image of the police offers an overview of the public's perception of the police. It is useful because they provide a summary measure of the level of overall favorableness or support that the public holds for the police. Negative attitudes about the police by disadvantaged persons appear to be part of a more diffuse alienation from government, law, and the political process generally.

There is an unfortunate tendency for the people to blame the police for everything that goes wrong in the community. It is admitted that the causes of public indiscipline in all walks of life manifested are deep-rooted and inherently social and economic in character. It is admitted that there is a high incidence of public indiscipline, creating a law and order situation affecting public life; people are quick to condemn the police and attribute the resultant chaos to police management and inefficiency.[21]

---

[21] Shah, G.R. 1993. *Image Makers: An Attitudinal Study of Indian Police*. New Delhi: Abhinav Publication.

One dominant and recurring theme found in the modern literature on the subject is that no law can be enforced effectively without the active support and cooperation of the public. Before the police as a formal organized institution came into being, the task of policing in most countries was a "cooperative community effort."[22] During the Medieval Age in England, for instance, most of the policing was done through the "mutual pledge" system, which encouraged responsibility among local citizens and their associations to maintain law and order.[23] Citizens were required to stand their turn for "watch and ward" duties, which involved patrolling, raising "hue and cry" when a crime was committed, pursuing absconders, arresting lawbreakers, and so on.[24] The same is true of development of policing in many other countries. In fact, the principle that a policeman is merely a citizen paid to perform certain duties owes its origin to these practices.

G.R. Shah, defining the importance of public and government support in building the police image said: "The public support and backing by the government in the face of criticism is a far better weapon than rifle and machine gun, but for procuring such support, public is also to be educated about the onerous duties and difficulties of the police."[25]

Problems of policing remained relatively simple for a long time. The reason for this was that the interactions between the police and the public occurred within the framework of the society, which was more or less homogeneous and in which a large number of people believed in the "common conscience" of the community. The institutions of family and religion played an extremely important role. All this has changed. Incredible advancement in science and technology, tremendous increase in population, a loosening of the hold of religion and family, a decline in the standards of private and public morality, erosion of the dominant values, a very high spurt in crime rate, and the emergence of new forms of criminality, have all combined to produce a very high degree of chaos in the modern society. The task of policing such a society has naturally become more complex.

---

[22] Olmos, R.A. 1974. *An Introduction to Police Community Relations*. Springfield, Illinois: Charles C. Thomas Publisher.

[23] Devlin, J.D. 1966. *Police Procedure, Administration and Organization*. London: Butter-Worth.

[24] Government of USA. 1967. The President's Commission on Law Enforcement and Administration of Justice. *Task Force Report: The Police*. Washington DC: US Government Printing Office, p. 3.

[25] Shah, G.R. 1993. *Image Makers: An Attitudinal Study of Indian Police*. New Delhi: Abhinav Publications.

Results of recent surveys have shown that only a small percentage of police work involves law enforcement per se.[26] Whatever be the role, the important thing from the police–public relations point of view is the manner in which the role is performed. As the most visible symbol of law, the way the police exercise their authority shapes their image in the mind of the public and results in inspiring or marring the general respect for law itself. As long as the public attach a sense of legitimacy to the acts of the police, the tasks of policing become comparatively easy. Legitimacy is, thus, an absolute necessity for successful policing in a democratic society. Thus, it is extremely important to highlight the important factors, which undermine the legitimacy of police action as viewed by the public.

Court Outlook

Here, few instances of court outlook can also be mentioned. Even the courts do not hold very good opinion about the police who are regularly in direct contact with the public. The Delhi High Court on May 20, 2003, while suggesting on the dowry offences, said that the provisions of the Indian Penal Code (IPC) were an easy tool in the hands of investigating agencies like the Crime Against Women Cell to hound people with the threat of arrest because dowry offences had been made cognizable and non-bailable. "These provisions have resulted in a large number divorce cases." The court recommended that the power to investigate these offences be vested in civil authorities like executive magistrates and cognizance be taken only after they reached a conclusion. "Till such a mechanism is evolved, no police officer below the rank of Additional Commissioner of Police (ACP) for offences under Section 498-A/406 IPC and Deputy Commissioner of Police (DCP) for the offences under section 304-B should be vested with (powers of) investigation" the court ruled.[27] Justice A. N. Mullick had once said in his verdict that police is an organized bunch of Rogues.[28] The apex

[26] Johnson, D. and R.J. Gregory. 1971. "Police Community Relations in the USA: A Review of Recent Literature and Project," *Police Science*, March, 62(1).

[27] Shukla, Amitabh. 2003. "Dowry Law Being Abused: H.C.," *Hindustan Times*, Bhopal, May 23.

[28] *Navbharat Times*. 1995. *Navbharat Times*, Bhopal, September 13.

court of India, the Supreme Court has adversely commented on Gujarat Police on the gangster Sohrabuddin's killing by the Gujarat Police.[29]

Five judges bench of Supreme Court, in a landmark judgment, observed that in order to protect their turf and save the skin of their delinquent politicians and *babus*, state governments have opposed CBI probes in any matter without their explicit consent. The apex court observed that:

> ... where it becomes necessary to provide credibility and instill confidence in investigations or where the incident may have national and international ramifications or where such an order may be necessary for doing complete justice and enforcing the fundamental rights.... The Supreme Court and high courts can also exercise their constitutional power of judicial review and direct the CBI to take up the investigation within the jurisdiction of the State.[30]

This depicts the lack of trust of the apex court in the political system and the local police investigation credibility.

---

[29] *Times of India*. 2010. "Gag Order Against TOI Dismissed," *Times of India*, Ahmedabad, February 7.

[30] Thomas, Abraham. 2010. "Higher Courts too can Order CBI Probe: SC Bench No Need to take Government's Consent," *The Pioneer*, Bhopal, New Delhi, February 18.

4

Management Gap
A Hindrance to Participative Policing

Does the word policing go well with the word participation? This is a pertinent question, which might come into anybody's mind. Participative policing sounds very attractive; however, it is loaded with lot of doubts. Participation in police activities, in real terms, looks quixotic. In the recent past, it has become trendy to talk about involving the community in police action. However, to what extent the desire has been actualized the way it has been conceived needs to be reviewed. What has been seen in the past is that the participation has been more dictatorial and directional, both coming from the police's end, than being democratic. More or less, the community invited to participate has been restricted to the needs of the police rather than the requirement of the community. It is a partnership structured on a wrong foundation.

Perhaps, it becomes a necessity to find out answers to a few relevant mysteries:

- Why do the best of initiatives fail to gain the desired ground?
- Despite consistent effort to draw them to closeness, why does the community's alienation persists?
- Is there a management problem within the organization, which adversely contaminates the intention?
- Is there an intentional dichotomy in the community, for whatever reasons?

Management Issues

If we try to locate the gap in intention and actualization, we find that there is a faulty and distorted use of management principles in the police organization. At the very onset, we need to evaluate if the police is following organizational principles in true spirit.

POLICE AS AN ORGANIZATION

On the Wikipedia website, the definition of an organization is given as: A social arrangement which pursues collective goals, controls its own performance, and has a boundary separating it from its environment.[1] Organization is the activity or result of distributing or disposing persons or things properly or methodically. Another definition describes organization as:

> Social unit of people, systematically arranged and managed to meet a need or to pursue collective goals on a continuing basis. All organizations have a management structure that determines relationships between functions and positions, and subdivides and delegates roles, responsibilities, and authority to carry out defined tasks. Organizations are open systems in that they affect and are affected by the environment beyond their boundaries.[2]

There is no doubt that the police are an organization. It perfectly fits in the definition of an organization as it is a social unit of people who are pursuing a collective goal of enforcing the law, maintaining order, and providing security. This organization has a hierarchical structure with defined duties and responsibilities to carry out the defined tasks. As the police are structured to serve the society, as any other open system, it is exposed to the changing environment and is also expected to change itself as per the need of the external system.

What sort of an organization is the police? Over the years there has been a shift in the role of this organization. The role has shifted

---

[1] Wikipedia. "Organization." http://en.wikipedia.org/wiki/Organization as visited on February 10, 2010.

[2] Businessdictionary.com."Organization." http://www.businessdictionary.com/definition/organization.html bas visited on February 10, 2010.

from being a suppressive organization to being a welfare-oriented one. The police have to realize that they are a "service-oriented" organization. Even the legal books call them "public servants." So, their role is that of a service provider and the community/public are their clientele/customers. Community policing is a true reflection of this server and clientele relationship.

The management gap exists because the attitude of the organization does not commensurate their overall goal of customer contentment, which is ultimately in opposition to the concept of community policing. There is a drift from their major role and responsibilities.

POLICE ORGANIZATION AS A SYSTEM

Organization, in a systemic form, can be understood as a collection of parts that are highly integrated in order to accomplish an overall goal. The system has various inputs, which are processed to produce certain outputs that together accomplish the overall goal desired by the organization. There is an ongoing feedback among these various parts to ensure that they remain aligned to accomplish the overall goal of the organization.[3]

Systems have inputs, processes, outputs, and outcomes. To explain, inputs to the system in the police organization include people, resources, complaints they receive, jobs assigned to them, and so on. These inputs go through a *process* where the unit entrusted with the job align, move along, and carefully coordinate, ultimately to achieve the goals set for the system like investigation of cases, and so on. Outputs are the tangible results produced by processes in the system, such as number of cases solved and put for prosecution, culprits apprehended, maintenance of law and order, and so on. Another kind of result is outcomes like sense of security provided to the community, feeling of satisfaction in the community, their clientele/customers.

In any system, for its efficiency and effectiveness, it is necessary to establish a strong network of feedback. *Feedback* comes from, e.g., the employees who carry out processes in the organization and the community whom the organization serves. Also, the feedback comes from the larger environment of the organization, e.g., influences from government, society, economics, and technologies. As the organization

[3] Carter, McNamara. "Organisation as Systems (of Systems of Systems)." http://managementhelp.org/org_thry/org_defn.htm as visited on February 11, 2010.

is a part—or a subsystem—of the bigger system of the environment, its operation depends on the constructive interaction it has with other subsystems at large and the feedback it gets from within and outside.

If this feedback technique is properly put into place then a *reverse planning process* in the system can be effectively introduced, which may help the organization to utilize their inputs to the optimum level by chalking out a process for maximum output with minimum energy consumption. It would help in: establishing overall goals; associating smaller goals or objectives (or outputs?) along the way to each goal; designing strategies/methods (or processes) to meet the goals and objectives; and identifying what resources (or inputs) are needed, including who will implement the methods and by when.[4]

The management gap exists in police because they fail to comprehend the very basic goal of being service providers. Though they are public servants, they behave like masters. Clientele satisfaction is never their priority. The reverse planning process fails miserably as the goal set does not correspond to the current demand of the organization.

ARCHITECTURAL ARCHAISM OF MANAGEMENT STRUCTURE

The former architects of the management structure of the police, particularly in India, had different interests and goals to pursue. The concepts and their implementation were suiting the time of its development. They have become archaic but they are still in existence, normally causing a rift between need and deliverance. There is a lack of a well thought strategic management process in place in the organization. The essence of good strategy-making is to build a position strong enough and an organization capable enough to produce successful performance despite unforeseeable events, challenges, resource crunch, and other surprises.[5] In the following discussions, some organizational principles are discussed.

---

[4] Carter, McNamara. "Organisation as Systems (of Systems of Systems)." http://managementhelp.org/org_thry/org_defn.htm as visited on February 11, 2010.

[5] Thompson, J.R., A. Arthur, and A.J. Strickland III. 2003. *Strategic Management Concepts and Cases*, Thirteenth Edition. New Delhi: Tata McGraw-Hill Publishing Company Limited.

Organizational Principles

There are certain organizational principles which have to be applied properly for the organization, as a part of the system, to work appropriately. Now, we will discuss these principles and analyze in what way the police organization has distorted its usage.

HIERARCHY

A hierarchical organization is an organizational structure where every entity in the organization, except one, subordinates to a single other entity. This arrangement is a form of hierarchy. In an organization, the hierarchy usually consists of a singular or group of power at the top with subsequent levels of power beneath.[6]

Here, in the definition, it is very clearly marked that the subordination is within the organization. The power assigned to each level is restricted to the domain of work within the organization. However, this hierarchical structure is too strict and inflexible in the uniformed services including the police. When we say strict, it means that the observance of hierarchy gets beyond the boundaries of the organization and crosses the limits of personal life. The other principles of organization, which are a sequel of hierarchical structure and help in disbursement of duties, get translated in different terms due to the strict hierarchy.

As mentioned earlier in this chapter, for the system to work smoothly and effectively, feedback plays a very important role. The very first casualty of inflexible, strict hierarchy is the feedback technique. Strict hierarchy does not promote feedback mechanism. Feedback would always demand free access within the system and with the outside environment. Unnecessarily clinging to the hierarchical structure leads to the breaking of that feedback process; resultantly what is desired is not met.

Many management experts advocate the promotion of an informal meeting of rank and file of the organization where the hierarchy is dissolved and honest feedback is shared. In the police organization also, vertical interaction courses, *badakhana*, *durbar*, and so on, are some

---

[6] Wikipedia. "Hierarchical Organization." http://en.wikipedia.org/wiki/Organizational_ hierarchy as visted on February 14, 2010.

initiatives but due to persistence of rigid hierarchical attitude, even these gatherings fail in the intention for which they are designed. One of the pioneers in opening up the organizational system, a Japanese model, propagated having offices with glass panes and visibility being maximum with small-walled cabins. This encourages the hierarchy to be limited just to distribution of work and responsibility and nothing beyond that.

Let us now understand the hierarchy of the police organization based on the frequency and nature of interaction they have with society. It is a "three-tier" system based on their level of interaction (Figure 4.1).

As depicted in Figure 4.1, there are three levels in police hierarchy: "cutting edge level," "supervisory level," and "administrative level." The lower level has been called the cutting edge level because this is the level which is in continuous and regular contact with all sections of the society. This level is comprised of police personnel from Constable (C) to Deputy Superintendent of Police (DSP). They are in direct contact with the people because they are the investigating and inter-rogating officers, patrolling officers, protest confronters, information gatherers, messenger of community policing, protocol officers, and direct law-and-order enforcers. The way they act, talk, behave, re-spond, and to some extent, the way they live, is very keenly observed by everyone in the society. The image of the police that is perceived by the society is more or less the image of this level of police officers. How-ever, including officers with the designation of DSP in this category is debatable as these officers are regarded as supervisory officers. Here, I have deliberately included them as cutting edge level officers due to some very important reasons based on the existing situation in Madhya Pradesh described above.

First, the Deputy Superintendents of Police are entrusted with the investigating job. They investigate cases of dowry deaths, atrocities against Scheduled Caste (SC)/Scheduled Tribe (ST), and some very important heinous-offence cases handed over to them by the Super-intendent of Police (SP) in the district. The number of registration of such cases has gone up tremendously. As a result—now it can be seen in every district—DSPs are investigating more cases than regular inspectors in charge of police stations. Investigation and associated interrogation means that the officer needs to be in direct contact with all sections of the society. Second, DSPs are included in the cutting edge level because, often, the office of the DSPs is located in the

FIGURE 4.1
The Hierarchy of Police: A Three-tier System

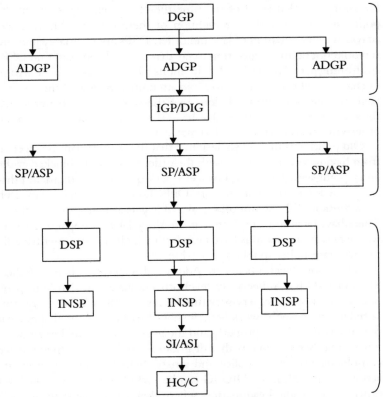

Notes: ADGP—Additional Director General of Police
ASI—Assistant Sub-inspector
ASP—Assistant Superintendent of Police
C—Constable
DIG—Deputy Inspector General
DSP—Deputy Superintendent of Police
HC—Head Constable
IGP—Inspector General of Police
INSP—Inspector
DGP—Director General of Police
SI—Sub-inspector
SP—Superintendent of Police

premises of the police station or somewhere nearby. Also, they are closely associated with the ongoing activities of the police station. It has been seen that most of the time the crime gets registered in the police stations after the intervention of these officers. Third, nowadays, in every situation of law and order, DSPs are invariably present. It would not be an exaggeration to say that normally one can find DSPs controlling petty law-and-order situations where the local police station in charge, anyhow, manages to avoid attending. In view of these stated factors, it becomes quite obvious that these officers are better suited for the category of cutting edge level than supervisory level which, otherwise on paper, they are designated as.

Old police stations are so designed that the complainant is screened from having direct audience with the officers. They are blocked at the entry point with lower level officer's desk questioning them and discouraging interaction with seniors. Only those with clout or who catch the attention of the senior officer available gets a chance to meet them. There have been some projects, e.g., in Ahmedabad, Bhopal, and so on, where new police stations have been built which are customer friendly to encourage police–public partnership.

Supervisory level officers are Additional Superintendent of Police, SP, and DIG/IG. Supervisory level officers have a dual role to play: one is their normal supervisory function where these officers are supposed to supervise the work of their subordinates to ensure that normal policing work is done properly and the goal set by the higher authorities is met. Second role is that of grievance redressal, as they receive complaints against the police and satisfy them by taking appropriate action to their plea. So, DIG/IG can be included in supervisory level officers only at the headquarters where they are available to play the role of grievance redressal officers by listening to the complainant directly. Otherwise, Additional Superintendent of Police and SP play the actual role of supervisory level officers in the district.

Officers at this level of the hierarchy have a very crucial role to play in building the police's image because they are the officers who can salvage the damage, whatever has been, done by the cutting edge level officers. Their role is mainly to keep the morale and motivation of the lower offices high by setting exemplary precedence, acting buffer to the political and other administrative pressures, and providing a favorable atmosphere to work. Though this level normally passes on the buck on cutting edge level officers for poor image of police but, actually, indirectly they have a governing role in that direction. First, they have to instill confidence in their subordinates by protecting them, guiding them, and keeping their morale high, so that they do not shift their loyalty to any other agency to serve their personal interest, leading to partial behavior in favor of the influential, which is the main cause for poor image of the police. Second, when a common person comes to seek their support, assistance, and sometimes to complain against their own men, the behavior of these officers solidifies or erases the image that has already been perceived. Here, one important factor that needs to be comprehended is that their action is going to affect the image of the police organization as a whole. Tragically, to bolster their own image, these supervisory police officers resort to abusing the errant officer, they start grumbling on the system, and start boasting about their own achievements. Diplomatic approach and a sincere effort to satisfy the complainant should be made so that the faith of the complainant is restored in the system and other officers. They should shun from working on increasing their own fan following.

Administrative level officers are those officers who sit in the police headquarters and are responsible for the administration of the whole police functionary. They are from the designation of DGP to the officers below in the hierarchy. They devote more time to policy decision-making and decide the course of action to be taken on a priority basis rather than normal police work.

This hierarchical distribution has been done on the basis of their level of interaction with the community but in actual practice within the system, every level of hierarchy is very strictly observed. There is a lack of openness and freedom in interacting at all levels, between the cutting edge level, supervisory level, and the administrative level. The strict hierarchical structure does not promote two-way communication within the organization. The channel of information sharing and grievance redressal is so cumbersome and impractical that the higher ups, unless personally interested, lose hold over the ground realities. They tend to live in the past, when they were in action, and fail to keep up with the changing and demanding current scenario. The cutting edge level in the police, which is the major chunk of the force and in continuous contact with the community/customer/clientele, get frustrated due to lackadaisical attitude of their seniors. As the nature of the job is very stressful and strenuous, the pent-up frustration finds a way to vent out while interacting with their clientele. Being averse to open interaction, blocking accessibility leads to a *communication gap* between the police and the community. The culture of inaccessibility trickles down the line and is reflected while interacting with the public as we described taking an example of the police stations.

Police in India is still clinging on to the British legacy of being opaque to the public and discouraging transparency. That system during the British colonial rule served its purpose of being an oppressive, repressive, and suppressive organization meant to serve its vested interest of exploiting the locals. The police organization, basically, are following the rule "Don't Change" as that suits them, though in a negative sense and keeping the 1861 Act in operation.

COMMUNICATION GAP

The major functions of communication are to control, motivate and act as means of emotional expression, and sharing and gathering of information. For effective communication, it should move in all directions: downward, upward, and crosswise. This means that the channel of communication should be opened and established according to the need of the situation. In normal conditions, the hierarchical structure should be followed—as its importance cannot be undermined—to encourage proper delegation of work and ensure responsibility and accountability lying at right places; however, that should not forbid the subordinates' interaction with the seniors. For communication to be complete, a system should be developed to provide a chance for both formal and informal communication.

While communicating with the community, certain communication barriers hindering participation at the desired level are: selective perception of both communicator and receiver; different languages and emotions manifested; and filtering of communication because of varied perspective. The key communication skills required for noise free communication are that both the ends of the communication chain—the communicator and the receiver—should have strong listening skills, there should be a proper feedback mechanism to correct any digression, and the presentation skill of the communicator should be good enough to attract the receiver to accept it wholeheartedly, without reservations.

Many of the problems that occur in an organization are the direct result of people failing to communicate. Faulty communication causes most of the problems. It leads to confusion and can cause a good plan to fail. Communication is the exchange and flow of information and ideas from one person to another. It involves a sender transmitting an idea to a receiver. Effective communication occurs only if the receiver understands the exact information or idea that the sender intended to transmit.

Enhancing the skill of the communication process is important because coordination, counseling, evaluation, and supervision happen through this process. It is the chain of understanding that integrates the members of an organization from top to bottom, bottom to top, and side to side. Improved communication becomes the backbone of participative policing efforts.[7] They should follow the "rules of engagement:" engage the community and the hierarchical levels within the organization in active communication.[8]

FEEDBACK

The importance of a feedback and the necessity of enriching the feedback skills has already been talked about earlier in this chapter. The purpose of a feedback is that in case of a misunderstanding or the message being altered in the process of communication, the second communicator understands the intention of the original communicator.[9] Feedback from known and sometimes even anonymous sources is the best instrument that a leader has to correct his/her mistakes and calibrate his/her performance.[10]

> *No one would talk much in society if they knew how often they misunderstood others.*

> —Johann Wolfgang von Goethe

Feedback includes both verbal and nonverbal responses to another person's message. To deliver the full impact of a message, use nonverbal responses to raise the channel of interpersonal communication.

[7,8] Butler, Gillian and Tony Hope. 1996. *Managing Your Mind*. New York: Oxford University Press; Mehrabian, Albert and Morton Wiener. 1967. "Decoding of Inconsistent Communications," *Journal of Personality and Social Psychology*, 6: 109–14.

[9] Friga, Paul N. 2009. *A Powerful Toolkit for More Efficient and Effective Team Problem Solving: McKinsey Engagement*. New Delhi: Tata McGraw Hill Publishing Company Limited.

[10] Murty, N.R. Narayana. 2009. *A Better India A Better World*. Allen Lane by Penguin Books India.

The nonverbal responses include:

- Eye contact: It signals interest in others and increases the speaker's credibility. Eye contact opens the flow of communication and conveys interest, concern, warmth, and credibility.
- Facial expressions: Smiling is a powerful cue that transmits happiness, friendliness, warmth, and liking, encouraging people to react favorably. It increases comfort in communicating.
- Gestures: If you fail to gesture while speaking you may not be heard. A lively style of speaking captures the listener's attention, makes the conversation more interesting, and facilitates understanding; otherwise the communicator may be perceived as boring and stiff.
- Posture and body orientation: The way of talking and moving reflects if the speaker is approachable, receptive, and friendly, or disinterested.
- Voice: This includes the vocal elements like tone, pitch, rhythm, timbre, loudness, and inflection. The usage of these six elements displays the passion and interest of the communicator.[11]

How well the police personnel are aware of these nonverbal skills of communication and feedback is not hidden. More often than not, even the best of plans and initiatives lose steam just because of improper application of nonverbal as well as verbal communication and feedback skills. "Speak comfortable words," is what William Shakespeare says. Mehrabian myth indicates that the content of the message is composed of: 55 percent visual component; 38 percent auditory component; and 7 percent language.[12] Police, visually, always look overstressed, irritated, disinterested, and overbearing. The auditory component too is non-conducive as their intonation is too strong, harsh, and blunt. Abusive language is synonymous with the police. So, in general, the police do not know how to communicate. If they are soft and well behaved, society comments, "You don't look like a policeman." Poor communication skills are an inherited quality of the police.

[11] Mehrabian, Albert and Susan R. Ferris. 1967. "Inference of Attitudes from Nonverbal Communication in Two Channels," *Journal of Consulting Psychology*, 31: 248–52; Pearson, J. 1997. *Interpersonal Communication*. Glenview, Illinois: Scott, Foreman and Company; Pinker, Steven. 1983. *How the Mind Works*. New York: W.W. Norton & Company.
[12] Shovel, Martin. 2009. "Mehrabian Nights: An Informative Tale about (Mis)communication," http://www.trainingzone.co.uk/item/184720, as visited on June 9, 2011.

The success of any organization depends on its adaptability to situation, need-based programs, and superiors knowing what to do. Operational flexibility is a must for any action thought of at a higher level to be successful. Lack of feedback will result into non-application of the principle of flexibility also.

DELEGATION

In any organization, no one can perform all the tasks alone. In order to meet the targets, down the line of hierarchy, there is a delegation of authority. Delegation of authority means division of authority and powers, downward to the subordinates. Delegation is about entrusting someone else to do parts of your job. Delegation of authority can be defined as subdivision and suballocation of powers to the subordinates in order to achieve effective results. Authority always flows from top to bottom. It explains how a superior gets the work done from his/her subordinate by clearly explaining what is expected of him/her and how he/she has to go about it.

Authority should be accompanied with an equal amount of responsibility. Responsibility is the duty of the person to complete the task assigned to him/her. Responsibility without adequate authority leads to discontent and dissatisfaction in the person. Responsibility flows from bottom to top.

Delegating the authority to someone else does not imply escaping from accountability. Accountability still rests with the person having the utmost authority. Accountability cannot be delegated. Accountability, in short, means being answerable for the end result. Accountability cannot be escaped. It arises from responsibility. Therefore, every delegator has to follow a system to finish the delegation process. Equally important is the delegatee's role, which means his/her responsibility and accountability is attached with the authority. Hence, it is said that authority is delegated, responsibility is created, and accountability is imposed. Accountability arises out of responsibility and responsibility arises out of authority.[13]

One of the most important aspects of delegation is that the subject of delegation should be very clear. The delegatee and the delegator

[13] Managementstudyguide.com. "Delegation of Authority." http://www.managementstudyguide.com/delegation_of_authority.htm as visted on February 14, 2010.

should have as strong two-way communication. As the accountability is not transferred, hence, there should be a continuous feedback. The delegation is to facilitate efficiency and enhance effectiveness. In the police organization, the delegation of authority is by choice. The issues are vague and not well defined. It is a good idea to map out a program of work to be followed. Such a program is not only valuable to the subordinate as a guide, but it can greatly help one stay on top of what is going on. As a management philosophy, Laissez-faire hardly ever works for long.[14]

With the much desired delegation and decentralization of police functions, the workload would diminish and specificity of work allocation will be possible. Effective control and supervision over the subordinates will improve competence and efficiency of the force. Similarly, friendly behavior of the policemen will improve the overall image of the organization, which will enable it to develop police–community relations in a more effective and positive manner.

PRINCIPLE OF SPECIALIZATION

According to this principle, the work of concern should be divided amongst the subordinates on the basis of qualifications, abilities, and skills. It is through the division of work based on specialization that an organization becomes effective. Police is an organization where the input, process, and output have a direct relation with the people—human beings. To be precise, it is basically the human beings who are involved intensively at all stages. In such a situation, when we talk about specialization, the definition would be different. It is not merely the skill of investigation, use of modern technological know-how, and expertise in weapon handling, but dealing with the people, being sensitive and empathetic, and knowledge of local sociocultural milieu.

However, these latter factors are never considered to be a part of specialization traits. Consequently, the humane factor in interaction is missing, making it unable to establish the necessary rapport with the customers—the community they serve. A long argument is still pending on the issue of considering the police a specialist or generalist. The *specialist* and *generalist* tirade has affected professional development

---

[14] Given, William B., Jr. 1980. *How to Manage People: The Applied Psychology of Handling Human Problems in Business.* Delhi: Vikas Publishing House Pvt Ltd.

of the police personnel. Specialists are those who are masters in a particular profession. Police work needs specialized professionals but, at the same time, needs a generalist attitude. It is quite pertinent when the police are said to be "jack of all trades and master of none." The training of police personnel in states, particularly the cutting edge level officers, right from DSP to constabulary, is managed in a very casual way. Whereas looking at the responsibilities and nature of their work, they need an intensive, exhaustive, and a multidisciplinary module with a scientific approach. With exposure to techniques of investigation, law and order maintenance, and other legal aspects, they have to be given strong exposure to the socio-cultural and political milieu, economic atmosphere, and they need to be psychologically strengthened to face any crisis. Other than crime-related activities, they have to take up social and other services as well. It is even believed that the definition of the role of the police has expanded to the extent that no walk of life is left untouched by police action. Child–parent disputes, marital disputes, neighborhood disputes, runaway, character verification for getting recognized by the state, many other family and child services, and municipal services, everything fall within the ambit of police function.

PRINCIPLE OF FUNCTIONAL DEFINITION

According to this principle, all the functions in the organization should be completely and clearly defined to the supervisors and subordinates. This can be done by clearly defining the duties, responsibilities, authority, and relationships of the people toward each other. Clarifications in authority—responsibility relationships—help in achieving coordination and thereby organization can take place effectively.

Police is an organization where this functional distinctiveness is clearly marked. However, while functioning, due to varied interests, exigency of time (as mostly it is crisis management), and inflated ego derived from unquestionable power, the functional distribution is overlooked and diluted. The subordinate, as a result, endures the most of the wrath of seniors. Over the years, due to the attitude of the seniors to save their skin, the positions have been degraded and authority and responsibility merged. Actually, which would have been the job of a C is now taken care of by the sub-inspector (SI) and that of Inspector by DSP or Assistant Superintendent of Police (ASP). Due to informal shifting of authority and responsibility, a chaotic situation has evolved and human resource management is at its worse with sheer wastage of manpower in the field. Diluting the roles and duties challenges the defined authority and responsibility, leading to overlapping of functions, thereby creating confusion in supervision and redress mechanism.

PRINCIPLE OF PRIORITIZATION

The police should be educated in the principle of prioritization. As the police, most often, are involved in crisis management, prioritizing their work becomes quite impractical. The situation changes every minute. A crime may draw the police's attention at one time, and a sudden law-and-order situation may distract them from the issue. It is then presumed that prioritizing in such conditions is not possible. But, in actuality, when the conditions are not predictable, prioritization becomes more important. Unless which one needs attention first is not known, the police personnel will be clueless and the state of affairs will be chaotic. The personnel should be well trained and prepared to distinguish between tasks, and should set them on priority basis.

PRINCIPLE OF HIRE AND FIRE, CARROT AND STICK (PART OF HUMAN RESOURCE DEVELOPMENT)

A very interesting fact in India is the desire in the society, particularly in the middle-class and lower middle-class, to get a government job. It is thought of being the most stable and secure prospect. In states, where dowry system is still prevalent, like Bihar, a simple clerk in a government unit would bid more than a manager in the private sector. The perception of the society is that in private institutions, the buzzword is *khun pasina neechod liya jata hai* (private institutions squeeze the blood and sweat out of their employees). The explicit opinion is that private institutions have hard task masters. The general opinion of a government job is that it is hard to get and equally hard to be removed from the job. Permanency is the keyword of government sector.

The principle of "hire and fire and carrot and stick" method is normally to motivate people, make certain that output is given, and ensure that loyalty of the employee does not shift. They act as motivator to the workers and threat to underachievers. A position in the organization is in accordance to one's performance. Government organizations (including police) totally discard these in their policy approach.

A very interesting and sarcastic factual description of usage of corporate strategy in government institutions is quoted below. This holds water even for the police organization. Corporate Strategy as applied in government institutions:

> *When you discover that you are riding a dead horse, the best strategy*
> *is to dismount and get a different horse.*

—Conventional Corporate Strategy

However, in government departments, more advanced strategies are employed more often, such as:

1. Buying a stronger whip.
2. Changing riders.
3. Appointing a committee to study the horse.
4. Arranging to visit other countries to see how other cultures ride dead horses.
5. Lowering the standards so that the dead horse can be included.
6. Reclassifying the dead horse as "living impaired."
7. Hiring contractors to ride the dead horse.
8. Harnessing several dead horses together to increase speed.
9. Providing additional funding and/or training to increase dead horse's performance.
10. Doing a productivity study to see if lighter riders would improve the dead horse's performance.
11. Declaring that as the dead horse does not have to be fed, it is less costly, carries lower overheads, and therefore contributes substantially more to the bottom line of the economy than do some other horses.
12. Rewriting the expected performance requirements for all horses.
13. And, finally, of course, promoting the dead horse to a supervisory position.

The hire-and-fire strategy obviously cannot be applied to the police as to the corporate system because the evaluation of performance is quite subjective. Quantifying the accomplishment is not an easy job. But total ignorance and indifference to this system invites ineffectiveness, lethargy, and indiscipline in the force.

PRINCIPLES OF SPAN OF CONTROL/SUPERVISION

According to this principle, the span of control is a span of supervision which depicts the number of employees that can be handled and controlled effectively by a single supervisor/manager. According to this principle, the number of employees to be handled by a manager should be decided.[15]

Let us broaden the spectrum of this principle when looking from the point of view of the police organization. Despite the police organization being a service-oriented organization, the community whom they are supposed to serve is not merely the "output or outcome" factors of the system. Because of the nature of their job, the same community also acts as "inputs" for this organization. Ironically, the population in the area under a police station has multiplied with further multiplication of other input resources as vehicles, buildings, other infrastructures, and so on, which are to be supervised, security ensured, and services catered to; but the strength of personnel has remained more or less same over decades. Hence, the span of control or supervision has widened to an unmanageable level. To add to the mismanagement, the expectations too have grown immensely. In such a situation, when a communication is attempted to achieve with the community, the beforehand perception of inadequacy and ineptness of the police plays a spoilsport.

PRINCIPLE OF UNITY OF COMMAND

It implies a one-on-one subordinate–superior relationship. Every subordinate is answerable and accountable only to one boss at one time. This helps in avoiding communication gaps and feedback and response is prompt. Unity of command also helps in effective combination of resources, i.e., physical and financial resources, which helps in easy coordination and, therefore, effective organization.[16] In police, the unity of command becomes more or less mandatory because it reduces the reaction time. As most of the time police are managing

---

[15] Managementstudyguide.com. "Principles of Organizing." http://www.management studyguide.com/organizing_principles.htm as visited on February 15, 2010.
[16] Managementstudyguide.com. "Principles of Organizing." http://www.management studyguide.com/organizing_principles.htm as visted on February 15 , 2010.

crisis, duality or multiplicity of chain of command would lead to chaotic situations and would lead to blatant blunders. This is the reason why police has their control room in every district and all the concerned authorities give direction via control room so that it is known to others what prior instructions have already been passed. There are a number of cases to be cited where multiple command has resulted into disasters. There have been accusations that during the 26/11 attacks in Mumbai, lack of unity of command in control room took its toll in the form of demise of valiant police officers in the field; two very senior commanding officers were in confusion regarding the location of their counterparts, resulting in failure to provide support during the need of hour.

Police is an organization, which just cannot juggle with this principle, but in day-to-day action making, compromises are glaringly visible. Even during investigation, investigating officer (IO) finds himself caught between different instructions combing from different levels of supervision. It makes mockery of the system and the organization as such loses the credibility before the community at large.

MOTIVATION

Motivation is the word derived from the word "motive" which means needs, desires, wants, or drives within the individuals. It is the process of stimulating people to actions to accomplish goals. In the work-goal context, the psychological factors stimulating the people's behavior can be desire for money, success, recognition, job satisfaction, team work, and so on.

One of the most important functions of management is to create willingness amongst the employees to perform to the best of their abilities. Therefore the role of a leader is to arouse in his employees' interest in their jobs which is directly proportional to their performance. Therefore, we can say that motivation is a psychological phenomenon which means that the needs and wants of individuals have to be tackled by framing an incentive plan.[17]

Abraham Maslow's motivational theory, hierarchy of needs, finds five major needs which motivate a person. They, in ascending order, are: biological and physiological needs (basic needs of life—food, drink,

---

[17] Managementstudyguide.com. "Organizational Behaviour." http://www.management studyguide.com/what_is_motivation.htm as visited on February 15, 2010.

shelter, sex, sleep, and so on); safety needs (protection, security, order, law, limits, stability, and so on); belongingness and love needs (family, affection, relationships, work group, and so on); esteem needs (achievement, status, responsibility, and reputation); and self-actualization (state of being mentally content, having a sense of fulfillment).[18]

Herzberg's two-factor theory of motivation showed that certain factors truly motivate ("motivators"), whereas others tended to lead to dissatisfaction ("hygiene factors"). Job satisfiers deal with the factors involved in doing a job, whereas job dissatisfiers deal with the factors which define a job context. Examples of Herzberg's "hygiene" needs (or maintenance factors) in the workplace are: policy, relationship with supervisor, work conditions, salary, company car, status, security, relationship with subordinates, and personal life. Herzberg's research identified that true motivators were other completely different factors, notably: achievement, recognition, work itself, responsibility, and advancement.[19]

In both the major theories of motivation, it can be seen that recognition, achievement, content of work, advancement, and reputation provide a high level of motivation for anybody in the society or organization. There has been, over the years, a decrease in the motivational factors from within and outside for the police personnel.

The community takes a lot of time and energy to recognize and appreciate the efforts of the police. Their achievements are undermined and mistakes blown out of proportion. A simple fact of the success of the police is that despite population explosion, high degree of contamination of the mindset of the people, high degree of dilution in values, cultural erosion, progression of individualistic attitude, avarice, and shift toward materialistic desire, the society is, by and large, living in peace. The anarchy that the media blares about dominates the image-building process. Community, to be honest, does not know what anarchy is or else this word would have never been on print or uttered.

The crime rate is always compared to the previous year's chart and assumed that situation is getting out of control, though the significant pace of change in other pressured areas is neglected and discounted.

---

[18] Chapman, Alan. "Abraham Maslow's Hierarchy of Needs Motivational Model." http://www.businessballs.com/maslow.htm as visited on February 17, 2010.
[19] Chapman, Alan. "Frederick Herzberg's Motivation and Hygiene Factors." http://www.businessballs.com/herzberg.htm as visited on February 17, 2010.

This is an unrealistic and illogical comparison. The hard work put in by the police to negate the upsurge in bad elements is not appreciated. Media is full of criticism with funny titles. The assumption amongst the police personnel is that the police job is a *thankless job*.

Within the organization, the motivational factors are missing. Personnel Management is in shambles. Police do not view the employees in toto. The external pressure is so strong that supervisors tend to keep their subordinates on the toes 24×7. They always push them to work incessantly, without giving breaks for social and family life. There is no space left for unwinding and rewinding. The higher management does not understand the environment from where the personnel come, his/her personal problems, work culture, basic needs, resource limitations, and mental health. The orders passed are expected to be complied with irrespective of its logicality and feasibility.

The requirement of the job calls for confrontation with vices of the society day in, day out. Police personnel are exposed to the negativity of life all times of the day. This negativity of the job seeps so deep into the mind and behavior of the police personnel that sooner or later they become victims of "police syndrome," looking at everyone suspiciously and doubting them to be the accused unless proved otherwise. The worst part is that they never realize that they are suffering from an ailment and are fitting patients of a clinical psychologist. They derive from that police syndrome a peculiar kind of mental power, which encourages brashness and high-handed attitude. Various psychopathological consequences including coercion, suspicion, alienation, cynicism, authoritarianism, and the likes are inevitable characteristics of a policeman's occupation.[20] The police subculture, which is a binding force within the organization, pushes them into isolation, away from normal life. Police subculture and police syndrome both are the result of a management gap in the organization. These two have a vital role to play in alienating them from their clientele/community, eventually jeopardizing the participational prospects for the community. The gap in proper implementation of management principles results into increasing the chasm between the community and the police.

[20] Bittner, E. 1980. *The Functions of the Police in Modern Society*. Cambridge: Oelgeschlager, Gunn and Hain; Niederhoffer, A. 1967. *Behind the Shield: The Police in Urban Society*. New York: Garden City, Doubleday; Skolnick, J.H. 1975. "Introduction: Professional Police in a Free Society," in J.H. Skolnick and T.C. Gray (eds), *Police in America*. Boston: Educational Associates; Westley, W.A. 1970. *Violence and the Police: A Sociological Study of Law, Customs and Mortality*. Cambridge: MIT Press.

Another major causative factor is the deplorable working conditions of the police and the manner in which the public and the seniors treat them, which develops poor self-image and low self-esteem in average policemen. This results in their taking out the pent-up frustration on the hapless public. The pay structure, prerequisites, working conditions, and prospects for career advancement of the police personnel at the lower ranks are not sufficient to attract proper recruits with right attitudes. Their daily interaction with the basic human instincts, the adversarial role in which they are placed vis-à-vis the public, and the conflicting expectations from them have a serious dehumanizing effect on them. This occasionally manifests itself in brutal ways. The repetitive nature of their work, boredom, long hours of duty, separation from family, high stress, pent-up frustrations encountered in a society having no respect for law, and so on, reinforce these negative feelings.[21]

The system in which the police personnel work is an impersonal system. There is no scope for sympathy, forget about empathy. They are rule-bound and governed by the law of the country. Contrary to that, Barrack Obama, in his book *Audacity of Hope*, writes that *empathy* is his golden rule, in personal and political life. Due to the police being bereft of empathy, they are taunted, *policewale apne baap ke bhi sage nahin hote* (policemen are disloyal even to their fathers). They are considered to be so bound by law that a saying goes: *policewalon se na dosti achi na dushmani* (you should neither be friends nor enemies with the police). However, this has positive as well as negative overtures. Positive because it reflects that the police are impartial and unbiased, law abiding, and law enforcing. Negative because they are accused of abusing the law-enforcing tactics to settle scores with the discordant lot.

The negative attitude makes the police personalize a crime. As Mahatma Gandhi said, "Hate the sin not the sinner," the police should believe in the principle of "hate the crime not the criminal." But, in actuality, the police get insensitive to both, the victim and the accused. So, the basic concept of policing of the present time, i.e., being proactive and reformatory, gets belied. This offensive attitude has led to drifting away of the community from the police, and the community are averse to participation as coming closer would purport getting caught in the radar of the police and embarrassment in the long run.

---

[21] Devarajan, M.K. 2000. "Attitudinal Changes for Better Policing," *S.V.P. National Police Academy Journal*, 52(1) (Jan–June): 50–56.

Customer Relations Management (CRM) is no doubt a novel idea, but to expect from the force of an organization which is over exerted, over stressed, and down in spirits, working in contradictory conditions is not fair. To expect them to put on the cosmetic makeup of "May I help you" for long is an impractical approach. Until proper care is taken to first put in order the anomalies within the organization, bringing drastic change in the attitude of the force overnight, just because on papers someone sitting in some comfortable office room has desired it, is asking for too much.

The quality of interaction that the public have/had with the police determines the direction, salience, and intensity of their attitude toward the police. It may be restated that, among all the sectors of criminal justice system, the police are most visible. Not only do they extensively interact with the public, but also whatever they do or do not do is invariably in full view of the public. From this stems the fact that the police are also much talked about. In the media, neighborhood gossips or person-to-person conversation, police inevitably come up for discussion which ultimately influences people's behavior and perception toward police which in turn affects the organizational climate of police. It is the psychological feel of a workplace or an organization unit and the organizational norms that seem to correspond to this feel.[22]

LEADERSHIP

When you boil it down, contemporary leadership seems to be a matter of aligning people toward common goals and empowering them to take the actions needed to reach them.

—Sherman, 1995[23]

According to Keith Davis: "Leadership is the ability to persuade others to seek defined objectives enthusiastically. It is the human factor which binds a group together and motivates it towards goals." Leadership is

---

[22] Mishra, R. and S. Mohanty. 1992. *Police and Social Change in India: History and Development of Police*. New Delhi: Ashish Publishing House.

[23] Sherman, Stratford. 1995. "How Tomorrow's Leaders Are Learning Their Stuff, Leadership Can't Be Taught, But Can Be Learned. Winning Companies are Creating Programs to Help People Grow." http://money.cnn.com/magazines/fortune/fortune_archive/1995/11/27/208026/index.htm as visited on February 4, 2010.

a process by which an executive can direct, guide, and influence the behavior and work of others toward accomplishment of specific goals in a given situation. Leadership is the ability of a manager to induce the subordinates to work with confidence and zeal.[24]

Bureaucrats, who are the leaders of government organizations, were once blamed of being subservient to the political masters. A term "committed bureaucracy" was coined, which flared up a lot of controversy in the circles. To placate the administrative thinkers, it was defined as being committed to the policies of the government, which is decided by the political party in power. This definition does have some relevance but would this be able to wash out totally the blame that the administrative structure has bowed down before the powerful political leaders is debatable. Now having upright, strong leaders is an exception. Being compromising, pliable, and moldable according to the demands laid down, taking along everyone to avoid unruffling of feathers even if it dilutes and challenges the legal status has become the desired traits of a leader. Now the situational leadership definition has changed.

Organizational leaders are supposed to be the trendsetters. Their action becomes the precedence and a guide for others to follow. Due to weak leadership, down the line, the system has become weak. Only those leaves of the rule book are opened which suits the interest of the powerful. Naturally, even while communicating with the public, this attitude dictates and conditional interface is invited. Collaboration is decided after gathering knowledge of have and have-nots. Filial affiliations dominate the rule book, and bending the rules with mala fide construes to the weakening of the accountability chain. Nepotism and favoritism is a mark of leadership now-a-days.

One of the failures on the part of the police is lack of good leadership. A police leader should be a philosopher, guide, and friend of his men. They should acquire knowledge and skills to impress their followers. All negative traits and attitudes must be eschewed. The leader should be a good human being and win acceptability amongst his men. Good leadership is to sacrifice for the betterment of the organization and subordinates' welfare. While fighting for a good, genuine, and legitimate cause, the leader should not worry about his present position or future placement. Some qualities of leadership are ability to communicate, level of confidence and credibility, ability to give acceptable

---

[24] "Leadership Basics." http://www.managementstudyguide.com/leadership_basics.htm as visited on February 18, 2010.

motivational advice, ability to assess changing needs, and ability to perform at an expected level. The police department is characterized by rigid hierarchy and strict discipline. Hence, the quality of leadership plays a tremendous role in the police's work culture. An officer with clarity of thought, proper understanding of his duties, and is welfare-oriented can provide excellent leadership. A harsh, overbearing, and heartless kind of an officer can make life miserable for his subordinates. Love rather than force, humility rather than ego would enhance the command of the leader and would help him stand out as a unique person.

The need for professional leadership will be more acute in a complex future where the only constant thing is change. Nineteenth-century leadership styles and skills will not be able to cope with the complexities of a society, entering the Cyber Age. The transition from the colonial era and a social revolution is sweeping aside traditional power centers and value systems, releasing dynamic energies that are transforming the Indian society. Traditionally, "soft" issues like environment and human rights are now major factors in governance, transcending national frontiers. The paramilitary administrator-bureaucrat was an adequate archetype for colonial policing, when the role of the government was limited and paternalistic, and expectations of the people were restricted to subsistence and security of life and property. Yesterday's paradigms of police leadership are crying out for change. The leader of the future will need the boldness to experiment with organizational and technological innovations at a local level, yet be aware of the need to carry along those who cling on to convention and precedent. Subject to the intense pulls and pressures of the field, the leader will need to define a baseline of professional ethics and personal values.[25]

The first task of a leader is to energize his people, creating a grand vision—a purpose which is noble, lofty, and aspirational—that would excite and energize everybody in the organization and the community. Having defined a powerful and attractive vision, the power of the vision has to be communicated to a large number of people in the organization.[26]

---

[25] Choudhury, J.N. 2000. "Indian Police Leadership: Can it Meet the Challenges of the 21st Century," *S.V.P. National Police Academy Journal*, 52(2) (July–December): 77–84.
[26] Murty, N.R. Narayana. 2009. *A Better India A Better World*. Allen Lane by Penguin Books India.

While discussing with a very senior police officer of Madhya Pradesh, a very important viewpoint came into fore. It was on the issue of application of management principles in the police organization. The opinion shifted from management principles, as such, to the need of leaders or managers in the police organization. He made a very clear distinction between leaders and managers. Leaders are those who are trendsetters, who lead from the front, who set examples for the followers to emulate. Managers are those who would ensure that things are properly managed, to bookish precision, and follow the letters of rules. Leaders are practical and show their true colors when they are managing a crisis situation. Managers would prefer to use hire-and-fire method of motivation and human resource management whereas leaders would motivate by setting standards by exemplary personal achievements and would prefer guiding than threatening.

I fully agree with my senior about the difference in the nature of the job of the police organization and a multinational company, but what still holds is that we cannot do away with management principles and sustain. The application of management principles is a must for the police to prove themselves as service providers, to effectively perform even with limited resources, and to coordinate with all parts of the system in this multidisciplinary environment.

Another aspect, which came up for discussion was that all leaders are managers but not all managers are leaders. Here, I differed. I had seen leaders who were good when it came to motivating the team in the field, particularly in the police, but failed miserably when it came to managing affairs with the available men, material, and money in normal conditions. Hence, I think an appropriate blend of leadership and managerial qualities is required for an effective and efficient policing system.

5

Police Syndrome

To understand the term "Police Syndrome," we need to know what syndrome means, technically, and what are its causes and effects. In medicine and psychology, the term "syndrome" refers to the association of several clinically recognizable features, signs (observed by a physician), symptoms (reported by the patient), phenomena, or characteristics that often occur together, so that the presence of one feature alerts the physician of the presence of the others. In recent decades, the term has been used outside the domain of medicine to refer to a combination of phenomena seen in association.

The term "syndrome" derives from the Greek and literally means "run together," as the features do. Most often it is used to refer to the set of detectable characteristics when the reason that they occur together (the pathophysiology of the syndrome) has not yet been discovered. A name given to a familiar syndrome often continues to be used even after an underlying cause has been found, or when there are a number of different primary causes that all give rise to the same combination of symptoms and signs.

Many syndromes are named after the physicians credited with first reporting of the association; these are eponymous syndromes. Otherwise, disease features or presumed causes, as well as references to geography, history, or poetry, can lend their names to syndromes.[1] In plain words, a "syndrome" is strong signs or characteristics, which a person reflects physiologically or mentally.

---

[1] Wikipedia. "Syndrome." http://en.wikipedia.org/wiki/Syndrome as visited on December 18, 2009.

Police Culture

The sociocultural conditioning plays an important role in the development of a syndrome. "Culture-bound syndrome" is a set of symptoms where there is no evidence of an underlying biological cause, and which is only recognized as a "disease" of a particular culture.[2] The field officers in the police suffer from "Police Syndrome." The characteristics displayed are cynicism, rudeness, irritation, negative attitude, and insensitivity. They are culture bound.

An organization's current customs, traditions, and general way of doing things are largely due to what it has done before and the degree of success it has had with those endeavors. This leads us to the ultimate source of an organization's culture.[3] Organizational theorists acknowledge the important role that culture plays in the lives of the organization members, affecting an employee's attitude and behavior leading to institutionalization.[4] According to one thinker, culture consists of those shared assumptions which have an active, shaping influence upon ideas, attitudes, and experience. In this sense, culture is a signifying system, which represents a "whole way of life of a social group or whole society."[5] Organizational culture refers to a system of shared meaning held by members that distinguishes the organization from other organizations.[6] Other authors stress that the police's behavior is determined through informal customs where they need to deal with the public instead of formal laws and regulations.[7] Generally, the police are

---

[2] Wikipedia. "Syndrome." http://en.wikipedia.org/wiki/Syndrome as visited on December 18, 2009.

[3] Schein, E.H. 1983. "The Role of the Founder in Crating Organizational Culture," *Organizational Dynamics*, 8(3): 221–38.

[4] Selznick, P. 1948. "Foundations of the Theory of Organizations," *American Sociological Review*, 13(1): 25–35.

[5] Brooker, Peter. 2003. *A Glossary of Cultural Theory*. London: Edward Arnold Ltd. http://analepsis.files.wordpress.com/2008/03/brookerculture1.pdf as visited on November 15, 2009.

[6] Becker, Howard S. 1982. "Culture: A Sociological View," Yale Review, 71(4): 513–28; Schein, E.H. 1992. *Organizational Culture and Leadership*, 2nd ed. San Francisco: Jossey Bass.

[7] Bittner, E. 1967. "The Policeman on Skid-row: A Study in Peacekeeping," *American Sociological Review*, 32(5): 699–715; Brown, M. 1981. *Working the Street: Police Discretion and the Dilemmas of Reform*. New York: Russell Sage; Reiner, R. 1983. *The Politics of the Police*. Toronto: University of Toronto Press; Reuss-Ianni, E. 1992. *Two Cultures of Policing*. New Brunswick, NJ: Transaction Books.

described as having their own subculture, their behavior more significantly structured by informal norms than by formal rules.[8] Police culture is a mentality or cognitive orientation involving how people see themselves and see others. Police are said to have a "we–they" or "us–them" worldview. This in-group, we (police) vs. they (civilians), solidarity is associated with the idea of the police subculture, but in practice, the more general term "culture" is commonly used to describe everything the police share in common.[9]

Police are typically viewed as a distinct subgroup, with a particular ethos that strongly influences their daily practices. Some author suggests that the police feel a rupture between themselves and the general public, which leads to a "we versus them" mentality that affects their social network.[10]

The nature of their job is such that it promotes non-socialization. Policemen, due to non-conducive working conditions, gradually drift away from the society. They are unable to disburse their social obligations and even the basic family responsibility remains unattended. They are trapped in the *police culture*, which drags them away from their normal social life. In the case of policing, e.g., the belief that you are never off duty would be a theme constraining a full interactive life with the general public.[11] The family becomes the victim of working culture lapses. The families of the policemen (women and children) get a raw deal and are neglected in the process. It will not be an exaggeration if it is said that the *policemen eat, drink, walk, and sleep policing*. Over the years they have got so deeply entrenched inside the world of crime, law, and order that their every walk of life is influenced by it. Even a normal discussion would end up on that note.

Another thinker describes the police's cultural characteristics of isolation (blue wall), brotherhood (an attack on one is an attack on all),

---

[8] Crank, John P. 1998. *Understanding Police Culture*, Cincinnati: Anderson Publishing House. http://www.springerlink.com/content/0r7h1327k6nj11q8/ as visited on December 18, 2009.

[9] Stevens, Mark. "Police Culture and Behavior." California State University. http://faculty.ncwc.edu/mstevens/205/205lect02.htm as visited on December 18, 2009.

[10] Kappeler, V., R. Sluder, and G. Alpert. 1984. *Forces of Deviance: Understanding the Dark Side of Policing*. Prospect Heights, IL: Waveland Press; Neiderhoffer, A. 1967. *Behind the Shield: The Police in Urban Society*. Garden City, NY: Doubleday; Skolnick, J. 1966. *Justice Without Trial: Law Enforcement in a Democratic Society*. New York: John Wiley & Sons; Westley, W. 1970. *Violence and the Police: A Sociological Study of Law, Custom and Morality*. Cambridge, MA: The MIT Press.

[11] Stevens, Mark. "Police Culture and Behavior." California State University. http://faculty.ncwc.edu/mstevens/205/205lect02.htm as visited on December 18, 2009.

and action (the ability to recognize danger and symbolic assailants).[12] This depiction of police solidarity is also described as responsibility toward fraternity. It is presumed that under the garb of solidarity, the police create a shield of protection and work with impunity. Many thinkers have described it as the Blue Code of Silence (or Blue Wall of Silence). It is an unwritten rule among police officers worldwide that no officer will report of his/her colleague's errors, misconducts, or crimes. If questioned about an incident of misconduct involving another officer (e.g., during the course of an official inquiry), if following the Blue Code of Silence, it would be standard procedure to claim ignorance. Ironically, it is similar to the code of silence in an organized crime, like the Omertà. Studies demonstrate that most police officers feel that the code is applicable in cases of "illegal brutality or bending of the rules in order to protect colleagues from criminal proceedings," but not to illegal actions with an "acquisitive motive."[13] However, in the recent past, there has been much dilution of this code. We can witness incidents where whistle-blowers have brought to fore many issues which in past would have been happily kept under the wraps. But that iron curtain still exists and is not totally penetrable.

The working culture of police ultimately has become the *police culture*. The working culture and conditions, which supplement and complement each other, have been the root cause of this syndrome. Working conditions in the police are not very conducive. Policemen can be seen donkeying around day in, day out. To our consternation, the culture, so closely protected by the police, is the breeding ground for police syndrome.

Police Syndrome

Besides the working conditions, there are many other conditioning causes of the police syndrome.

There are unnumbered hours of work, routineless day plans, irregular eating breaks, and erratic sleeping habits throughout the career. Personal life is almost nonexistent for them. The day starts for

---

[12] Stevens, Mark. "Police Culture and Behavior." California State University, http://faculty.ncwc.edu/mstevens/205/205lect02.htm as visited on December 18, 2009.

[13] Wikipedia. "Blue Code of Silence." http://en.wikipedia.org/wiki/Blue_Code_of_Silence as visited on December 18, 2009.

them with a call in the bed about a news of some untoward incident like theft, murder, rape, assault, robbery, and so on; in the presence of sunlight they keep themselves occupied, besieged with the worst vices of the society and finally hit the bed at late hours in the night after pulling themselves out from a similar scenario each day. Day in and day out they spend time facing unruly mobs, criminals, and law violators. Most of the time, in consciousness, is consumed confronting the vices of the society and hunting for or interacting with the perpetrators. Negativity and vices is what falls into their kitty the whole day.

The investigation skill development training also has an impact on the attitudinal development of the police personnel. Ironically, the subject of training aggravates the situation. It reinforces the syndromic characteristic of cynicism. The basic philosophy of investigation focuses on suspecting one and all. It advocates doubting right from the victim to everyone else in contact, physically present or not. Then through deleting/weeding out mechanism, the investigator zeroes in on the main culprit. Hence, from very inception, a policeman is taught to distrust, be cynical.

Police is a closed and opaque organization. The organizational mismanagement also contributes, in some way, to the building of this syndrome. The wrongly applied organizational management principles like strict hierarchical setup and adverse to two-way communication leaves a lot of frustration at the lower echelons. The promotion and encouragement of yes-manship and unchallenged compliance to orders of the seniors puts policemen in the make belief world where they think their orders cannot be challenged by anyone. Due to hindered communication within the system, their frustration finds a vent out when in contact with a man in the street. It is very surprising that the organization is sustaining and feeding a culture, which is perpetuating a network for a disease like the police syndrome to flourish.

To be honest, most of the field officers are victims of the police syndrome and that suggests that most of the field officers are sick from a psychological point of view. To not comprehend the sickness is not a deliberate attempt but is skipped in ignorance. Police refuse to accept that they are sick. They refute the very idea of being branded as suffering from a disease. The reason is the misinterpretation of the ailment. What a doctor would interpret as illness is misconstrued by policemen as power and authority. Being impersonal and insensitive is looked upon in the police circles as professional competence. Rudeness and high-handedness is a sign of authority and power. It is presumed that the police have the license to kill. Impoliteness, indifference, and cynicism, which would call for immediate clinical attention, are looked upon as a personality of machismo, prerequisites of police work culture. Tenderness, politeness, sensitivity, being sweet tongued, and considerate, are all classified as feminine traits, unfit, and disqualifying for the police. Our negativity is hailed as professionalism. That is the irony of situation. The disease is being treated as strength. This denial mode is not only harmful for the organization and the individual, but for the society as well, whom they are assigned to serve. The predicament is that all know of their ailment but collectively deny to be cured.

One more noteworthy aspect is the public apathy. The society on one hand chooses to criticize the police's way of functioning and on the other hand opt to isolate or alienate them. This distance maintenance, chasm creation leads to the communication gap. Due to lack of consistent community participation, the good initiative taken up by the well-meaning police officers fail to get transformed from a personalized effort to an institutionalization of activities. This alienation eventually sucks up even the good headed into that culture of the police and syndrome symptoms take over.

Corrective Suggestions

The description of a syndrome usually includes a number of *essential* characteristics, which when concurrent lead to the diagnosis of the condition. These are a combination of typical, major symptoms and signs—essential to the diagnosis—together with minor findings, some or all of which may be absent.

In contrast to the major and minor findings, which are typical of the syndrome, there may be an association with other conditions; meaning that in persons with the specified syndrome, these associated conditions occur more frequently than would be expected by chance. An example would be Down syndrome, which has the associated condition of diabetes mellitus. Knowledge of associated conditions would dictate that they are specifically looked for in the management of the syndrome.[14]

---

[14] Wikipedia. "Syndrome." http://en.wikipedia.org/wiki/Syndrome as visited on December 18, 2009.

This explanation means that the need is to understand police culture, its formative process, and its perilous impact as the associated condition, which would help in diagnosing the police syndrome and methods for checking its perpetuation. Management of the police syndrome would require an inclusive and holistic approach. Some suggestions would include: unwinding to relax from the monotony and bring freshness in otherwise stale lifestyle. Compulsory leave (Compulsory Time Off [CTO]) for recreation and recuperation is advisable for that. Recurrent relaxing meditation program should be started, qualitative rather than quantitative working hours should be emphasized on, and effective man management technique should be put into place. The in-built nature of their job is already very demanding, hence, internal organizational and external pressures should be neutralized and minimized. The police and the community should participate, partner, and collaborate more intrinsically and exhaustively. That will help in offloading a lot of stress from the police and will enhance effectiveness and efficiency multifold.

6

Perspective Constrains

There have been some perspective constrains, which have hampered community participative activities. This chapter discusses some of those constrains to understand their influence on collaborative mechanism.

Image Distortion

The image of the police has always been at the receiving end. Studies have proved that the image of the police is not always built on the basis of their action. Many other contributing aspects that shape the perception are coming from secondary and tertiary sources. Secondary and tertiary sources include hearsays, folklore, historical legacy, media reports, rumors, and so on. Even the methods resorted by parents and family members like warning the children to toe their line else being handed over to the police, or by teachers and parents instructing them to keep at a distance from the police even in dire situations, and so on, go a long way in building the image of the police. The police's image is painted as being alien, inaccessible, brutal, corrupt, and touch-me-not. Consequently, when participative policing initiatives are put in place, the required involvement of the community is missing. Participation which is the basis of collaboration does not exist. On record, they do keep patting their own shoulders by boasting exemplary participation; however, verily, it is either coerced participation or handpicked participation. The very spirit of the initiatives is lost by this approach. Eventually, the desired results are never achieved.

General public is a victim of self-limiting beliefs.[1] This is the belief they have about themselves and their potential, which holds them back. Most of these self-limiting beliefs are not true. They are the result of information one has accepted without even questioning, often from early childhood. Even if they are completely untrue, if one stokes that belief, it becomes one's truth.

Displacement and Generalization Syndrome

The community and the police are suffering from displacement and generalization syndrome. Displacement syndrome means shifting of responsibility and onus from the actual person to others. If one is angry on A for his/her deeds and he/she expresses his/her unpleasantness on B, this means displacement. Similarly, if for some wrong has been done by A, the whole organization or the community is blamed for that; it indicates generalization. Both these syndromes are major impediments to participative policing.

This can be explained through the "halo effect" as well. Halo effect operates when a general impression is drawn about an individual on the basis of a single characteristic, such as intelligence, sociability, or appearance.[2] Research suggests that it is likely to be most extreme when the traits to be perceived are ambiguous in behavioral terms, when the traits have moral overtones, and when the perceiver is judging traits when he/she has had limited experience.[3]

In the police organization, both displacement and generalization syndromes are corollary of the police syndrome. Police syndrome makes the police cynical; doubting everyone coming in contact. Displacement syndrome results in venting out of the frustration of the system on hapless community members and generalization syndrome leads to the

---

[1] Brian, Tracy. 2008. *Change Your Thinking, Change Your Life: How To Unlock Your Full Potential For Success And Achievement.* Singapore: John Wiley & Sons (Asia) Pvt Ltd.

[2] Murphy, K.R. and R.L. Anhalt. 1992. "Is Halo a Property of the Rater, The Ratees, or the Specific Behaviors Observed?" *Journal of Applied Psychology,* 77(3): 494–500 ; Murphy, K.R., R.A. Jako. and R.L. Anhalt. 1993. "Nature and Consequences of Halo Error: A Critical Analysis," *Journal of Applied Psychology,* 78(2): 218–25.

[3] Bruner, J.S. and R. Tagiuri. 1954. "The Perception of People," in E. Lindzey (ed.), *Handbook of Social Psychology,* pp. 634–54. Reading, MA: Addison-Wesley.

belief that whole the community is noncooperative, non-recognizing to their hard work, having unrelenting expectations, doubting their acts, and complaining.

In the community, the displacement and generalization syndrome is deep-rooted. One erroneous act of a policeman, says, Constable Vijay (fictitious character), becomes a matter of hatred toward everyone in visibility. It is not seen as an error committed by Vijay, but becomes the fault of the police station and, when more generalized, the fault of the entire police organization. Custodial death incidents, misbehavior by a policeman, and so on, are some examples which invite the wrath of the community toward the whole police station or district force. Police personnel are never identified as a people by the community at large. The community always treats them as *vardidhari* and their opposition is against the entire police force. This is a *"look alike"* attitude. Meaning, people adapt the approach of being against the *policewalah* rather than blaming the individual perpetrator. This generalization widens the rift between the community and the police.

Anarchical Contradictory Interpretations

There are two dangers facing any society. These are autocracy and anarchy. Both are inherent in a system, which is based upon an imbalanced use of power. Too much use of power leads to autocracy whereas too little to anarchy. This imbalanced use of power results in a rule of tyranny, corruption, and injustice, all prejudicial to the well-being of the people. One very interesting contradictory claim of the two—the police and the community—is that both have different opinions about the police's existence.

In the newspapers, it is a common feature quoting that the police's presence has become meaningless and there is anarchy everywhere. The culprits are having a field day. Crime is uncontrolled and escalating without hindrance. At the same time, the police silently retort, within their circles, that peace and tranquility is by virtue of their services. They believe that the criticizers have too liberally interpreted the word anarchy. They categorically claim that to witness literal anarchy, there should be a declared withdrawal of the force. Due to this perspective contradiction, both fail to appreciate the importance and contribution in managing the affairs.

Participation Transmission

It is the process through which the efforts of participation are transmitted into ultimate objectives. It is basically a sort of black box, implying that while it can be known that participation efforts do influence output and results, it is not easy to ascertain how precisely it does. Perceptible benefits can be felt but quantifying the outcome is not feasible. The participation of the community in police activities is many a times hidden. Had there been a total vacuum in participation, the police would have miserably failed in its field. The success of police function can be unquestionably attributed to participation.

However, the extent of participation required and planned is not being achieved. The efforts for calling participation fail to attract enough support from the community. Due to lacunae in planning, improper and faulty procedures, failure in disseminating information about objectives and issues to the stakeholders, inappropriate implementation, wrongly chosen selective participants, and hidden agenda of the implementers, the participation transmission suffers the maximum. There is a big disparity between the desired results and achievement.

Performance Matching Expectation Scale (PME Scale)

The expectations of the community and the police from each other are again one of the factors of perspective constrains. The community's expectations from the police keep growing. They expect the police to do wonders. It is expected that the police has a magic wand and just by swinging it, they can solve all crimes. The mere presence of policemen raises the expectations, subconsciously, within the community that the problem will be solved. If the performance of the police does not match their expectations, the police are blamed of being inactive and insensitive. They brand the police as unwilling to serve or conniving with the lawbreakers.

Likewise, the police lay down their own utopian conditions for the community's assistance. Like an ostrich ignoring the predator by burying its head in the sand, they tend to forget their image in the community and expect the members of the community, both male and female, to come forward and support them in whatever way they want. When the performance of the community does not match their expectation, they land up looking at the community as non-supportive.

This performance-matching expectation scale should be a realistic one. On PME scale when the performance falls within the "circle of expectation," the participation of the stakeholders increases. This circle of expectation expands and contracts, depending on the honesty and transparency developed between the parties. More the communication, more realistic and logical will be the expectation. With the increase in trust and confidence, the circle of expectation grows and more participation comes forth.

On this scale, both sides of the scale are revealing a mismatch. When there is less performance, the community loses confidence in the police organization and starts doubting their potential, eventually withdrawing themselves and leaving the police isolated. When the performance is more than expected, the police get overconfident and tend to neglect and overlook the community's importance and contribution. They start patting their own shoulder, claiming all credit for their success, undermining the contribution of the community. This ultimately alienates their indispensable partner, i.e., the community.

FIGURE 6.1
PME Scale

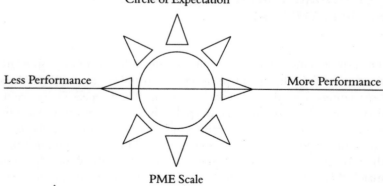

The police–community partnership tend to run out of the *circle of expectation* toward mismatch end either because of low or more performance, though the chances of the former seem to be more plausible.

Why does this mismatch exists? To understand this, it is necessary to analyze the process of expectation building.

Knowledge-based Expectation (KBE)

When you know something, say what you know. When you don't know something, say that you don't know. That is knowledge.

—Kung Fu Tzu (Confucius)

Expectations are always based on the knowledge one has about the potential of the performer. Many a times, the knowledge of a person, community, or organization is developed without knowing it fully. All that glitters is not gold. It is necessary to have proper understanding before claiming to be well-versed in the subject. "Little knowledge is dangerous;" this adage fully applies to the relationship between the community and the police. Reason for the strong mismatch of performance and expectation is because of shortage of knowledge about each other—confined knowledge.

KNOWLEDGE ABOUT POLICE

It is a proven fact that the police's negative image, as perceived by the public is not merely because of the treatment meted out to people in police stations. A study sponsored by the National Police Commission (1978–81), held that 82 percent of the respondents were of the view that the police did not discharge their duties in a straightforward manner. Criticism was directed more against the lower ranks for corruption and susceptibility to political influence.

More often than not, they interact with the police more on roads or other public places than they do in police stations. Policemen, who are nowadays omnipresent, are looked upon for assistance whenever a person is in a fix. The help-seeking person's problem may vary from asking an untraceable address to seeking assistance to hunt or stop a taxi or an auto rickshaw. It is the presumption of every common man that a cop in uniform is the solution to all his/her silly, petty problems. The impression that people carry about the police is mostly because of this small interaction they have with the police. We will have to take this fact very seriously. It is important to understand the role of policemen, particularly lower echelons, who normally man the intersections, stations, or any other public place.

The knowledge of police working and their powers is very restricted to a layman. The work of many other agencies is thought to be the responsibility of the police. For example, the community at large cannot distinguish between bailable and non-bailable offences and cognizable and non-cognizable offences. Any accused bailed out on a bailable case is seen as not being apprehended. Bailed out offenders from the court are also thought to be left out by the policemen. Bailed out under section 151 IPC is seen to be done by the policemen. In India, the police force is insufficient to carry out normal policing. The national average is just 126 officers per 100,000 people. Even the UN norm says that it should be 222.[4] Hence, we fall short to almost half the prescribed international level. This shortage of manpower, population to police, is not understood by a common man. The police are expected to be omnipresent; prophecy being their gifted wisdom. Resource crunch is never brought to the knowledge of the public. Resultantly, their expectations never wane. They presume the police to be fully powered, to do anything under the sky, and solve all the problems cropping up.

In a democratic setup, particularly in an organization like the police, perceived organizational climate would definitely play an important role in shaping behavior, attitudes, and coping styles. Work-related attitudes are job satisfaction, work identification, intrinsic motivation, and job involvement. These are directly related to the work a person does and are generally termed as "job attitudes."[5]

In our country, an important factor responsible for episodic outbursts of the police violence and brutality is the deplorable conditions under which the police work. The duty hours of the police are relatively longer and irregular, housing conditions are poor; in many police stations the police personnel live in houses which have been declared unfit for human habitation. A study carried out by the National Productivity Council had shown that a policeman has to work 16 hours a day and seven days a week; the recuperation time to regain mental balance is short and facilities for healthy recreation are minimal, if not

[4] Khara. M.S. 2009. "Community Participation in Security against Terrorism," *The Indian Police Journal*, LVI(2): 8–15, April–June.

[5] Mishra, R. and S. Mohanty. 1992. *Police and Social Change in India: History and Development of Police*. New Delhi: Ashish Publishing House.

nonexistent. Another factor, which provokes the police's aggression, is the murder or grievous hurt inflicted on the police personnel by the criminals and antisocial elements. Deprived of solicitude from members of the public, the police feel that they have to strike hard against their enemies and it is not always possible to follow the rules of the game.

During the British regime, discipline in the states was strict and almost entirely controlled by the police hierarchy. Outside interference was extremely rare and was generally counterproductive. Every police officer could initiate disciplinary enquiry in case of any lapse. Dereliction of duty was more or less certain to detect. In most cases, the word of the Superintendent was final and outside interference was severely scotched. In matters relating to transfer, posting, promotion, and punishment, the view of the IGP were routinely accepted. Today, the outside interference, frequently assuming the garb of government directive, has become endemic as it is not uncommon for officers such as the District Magistrate, DSP, and staff even at the police station to be posted on recommendations of influential persons, mostly related to political field. Unless political will is shown in bolstering the system for maintaining discipline in the police, its image is likely to be further tarnished.[6]

The police personnel are frequently asked to perform contradictory and inconsistent services in the front line of our troubled and violent society. Whenever there is an upsurge of crime, there is an outcry against the police to control crime without realizing that the police alone cannot play a decisive role in reducing crime. According to one estimate, the police personnel in our country spend only 37 percent of their time in investigation of cases. Very Important Person (VIP) duties, law-and order-problems, and other miscellaneous commitments occupy the major portion of their time.

In an organization, job attitude of employees has tremendous impact on their performance, interpersonal relations, mental health, and the decision to leave the job. It is observed that positive job attitude has positive effects on performance, attitudes, and interpersonal relations at work. On the other hand, negative job attitude has adverse negative effects on mental health and the decision to quit.[7] Kirkham, a criminologist, tried to assess the role of the police as a participant observer. He joined the police and, during his work, he found that the thankless

[6] Tripathi, S.V.M. 2001. "Discipline and Police," *The Indian Police Journal*, XLVIII(3): 13–20, July–September.

[7] Sutaria, R. 1979. "Effects of Job Attitudes and Personality Characteristics," *Indian Journal of Industrial Relations*, 14(4): 535–44.

and strenuous job of policing generated anger and impulsiveness in him.[8] In spite of doing patrolling and other jobs day and night, the people were never sympathetic and never tried to understand the problems of a policeman.

One of the sociological paradigms, as propounded by Skolnick, elaborates that the organizational tension in the police department is primarily due to the internal contradiction between the legal system and the bureaucratic pressures.[9] Democratic bureaucracy puts more emphasis on initiative during the process of public administration whereas the rule of law entails strict adherence to the provisions of the law. Thus, Skolnick highlights the tension between the operational consequences of the parameters of order, efficiency, and initiative on one hand, and strict adherence to legality on the other hand.

KNOWLEDGE ABOUT COMMUNITY

In the same way, the police try to sweep the whole house with the same broom. Their expectation from the community never corresponds to the local potential. The police's expectation from the local populace should be carved area-wise, and based on inhabitants. However, the initiatives planned are not need-based, worked out after proper analysis of the demand. Somewhere top-up initiatives are planned and pushed down the line to be implemented, a typical intuitive approach. In case of a fiasco or underperformance, the community is accused of showing disinterest toward their honest collaborative approach. When there is gap in expectation and deliverance, the faith and trust on the deliverer is lost. This can be said as faith–trust deficit (FTD). And the victim of this deficit is participation.

A warm, smiling, and interactive response from the policeman, luck smiling upon the face of the person in need, and if the person receives correct guidance, this will leave an indelible impression on the person. The good made does not end here; it gets carried to long distances, to many people, when the person speaks to others about his

---

[8] Kirkham, G.L. 1964. "The Criminologist as a Policeman: A Participant Observation Study," in Donal Mainamara and Marc Ridel (eds), *Police: Perspectives, Problems, Prospects*, pp. 35–42. New York: Praeger Publishers.
[9] Skolnick, J.H. 1975. "Introduction: Professional Police in a Free Society," in J.H. Skolnick and T.C. Gray (eds), *Police in America*, pp. 60–68. Boston: Educational Associates.

good experience. In fact, this one pleasant interaction may motivate and encourage him/her to approach the police whenever in need. This subject has been discussed in detail in Chapter 3, under the topic of police–public interaction.

The Three E-process of Police Management

The three E-process of police management, in a very simple way, can explain about how illiterate one is about the police management by taking an example of traffic management and second, using it as a simile to describe the police management as a whole.

One of the main issues in policing is traffic control. This is one aspect of policing which attracts attention of one and all. The state of affairs of traffic plying on the roads leaves an image of the police's efficiency. This is a very interesting fact that can explain the phenomena of image-building of an institution. Traffic management is a collective responsibility, which involves three phases: Engineering, Education, and Enforcement.

- Engineering is the development of infrastructure, good roads, diversions, dividers, necessary speed breakers, and removal of unnecessary speed breakers.
- Education would involve disseminating of information and imparting knowledge of rules and regulations to the enforcers and abiders both.
- Enforcement of rules and regulations by the law-enforcing agency, which is the police.

The role of the police is that of enforcement, and that comes into play only once the other two become operational. It is a fact that most of the problems in traffic management are because of poor engineering including bad roads, unwanted speed breakers, choked crossroads, unmanageable rush, improper signposts, and all other engineering misdeeds. Adding to this is almost a lack of awareness of traffic rules and regulations by the users. However, the onus of traffic mismanagement is passed on the police. The irony of the situation is that the lastly responsible in the process is mostly criticized.

USING THE THREE E-PROCESS TO UNDERSTAND MANAGEMENT IN THE POLICE

This three E-process of traffic management can be used to understand the management of the police organization in simplistic terms. The engineering process can be compared to the policy and planning processes in policing. Education is the awareness and knowledge of the policy decisions by the field implementing officers and the community, and enforcement is the implementing of those policy decisions by the police personnel in the field.

The engineering, policy, and planning processes in the police organization is a victim of stringent and haughty hierarchical attitude. The natural fallout of strict hierarchical adherence or hierarchical snobbery in the police structure is the intuitive approach adopted in taking decisions, rather than using the data approach. Organizations using intuitive approach do not use customer research, or use it sparingly because they believe they know what their customers want.[10] In the police, due to this intuitive approach, often there are numerous seniors' pet projects promoted. And as soon as the individual leaves the scene, the projects are shelved. A research has showed that there is below average success rate for executive sponsored projects.[11] Data approach would involve research about the need, ground realities, and subordinates competence, and accordingly after analysis of all the data, projects would be decided.

In the police organization, subordinates follow orders verbatim without trying to understand the nitty-gritty of policies. The spirit and letters are never inculcated. More or less, subordinates prefer to do the needful on papers, as they call it: *kagaz ka pet bharna hai*. There is a lack of communication in the hierarchical setup. Communication gap can be reduced by ensuring that all people within the organizational system speak the same language and build a shared and consistent understanding of the domain. This leads to better specifications, flushes out incorrect assumptions, and ensures that functional gaps are discovered before the development starts. With these practices in place the input, process, and output can be coordinated in a better way that genuinely

---

[10] Prasad, B.V.S. and Kalai Selvan. 2007. *Customer-Centric Business Model, An Introduction*. Hyderabad: Icfai Books, The Icfai University Press.

[11] Cooper, G. Robert. 2005. *Product Leadership*, 2nd Edition. New York: Basic Books.

fits for purpose.[12] But due to hindered communication, the education part becomes limited for the personnel within the organization and the community who are major participants in input and output processes.

A consequential domino effect of poor engineering and education is that enforcement becomes difficult. What is perceived is not realized. The community remains in the dark about their role and expectations, whereas, the enforcers go more by the letters than by the spirit, and fail to get cooperation and collaboration, a must for realistic achievement.

---

[12] Adzic, Gojko. 2009. *Bridging the Communication Gap*. London: Neuri Limited. http://www.acceptancetesting.info/the-book/ as visited on February 18, 2010.

7

Police's Opinion about Their Jobs

First report of the National Police Commission, set up in 1977, under the chairmanship of Shri Dharma Vira (former Governor of Punjab), in its Chapter-II "The Constabulary," part 2.19 described the position of the constable. It said:

A job analysis conducted by the National Productivity Council has shown that the working hours of the subordinate police officers range from 10 to 16 hours every day of seven days in a week… without any respite. Long and arduous hours of work without facilities for rest and recreation, continuous employment on jobs under extreme conditions of stress and strain, both mental and physical, prolonged stagnation in the same rank without even one rank promotion throughout their service for a majority of them, constant exposure to criticism and ridicule by a demanding public, a totally inadequate pay structure with no compensation for the handicaps and privation they undergo in their jobs, low status and lack of involvement in planning and executing field jobs with a full understanding of the objectives set by the police organisation, etc., have all had their telling effect on the morale of the constabulary throughout the country. The increasing educational level of the Constables—a trend noticeable in the recent years—has sharpened the edge of their frustration with their existing lot within the police system … They function as automatons in situations where they are required to exercise their discretion and judgment. They function rigidly in circumstances, which require flexibility of approach and understanding of the opposite point of view. We are convinced that mere changes in their training schedule will not bring about the necessary improvement in their motivation or performance unless some serious deficiencies in their living and working conditions which have long been neglected are immediately taken up and remedied. We consider this exercise to be of primary importance in any attempt at police reform.[1]

In an interview, Rustamji, a former member of the National Police Commission, said that the police department was the "worst employer in the land" and that a constable who worked 13–15 hours a day, got no decent quarters to live in and got one-third of the pay of a sweeper in the government[2,3]. A syndicated study by SVPNPA (1974) in the states of Maharashtra, Madhya Pradesh, West Bengal, Orissa, Bihar, and Assam on "attitudes of subordinate policemen" found that majority of the subordinates (61 percent) thought that the rules of departmental proceedings allowed sufficient scope for fair play and justice. However, 32.5 percent disagreed and did not seem to have many expectations of fair play and justice out of the rules of departmental enquiries. With regard to the regulation of private life, 78 percent of the police ranks feel that there is much regulation of the private life of policemen by the department. This view has been uniformly expressed by the police officers of all ranks as well as from different backgrounds. The vast majority of the respondents (87 percent) desire to do only eight hours of work per day. The police ranks seem to be disillusioned with the long working hours and want to get their working hours reduced to the level of other government employees. Also, 50.5 percent of the respondents expressed the view that the police department did not provide good opportunities for promotion. However, 49 percent were of the opinion that the department provides opportunities for promotion. With regard to promotion and merit, 37.5 percent have expressed the view that the promotions in general go to those who do the best work. Although, 32.5 percent respondents were found doubtful

[1] Shri Dharma Vira. 1977 (November 15th). *First Report: National Police Commission* (Chapter II: The Constabulary, part 2.19), submitted to the Ministry of Home Affairs, Government of India, and published by its Resolution Number VI. 24021/36/77-GPA.
[2] K.F. Rustomji was one of the most decorated and respected police officers of India. He was member of National Police Commission. Pay issue is dealt in 3.21 section under Overtime Allowance, Chapter-III, PAY STRUCTURE OF FIRST REPORT NATIONAL POLICE COMMISSION, under Union Home Minister, New Delhi, 1977. Also see Government of India. *Report of the National Commission on Police.* New Delhi: Government of India.
[3] Mishra, R. and S. Mohanty. 1992. *Police and Social Change in India: History and Development of Police.* New Delhi: Ashish Publishing House.

and 29.5 per cent felt that the person who is best at work seldom is promoted in the organization.

This study revealed that 49 percent of the respondents were of the view that they would have definitely got promoted had they been working in some other organization, while 31 percent of the respondents considered long working hours as the main disadvantage of the police service; 18 percent of the respondents were of the opinion that too much political interference was an irksome feature of the police service. Too much harassment by superior officers (12.1 percent) and too much subordination (12 percent) in the police service were also found. Only 14.5 percent of the respondents were sure that they always get just and fair treatment, while 42.5 percent of the respondents said that they rarely get just and fair treatment from their superior officers. A majority of the respondents (51 percent) said that their seniors helped them only "sometimes," 14.5 percent of the personnel felt that their seniors never helped them when they were in some difficulty. The important reasons for noncooperation by the public, according to the police personnel, are the harassment caused to the public in the process of a court trial and rude behavior of the police and lack of confidence in the police. A majority of the police personnel (57.5 percent) were conscious of the fact that, in general, people do not think well of the kind of job they do. However, a smaller number of participants (42 percent) firmly believed that the people in general thought well of the police job. Most of the police personnel (86 percent) were very much interested in their work; however, at the same time, majority of the respondents felt that they very frequently failed to fulfill the expectations of their families because of the demands of their work.[4]

A study was conducted in Bhopal in the year 2001 to understand the opinion of the policemen whose image and attitude has been a matter of discussion for a long time.[5] To understand someone's attitude in totality, it becomes necessary that we hear their part of the story so that a clear and more authentic picture can be drawn. As respondents, 75 policemen were chosen for the study, ranging from constabulary to DSP level, as they are at the cutting edge for all practical purposes. They were those police personnel who were in direct and lively contact

---

[4] Mishra, R. and S. Mohanty. 1992. *Police and Social Change in India: History and Development of Police*. New Delhi: Ashish Publishing House.

[5] Mishra, V. 2004. "Changing Image of Police: An Empirical Study," PhD Thesis, Barkatullah University, Bhopal.

with the public, and whose every action and inaction had an immense value in establishing the image of the police.

On being asked about the common perception of the public, that police is inhumane, they had different reasons to quote. More than a half of them (around 60 percent) opined that this impression was spread by hearsays rather than supported by facts. While 30 percent response was that most of the time their behavior got impolite because of the stressful working conditions and long working hours. Other factors coming to light were like high expectation of the public from the police (35 percent). The services provided by them always fell short of public expectations resulting in increasing chasm between expectations and their fulfillment. Another factor was that the public was in a habit of drawing comparisons with the predecessors and other colleagues, which caused much irritation and jealousy resulting in undesired behavior (20 percent).

When asked if they were able to fulfill their family responsibilities, respondents agreed that their children had become a victim of bad companionship and they, to great a extent, failed in meeting their family obligations. When questioned about the cause, a very detailed response came forward. They were happy for this question as they felt that the issue was never addressed by anyone in the organization or by anyone else. More than one factor was attributed to this:

- Eighty percent held the opinion that the main cause of the failure to fulfill any family responsibility was the senior officers' attitude. Seniors were not at all concerned about their social and family life and, in fact with lot of pursuance, they used to get only a day or two days leave to attend to some important family work. They were expected to work round the clock.
- Forty percent of the policemen held the public responsible for their problem. According to them, the public do not appreciate the policemen as a family person. Policemen's little enjoyment with their family members was discouraged on the accusation that they are being indifferent toward their work.
- Regarding their children, 90 percent of the respondents said that it was because of unlimited working hours and odd working hours that they could not supervise their children's activities properly.
- Also, they get posted in such remote places (80 percent), many a times with no basic facility for education and no proper environment, that they are helpless.

- Frequent transfers (85 percent) and that too at inopportune times contribute to the children's diversion from concentrating on one thing; as a result, they get confused and get easily swayed by the unwanted elements of the society.

When questioned about the extent to which the expected duties affect their mental and physical health, 85 percent said that they were more worried about the immense mental stress associated with the job expectations than the physical stress. Mental stress was because of the fact that for their acts, without going into the spirit of efforts, they had to bear the brunt of both seniors and the public together (here politicians have been included in the public). Support was missing from all quarters. The agony because of the torture inflicted for one wrong act was so much that it felt like the lack of initiative was the key to success in the job. Seventy-five percent did respond by saying that though mental stress was the main cause of worry, there was also a lot of physical stress associated with job. Physical stress was because of long working hours and odd working hours. Here too 60 percent said that it would be better to ask them to toil for 8–12 hours continuously, but proper time should be given to rest and relax, so that they can re-energize their body. A big group of respondents commented that the working culture was the cause for policemen's all ailments.

When they were asked about how the public treated them and what sort of behavior did they expect from the public, their response was quite optimistic. Sixty percent of the respondents said that the behavior of the public was not good and they were criticized for every action. Appreciation was hard to come from the public. Eighty-five percent responses showed that the public had a dual character as they expected the police to act very sternly when it came to dealing with their problem but, at the same time, when it came to dealing with other's problems, they exerted on the police to respect human rights of every citizen. Interestingly, (80 percent) policemen believed that, intentionally or unintentionally, they are isolated. Even their family members are isolated. Besides the public, the police subculture is to be blamed for this, which automatically supports withdrawal from leading a normal life. However, 90–95 percent of the respondents strongly felt that their expectation from the public was that they should be treated as one of them and they must be supported in their work. Optimism was there; 40 percent said that because of the interaction beyond crime helped in improving the relations between the two.

When asked about the behavior and expectation from the seniors, 95 percent of the respondents said that the behavior of seniors was not at all up to the mark. Few were in fact too open to say that the seniors expected them to be subservient and, particularly in the name of discipline, misbehaved with them. Sixty-five percent of the respondents opined that seniors were hypocrites; on paper they expected something else and practically they were expected to function in a different way. According to them (75 percent), postings were politically motivated, and hence, the seniors now were too politically pliable; as a result, they could not bank on them any more. There was a common belief (85 percent) that seniors did not come to their support in time of need. They wished their seniors to be free from these quoted problems.

When asked that the core responsibility of the police is to "serve the public," even the motto of Madhya Pradesh Police is "Patriotism and Public Service," did their work fall within the zone of expectation? Almost all of the respondents agreed that the police do have a responsibility to serve the public; however, 60 percent said that they fulfilled their responsibility sincerely, while 40 percent of the respondents felt that they could not come to the expected level. The reason for this failure was none other than what they had stated, i.e., lack of support from the public, political interference, overburdened in job besides actual police work, dearth of strong police officers, and so on. What did they actually meant by "strong police officers" needs little deliberation? I tried to get an answer to that by questioning a few of the respondents directly. What they meant was as simple as it spelt. They wanted officers who could stand the pressure from all quarters and who could work with sincerity and extend sincere support in the time of need.

It is interesting to note that the respondents chosen were police personnel from a constable to the level of DSP. However, other studies have also established this fact that the image of the police as perceived by the public is the result of the behavior and attitude of offices of this level, i.e., the "cutting edge level," as they are in contact with the community at every moment. (It has already been explained about the cutting edge level in the preceding chapter.)

On the basis of the study, one interesting aspect was realized. The problem the police are facing had some psychological connotation in nature. They seemed to fail to differentiate between positive thinking and negative thinking. Most of them had the tendency to notice the empty half of the half-filled glass. Hence, they inhabited the tendency to crib and feel frustrated. It is an ironical situation, where rarely any policeman talks good about the job conditions or the nature of the job, but hardly anyone talks about quitting it (particularly at lower echelon). In fact, some confided that what attracts a policeman to stick to this job are all those actions and inactions, which are paying, otherwise considered to be illegal and objected by all.

While imparting training to the police officers, from constable to the level of ASPs at range headquarters and districts, during September–November 2003, on core-skill training areas including sensitization toward weaker sections, attitude and behavior of police, stress management, interview (interrogation) skills, and laws relating to SC/ST, I had chance to have a free interaction with them. Of the 120 trainees, almost all agreed that their attitude was not at all polite, at least toward them who wielded no clout. May be they candidly confessed because we were all police officers, sitting in a friendly atmosphere, and no senior officer (SP and above) was present who could have otherwise taken it ill. The trainees described the following reasons for such behavior:

1. Overload of work: Because of the additional assignments like protocol duties, law and order, rallies and protests, festival duties, and so on, the main work of the police, i.e., registration, investigation, detection, and prosecution have taken a back seat.
2. No family life/social life: Due to overload of work and additional duties they do not get time with their family.
3. Lack of time/long duty hours: Lack of time and long duty hours was also described as a reason for this behavior.
4. Lack of cooperation from public in their work: They are not looked upon as one of them by the public; they are isolated despite the fact that a few years back, before joining this service, they were one of them.
5. Sadistic attitude of seniors: Seniors enjoy troubling the force by calling for duty hours before it is needed. They take care of neither their food nor water when working for long hours at odd places, and at odd times. They enjoy scolding in public and sometimes without even getting to know of the reality of things, overact. Petty politicians, press representatives, or some nonentity are allowed to sit but at the same time even senior supervisory officers are not offered seats. They enjoy calling meetings in the middle of the night. These things are completely missing in all other departments.
6. Contradictions in expectation and orders of seniors: In fact, participants went to the extent of pointing out that it is taught in all trainings that we need to change our attitude. We are supposed to trouble no one. Interrogation must be in the form of an

interview (one of the important subjects of training), but at the same time under some operations (like Ankush, Shikanja, Elections, Festivals, and so on), seniors pressurize to arrest people under prevention sections. To ensure under pressure that warrants are executed to reach the target level, we are compelled to harass their relatives. To achieve target in property offences and to detect body offences, all sorts of measures have to be applied. Why is there such a big contradiction between what is desired in the field and what is taught in the classroom? There is a state of confusion presently as to what attitude has to be kept and how should they behave.

7. Noncooperation by seniors at the time of need: Orders are given mostly verbally and when a subordinate falls in trouble, seniors to save their skin just let them face the music. Sometimes they do not even think of taking moral responsibility in such situations, leave alone standing up to protect them.

8. Too much pressure from politicians or other pressure groups: They are so used to satisfying these people even unwillingly, that the frustration is vented out on the helpless complainants.

I have been a part of the training sessions ever since, and surprisingly have not found much change in the attitude and perception till date.

Some of the attitudinal problems that are faced could be attributed to the approach toward the job. Day in and day out, the police personnel work, talk, eat, and sleep police. Whenever policemen meet, they prefer talking police or job-related issues. They even carry their job home. The impact of such an attitude can be understood from the fact that, my co-trainers, psychologists, and sociologists, with 20–25 years of experience, did not know much about the law. Though it is presumed that once a law enacted and promulgated, lack of knowledge of the law is no excuse to get away from prosecution. However, most of the policemen's children and wives, irrespective of their level of literacy, can quote various sections of relevant laws. Police personnel normally get so engrossed in their jobs that they forget their social obligations. They prefer getting dissociated with the common man on the pretext of lack of time. In fact, they get so engrossed in work that they keep in contact with only those persons who matter professionally and serve their interests. Interaction is to meet selfish ends. In fact, the work culture is such that the police, as a social animal, are not accepted either by the seniors (police) or by the society. They are alienated by the organization blaming them to be too soft and, therefore, incapable of doing their job. At the same time, the society points them out saying that he does not look as a police officer. Police personnel gradually have to adopt all the ills of the police job for their survival and to rated high in the society as well as within the organization.

Normally, what a senior officer asks his subordinates is to be strict. Strictness is misconstrued as getting foul mouth and body blasting. It does not imply to them that it may be a synonym to impartial enforcement of law and no advantages should be given to anyone irrespective of his/her caste, class, creed, and political affiliations. Maybe in a few instances when due to administrative reasons supervisors digress from what they speak, it is interpreted as a rule to be followed. But the participants here very vehemently objected my opinion and reiterated that this justification would stand for what existed in bygone days; now there is no confusion that officers coming are *hypocrites*. They do not deviate but their every action can be regarded as a calculated move, according to what suits them.

A very interesting fact came to light while asking the trainees the meaning of interrogation. More than half the trainees invariably said that it is a method of extracting confessions by whatever means (obviously torture, as they said it in Hindi, *Danda aur Aatank*). What methods of interrogation the police are going to apply are paradoxically chosen by the accused because the accused, by deciding how fast they are going to confess, can avoid many unpleasant moments for themselves. They can save themselves by confessing immediately, the way the interrogator desires.

Most of the policemen, including the high-ranked police officers, lack interest in reading and writing. Even the column they read in the newspaper is that which contains something about the police. While browsing, they first look for news related to their own police stations, then about their districts, and then something of their interest in the state. They barely go beyond that. If anyone has any academic interest, he/she is branded as unfit for the police job. When compared to the other institutions, policemen find themselves lost, particularly the lower echelons, which constitute more than 90 percent of the police force. In fact, leaving aside the State, National, or International affairs, they are oblivious of what is happening within their district if it was not directly related to crime. When in Chindawara district, I asked them if they had any knowledge about Sashaktikaran Kendra (Empowerment Center), which was mandatory, 98 percent of the trainees (at the rank of inspectors and below) showed their ignorance while the Empowerment Center was established a year back and was operational in the police line to conduct training. In fact the success of that center, as a part of community policing, was possible only with the support of the police stations. Surprisingly, all the ignorant participants were from the police stations. It was a pain to witness that one of the major initiative to empower the weaker section was so ineffectively implemented; a total lack of conceptual literacy.

Thus, incompetent, untrained, and undisciplined policemen invariably provide unsatisfactory services, damage the reputation of their own departments, and promote unfavorable public opinion throughout the country. The "closed structure" of the police has resulted in growing isolation and gradual alienation of the police from the general community. It has created unnecessary dilemmas and inhibitions hampering the community's participation in the police work. Authoritarianism is frequently the all-encompassing attribute charged against the working police officer.

Studies have also indicated that the police personality is merely a reflection of the dominant cultural personality of citizens with whom the police primarily interact. In addition, policemen are overburdened with work and such pressure of work will cause a lot of mental and physical stress and strain. Finally, it is important to note that if the public has the right to define the behavior of the police and they expect the police to change their attitude, the police has also all the right to expect a particular behavior from public, which finally will be transformed into better services.

There are some relevant issues of concern in the third level of the tier system—the cutting edge level. This level of officers appears to have little faith in the public. They allege that the police work is done mostly under strong political pressure. They feel that undue restraint is put on them and they are made accountable for most of the social ills. Paradoxically, the police are accorded low status and respect by the community; however, they are expected to perform a complex job under conditions which are often frustrating.

Thus, the grievances of the police personnel against the public are diverse and variegated in nature, including organization of social, economic, and psychological factors. In a recent study, Nandy observed that the police officers are criticized by one group of the community for not enforcing certain laws, and are hated, and are sworn at by another group of the same community for enforcing those same laws.[6] This shared misunderstanding spirals conflict between citizens and the

---

[6] Mishra, V. 2004. "Changing Image of Police: An Empirical Study," PhD Thesis, Barkatullah University, Bhopal.

police. In fact, among the police, the image of public antipathy toward them is largely the product of their selective contact with the citizens.

The use of extralegal methods highlights the genuine moral dilemma faced by the police in achieving the unquestionably good ends through dirty means. This has been called the "Dirty Harry problem" by some American criminologists (the name is derived from the Warner Brothers film, *Dirt Harry*, and its chief protagonist, an antihero, Inspector Harry). But the danger lies in the fact that often the policemen lose their moral proportion, turn cynical, and see their dirty acts not as a means to achieve good ends but as ends in themselves.

Political and bureaucratic controls have created a situation of goal displacement and contradictions vis-à-vis the basic functions of the police as the law enforcers. The failure of basic institutions of the society, increase in population without the growth of proper human resource, and the lack of inherent social control, proper growth, equality of opportunities, proper diffusion of welfare ideologies, and so on, have created an environment where the political parties in power make use of the police to control the disadvantaged classes and to suppress their agitations when they air their grievances. The conflict between the role and goal has enhanced the tension levels and given birth to new contradictions. The stick (police action) and carrot (concessions) approach toward the less privileged and the glaring gap between them and the traditional elite has given rise to neo-elite in the society who are more political and opportunistic, i.e., exploitative in nature and fond of propagating "half-truths." This has also been an offshoot of the mismatch between the idealism presumed by our constitution and the legal enactments on one hand and the ground level organic reality on the other.[7]

The craving of the officers for achievements, which will bring them psychological and material rewards like fame, field postings, recognition through gallantry medals, out-of-turn promotions, monetary rewards, and so on, sometimes prompt them to resort to extralegal, but effective, measures like torture and killings in "encounters." The preoccupation with statistics, the peculiar mindset of an average policeman that he/she is responsible to cure all of the ills of the society, and the failure of the other wings of the criminal justice system often drive policemen to desperation and use of questionable methods.

---

[7] Maheshwari, A.P. 2000. "Crisis of Policing in India," *SVPNPA Journal*, 52(2): 124–30, July–December.

Another major causative factor is the deplorable working conditions of the police and the manner in which the public and the seniors treat them, which develops poor self-image and low self-esteem in average policemen. This results in venting out of their frustration on the hapless public. The pay structure, prerequisites, working conditions, and prospects for career advancement of the police personnel at the lower ranks are not sufficient to attract proper recruits with right attitudes. Their daily interaction with the basic human instincts, the adversarial role in which they are placed vis-à-vis the public, and the conflicting expectations from them have a serious dehumanizing effect on them. This occasionally manifests itself in brutal ways. The repetitive nature of their work, boredom, long hours of duty, separation from family, high stress, pent-up frustrations encountered in a society having no respect for law, and so on, reinforce these negative feelings.[8]

The image of the police is far away from the desired picture. It is high time that in order to regain the confidence of the public, in the indispensable institution of the police, they resort to some correctional methods. One important point to be made clear is that the police are no "cult" as they are normally treated. From time immemorial, in every society, there has been a mechanism to check action and inaction of members of the society, which does not fall within the set rules and regulations of the society. To enforce these laws, few selected members of the society were authorized to bring to book the defaulters. This, in fact, is technically termed as policing, depicting disciplined acceptance of law promulgated by the consent of the society. So, there always existed a system ensuring the abidance of law. These policemen, however, were used by the governing bodies of the societies according to their own interest. The colonial era witnessed the police as a subservient organization, which was hell bent to satisfy their masters by adopting all brutal methods. Unfortunately, even after independence, our subsequent governments could not do away with the archaic police acts. Consequently, despite the fact that the police were gradually vested with welfare-oriented roles, lack of conducive laws restrained them from doing justice to their new role. Their barbaric image which the police could not do away with is, to a great extent, because of reasons beyond their control. New police regulations as recommended by the police commissions should be brought into effect.

---

[8] Devarajan, M.K. 2000. "Attitudinal Changes for Better Policing," *SVP National Police Academy Journal*, 52(1): 50–56, January–June.

Training

There is a Chinese proverb, "If you want to plan for a year, sow rice; if for a decade then plant a tree; if you want to plan for your lifetime, train your manpower." Training is an inevitable part of human resource development. It is normally of two types: basic training, i.e., after induction into the unit and the in-service training when working in the unit. Basic training is to acquaint about the service conditions, expectations from them, and more knowledge about what they are supposed to do. It helps the trainees to cope with the needs of the service. In-service training is to give inputs about the new developments in the service. Mark Twain has rightly said, "Training is everything. The peach was once a bitter almond; cauliflower is nothing but a cabbage with a college education." Training is the key to success in any organization. The importance of training has been seriously taken up lately and lot many training programs are being organized.

The training condition of constables is pathetic. They are treated more or less like a machine than as an asset to the force. There is evidence of the age old colonial concept of military police deeply rooted in the minds of administrators. No effort is made to update the system as per the need of the community. What is required is to cater to their needs as civilian police rather than military police. Earlier, educational requirement for joining the police as a constable was 8th standard, now it has been changed to 10th standard. A close perusal of applicants' profiles show that not less than 25 percent of the applicants are graduates. Now, looking at the type of work assigned to a constable and the desirable attitude, it is advisable to have entrants with higher qualification. The need of the day is that policemen with better understanding of the public's psyche are required. With increased emphasis on participative policing and humane touch, un-thought of in bygone days, is required in every action. A person with high ability, intelligence, and competence can handle the situation better. Along with more qualified entrants, more advanced training methods are also required, which would make a constable professionally competent.

Today, the in-service training has become a buzzword for almost all institutions. The police department is no exception. If we seriously look into the scenario of the basic training of the new entrants, we find that the training of the Indian Police Service (IPS) officers conducted at Sardar Vallabhbhai Patel (SVP) National Police Academy,

Hyderabad, has been updated taking into consideration the need of the time, as well as the latest management concepts, along with the required training for a policeman is imparted. But not all states are taking equal interest in the basic training of officers of the state police service as well as for constabulary who constitute the cutting edge level and are major agents of opinion building of the police. The training skills of the trainers and their academic interest in most of the cases are not up to the mark. Moreover, the trainers posted at training institutions are those who have been shunted on the ground of disciplinary and administrative action. Consequently, their morale is very low and, in fact, they give a very negative picture of the organization and officers. They do not have any interest in either teaching or improving the environment of the academy. From day one the trainees are told about the ills of the organization and shortcut methods of survival under the garb of practical approach. This practical approach would always speak volumes about benefits of yesmanship and making a political godfather but hardly about garnering the community's support. In order to appreciate the great challenge of fostering core values of professional policing and equipping the police subordinates with knowledge and skills, one must understand that more than 90 percent of the police organizations in India comprise of officers of the rank of ASI or below. For the department to be professionally more competent, it is advisable to establish an agency "Knowledge Management Cell" for creation, dissemination, renewal, and application of knowledge toward organizational sustenance, survival, and progress, with a specific trained "Knowledge Management Officer" to take care of that cell. The knowledge would range from that required for policymaking to simple operational matters of day-to-day importance.[9]

[9] Jain, M. 2000. "Need for Knowledge Management in Police," *SVP National Academy Journal*, 52(1): 99–112, January–June.

8

Variables Acting as Hindrance to Participative Policing

Bounded Rationality

In the face of a complex problem, normally to respond, the problem is reduced to an understandable level. This is accredited to the limited information-processing capability of human beings, which makes it impossible to assimilate and understand all the information necessary to optimize.[1] People tend to *satisfice*, i.e., they seek solutions that are satisfactory and sufficient.[2] Because of the restricted capacity of the human mind to meet the requirements of full rationality, individuals operate within the confines of bounded rationality. They construct simplified models that extract the essential features from the problems without capturing all their complexity.[3] Keeping this concept of bounded rationality in mind, this chapter will provide an insight about some of the variables, which have been influencing the perception of the public, eventually governing their level of participation. These variables incorporated are first, the police's attitude-related variables and second, the variables of the society influencing their perception.

---

[1] Kahneman, D. 2003. "Maps of Bounded Rationality: Psychology for Behavioral Economics," *The American Economic Review*, 93(5): 1449–75.

[2] Robbins, Stephen P. and A. Timothy Judge. 2007. *Organizational Behavior*, Twelfth Edition. New Delhi: Prentice-Hall of India Private Limited.

[3] Simon, H.A. 1997. *Administrative Behavior*, 4th edition. New York: Free Press; Augier, M. 2001. "Simon Says: Bounded Rationality Matters," *Journal of Management Inquiry*, 10: 268–75, September.

Police's Attitude-related Variables

HIGH-HANDEDNESS AND RUDENESS

It is frequently alleged that the police personnel resort to brutal methods and practices in their dealings with the citizens or otherwise misbehave with them. This is a somewhat curious phenomenon in view of the fact that the police, as an organization and in its philosophy, appear to have become more enlightened and more humane than it was in the past. This is evident not only from the greater emphasis on the modern scientific approach to crime and investigation, which, to a large extent, eliminates the need to resort to third degree methods, but also from the increasing replacement of the lethal by non-lethal equipments by the police for dealing with riotous mobs.

Torture by the police is one of the main and frequent accusations leveled on the police. It is believed that the police's torture of prisoners is colonial legacy but in the independent India, resorting to torture has become more frequent than in the colonial era. In D. K. Basu case, 1997, the Supreme Court drafted guidelines to be followed by the police for arrest and interrogation. Later, the court directed the State Human Rights Commission to ensure that the guidelines were adhered to. Yet, complaints about the violation of norms are increasing day-by-day. A study conducted by Campaign for Custodial Justice and Abolition of Torture revealed that in Tamil Nadu alone, 36 complaints investigated were found correct between May and October 2002. The people alleged that they were beaten up and humiliated, and many women complained against the police officers for asking nasty questions. The police used abusive language against complainants, called them by their caste name; illegal detention being frequent.[4]

Kelley's study (1983) on 100 rape victims revealed that the satisfaction of the rape victims depends primarily on how they were treated by the police rather than whether the offender was punished, or whether compensation was paid.[5] The study also revealed that the rape victims' primary objections were that they were treated as witnesses and not as

---

[4] Viswanathan, S. 2003. "A Tale of Torture," *Frontline*, Delhi, August 15.
[5] Kelley, D.P. 1983. *Rape Victims' Perception of Criminal Justice*. Baltimore, Maryland: John Hopkins University.

people and that they were excluded from the deliberations and denied information about the case development.

Appointment of Public Relations Officers and initiation of more community relations projects by the police are again an indication of a growing desire on the part of the police to win the support, esteem, and cooperation of the public. What then is the raison d'être for the increasing complaints of the citizens against police misbehavior and for the wide gulf between the police and the public, which exists in various countries, including India? Though the organizational philosophy may have become more enlightened, the fact remains that the instances of individual policemen misbehaving with the public are not rare. This shows that all its members have not internalized the philosophy of the organization. Every force has some bad eggs that, by their misbehavior, bring a bad name to the whole organization and spoil its credibility. This happens because the public does not make any distinction between the organization and its individual members. To the public, every policeman is the police force. The good which the force does dies and the evil which the policeman does lives forever, producing a cumulative reaction of hostility and opposition on the part of the public. It is precisely for these reasons that the United States Commission on Civil Rights laid such great stress on the behavior of individual policeman.[6] Many studies have shown that young, inexperienced officers, in an attempt to show their presence, are more aggressive, intolerant, and use more force than required.[7]

DOUBTFUL INTEGRITY

Another important factor, which erodes the trust of the public in the police, is the doubtful integrity of the police. They are accused of being

---

[6] US Commission on Civil Rights. 1981. "The Report of the U.S. Commission on Civil Rights," Vol. V. Washington DC: Government Printing Office.

[7] Hunt, J. 1985. "Police Accounts of Normal Force," *Urban Life*, 13(1985): 315–41; Terrill, W. and S. Mastrofski. 2002. "Situational and Officer-based Determinants of Police Coercion," *Justice Quarterly*, 19(2): 215–48; Van Maanen, J. 1974. "Working the Street: A Developmental View of Police Behavior," in H. Jacob (ed.), *The Potential for Reform of Criminal Justice*, pp. 88–130. Beverly Hills, CA: SAGE; Van Maanen, J. 1978. "The Asshole," in P.K. Manning and J. Van Maanen (eds), *Policing: A View from the Street*, pp. 227–38. Santa Monica, CA: Goodyear; Harris, Christopher J. 2009. "Exploring the Relationship Between Experience and Problem Behaviors: A Longitudinal Analysis of Officers From a Large Cohort," *Police Quarterly*, 12(2): 192–213.

corrupt. Corruption is a taint, which deprives the force of the public esteem and cooperation. The problem of the police corruption is not of recent origin. The stigma has been attached to the police right since the early days. The Victorian catchphrase "If you want to know the time, ask the policeman" originated out of the belief that the policeman used to remove the watches from the pockets of drunken revelers. This popular image of the policeman has, somehow, persisted right up to the present age. However, the gravity of the problem is different in different countries; but no country, not even a policeman, denies the fact that corruption, in some form or the other, exists in almost all the forces.

Involvement of the policemen in crimes, particularly crimes which have had long-lasting effect on the national scene, has further tarnished the image of the police. The assassination of Indira Gandhi, the then Prime Minister of the country, resulted in the loss of faith in the police institution to a great extent. A lot of hard work had to be done to restore the lost faith, though even till date it is cited as an example to doubt the policemen.

Few incidents of senior police officers being dragged into controversies like rape and murder (few examples like R.K. Sharma (IGP) in Shivani murder case; one Inspector Y.N. Dixit arrested in the Madhumita murder case as accused by the CBI of suppression of evidence and illegal confinement of people; recent case of molestation of Ruchika by IGP, now retired DGP Rathode in Haryana) bring a bad name to the whole organization.

These incidents have an impact on the overall image of the police. No common person is bothered about the name of the perpetrator but everybody believes that the police, as an organization, are unreliable. Custodians looked upon as perpetrators of sin, dips the trust of people and ultimately the image gets a showdown. FTD widens. The police rely on their legitimacy with the public to perform their duties. Such legitimacy is embedded in the confidence the citizens have in their local police, which is damaged when the police behave poorly in their encounters with the public.[8]

---

[8] Harris, Christopher J. 2009. "Exploring the Relationship Between Experience and Problem Behaviors: A Longitudinal Analysis of Officers From a Large Cohort," *Police Quarterly*, 12(2): 192–213.

LOPSIDED LAW ENFORCEMENT

It is widely believed by the public that enforcement of law by the police is not equal. Filial affiliations dominate during the execution of law. "Show me your face and I will tell you the rule/law," has become a practice. Politoxication, criminal nexus, dominance of corruption, erosion of values, external and internal pressure, and above all, the survival instincts have drifted the policemen from traversing the path of law.

On the contrary, the justification that the police pass on the buck for the lopsided law enforcement on the community is by citing certain reasons. First, the police feel that expectations of the public are not always clear, consistent, and based on realistic considerations. Every member of the public wants effective and impartial law enforcement as long as he/she remains its beneficiary and does not become its victim. Second, the police do not exist and function in vacuum as they have to operate within the society. To build up a proper climate of trust between the police and the public, it is important that the public realize the limitations within which the police have to work. Third, the policemen feel that in spite of their difficulties, hardships, and problems, they have never received adequate recognition from the public and its representatives in power. Fourth, in a situation where the partiality is the order of the day in all sectors of the society, their impartiality is a utopian expectation. The feeling of discontent arising as a result of this is shared by policemen in almost all the countries.[9]

In the recent case against the retired DGP of Haryana, in Ruchika's molestation and suicide abetment case, the CBI in its appeal against the court verdict stated:

> Ruchika was a minor while Rathode was a high-ranking police officer of Haryana. It was a duty of the IGP to protect the vulnerable citizen but he himself committed molestation of a minor girl.... After submission of memorandum by the victim, Rathode unleashed a reign of terror on probable witness in order to refrain themselves from pursuing the matter further.[10]

---

[9] Joshi, G.P. 1985. "The Basis of Police Authority Cannot be Mere Law: It Has to be Public Trust Too," *Essays on Police Community Relations*, pp. 11–19. Hyderabad: SVPN Academy.

[10] Bhardwaj, Supriya. 2010. "Ruchika's Molestation Predetermined: CBI," *Times of India*, Ahmedabad, February 5.

The use of "touts" by the police and particularly by the investigating officers who extract money on their behalf from innocent persons on the threat of involving them in criminal cases and sometimes even getting innocent persons implicated in criminal cases is generating considerable anger, particularly in rural areas. Unless the supervisory officers break this racket and remove touts from the system, the police will fail to invite cooperation from the community.

To be ignorant of one's ignorance is the malady of ignorance. It is an irony that the most powerful are unaware of their power. Public forgets that they are the kingmakers, and nefarious designs of anyone can be confronted by voicing their opinion vehemently. It is needed that they rely more on facts and cross-check the truthfulness of statements and actions than believing in rumors. Rights have to be earned and for that, knowledge, alertness, and assertiveness are prerequisites. The prevailing ignorance is deterrent and detrimental in the proper understanding between two important sections of the society, law enforcers and law abiders. Common person's lack of knowledge is exploited to create chasm between the two. In fact, the hatred of the police engrained in the minds of common persons is so deep that victim looks upon even the interrogation and investigation as harassment. Under such conditions, cooperation in their effort is a far cry. The misconception that the police is a foe and not friend is the main hurdle, which has to be obliterated. Public is so averse that the overaction by the police invites a lot of hue and cry but less is done for inaction, other than issues having political importance. This is a harmful trend existing as it is necessary to realize that not failure but low aim is a crime. By action, at least the police are striving to serve. Policemen are also humans. To err is human, so if any action goes wrong, constructive condemnation must be coming with attempts on the part of the police to rectify the mistake committed.

The Government of India document of the year 2002 stated:

> ... there are innumerable complaints of misuse of powers by the police including arbitrary arrests and unnecessarily long detention in custody, not to mention the large-scale violations of human rights. The Criminal Justice System does not seem to operate evenly, as the rich and the powerful hardly get implicated, much less convicted, even in case of serious crimes. The growing nexus between crime and politics has added a new dimension to the crime scenario. Victims feel ignored and are crying for attention and justice. In sum, not only is the system slow, inefficient, ineffective, but also costly and corrupt. People by and large have lost

confidence in the Criminal Justice System and fear that the country is dangerously racing towards anarchy.

Could there be a more damning condemnation of our present system?[11]

A better police–public understanding can be ensured only through a meaningful interaction between the two segments during normal times rather than struggling at the time of conflict and crisis. Police officials need to remember that not even 1 percent of the public is criminal or criminal minded and hence, they are not to be tough looking with one and all. In fact, people normally get in touch with the police only in distress. As it is with the human psyche, in distress, one is not willing to hear others' woes, so they are not in a position to get enlightened with the constraints of the police, whatsoever it is. Therefore, it is not appreciable for the police officers to enlist their problems at that time. Such arguments could, however, be advanced at various forums in normal times.

A study by Rao indicated that lesser the awareness about the police work and the police constraints, more are the mistaken impressions of the students about the police. In this study, 2,071 adolescent students from nine different mega metropolitan cities of India were asked as to "whether they have met a policeman ever and talked to him/her." For this question, the response of 72 percent of the students was negative. In a city-wise analysis, students of Bangalore (85 percent) and Mumbai (82.2 percent) stated to have never or rarely met policemen. In comparison to male students (67 pecent), female students (78 percent) reported least contact. A further analysis of the impression of these students with least interaction with the police indicated that 75 percent of them spoke ill of the police and the police mechanism, while 60–90 percent students stated that the police are corrupt. Sixty-one to seventy-five percent students stated that people are afraid to lodge complaints to the police and 32–56 percent disagreed that the police are sympathetic to people. The basis of such impressions of young adults was nothing other than the media (63–70 percent), while 13–21 percent of them confirmed that they have had a personal experience. On the other hand, after a few interactive sessions with the students, it was found that with improved awareness about the police and their working mechanisms, the students improved their perceptions about

---

[11] Rizvi, S.K. 2002. "Delivery of Service by Police: Quality and Cost," *The Indian Police Journal*, IL(3): 96, July–September.

them. Such a proactive approach has been found to be very important because today's young children are tomorrow's citizen from whom the police expects cooperation and support.[12]

A similar study was conducted in Bhopal,[13] during 1998–99, on 250 students from different schools (varying from convent to public schools) hailing from cross sections of the society including all castes, classes, and religions. These students were chosen from both old Bhopal city with more·Muslim population and New Bhopal city with more Hindu population. This was deliberately done because Bhopal has been a communally sensitive capital, witnessing one of the worst communal riots in 1993. Since then, the police have become so over-sensitive that a simple incident has been very sternly dealt with. Lots of precautions are taken by changing the whole city into a cant area, deploying rapid action force, special task force, and special armed force companies in no time at the slightest apprehension of tension brewing. The students chosen were from class 8 to 12, as they were expected to be mature enough to comprehend the tension, if at all it mounted due to the police action or inaction. After analyzing the responses of the students obtained through the questionnaire, an interactive session with the students was organized to understand the cause of the feedback.

This study revealed that when the students were asked about the character of the police, 95 percent of the students' response was that they were brutal, corrupt, and inhumane. The few who spared were having their parents or some other first kin members in the police services, 85 percent of the students said that women, girls in particular, should not go to the police stations. When the students were asked why they think so, the common response was that there are fair chances of being ill-treated by the police. Sixty percent of the students thought that the police were responsible for all wrongs in the society because they believed that the police had enough powers to check whatever happens in the society and the crime that happens is with the police's consent. Similarly, when asked if the police can be an important agent of social change, surprisingly, 80 percent responded with affirmation. The answer again coming out of the same perception that the police have enough power and authority to do what they wish to.

[12] Rao, U.N.B. 2000. "Proactive Techniques Tried out for Improving Performance of Police," 52(1): 85–99, January–June.
[13] Mishra. V. 2004. "Changing Image of Police: An Empirical Study," PhD Thesis. Barkatullah University, Bhopal.

Most mind-boggling data that came to light and which calls for serious attention of the police officers was that 85 percent of the respondents said that what image they perceived was acquired from a secondary source. Mass media was the main culprit according to 88 percent of the participants. Entertainment media (movies, TV serials, and so on) and the press (electronic and print), which very often shows one-sided story, is the main source for building of a negative image of the police. Parents and other family members also play crucial roles in spreading this lopsided perception of the police. Ninety percent of the participants agreed that no one ever appreciated or encouraged interaction with the police, but in fact, they are always portrayed as a disgraced institution, which should be shunned. While asking about the role of school, students reiterated that schools encouraged them to avoid the police not only during the normal course of life, but also they were asked not to report cases of eve-teasing or any other such instances as that would bring a bad name to them and their family and, at the same time, they will be harassed by the police (85 percent). Another interesting fact that the study revealed was that hardly 5 percent of the students had come in direct contact with the police, other than those who had their family members in this organization. Those who did, there was hardly any instance to quote where these children, who were to step into adolescence, had experienced some bad interaction with the police. So, at least this study highlights one fact that the police solely cannot be held responsible for the negative image in the public.

Sociocultural–economic Variables of the Society Influencing Perception

There are researches which establish the fact that there are a number of variables which influence the individual's perception toward the police. Some of the factors are age, caste, religion and race, gender, socioeconomic status, and others as mentioned below:

- Age factor: Most of the research shows a positive relationship between age and attitudes toward the police. The youth seem to be more alienated from the police than oldies.[14] Research findings suggest that as people age, their satisfaction with the police continues to increase, until a certain age level, beyond which attitudes toward the police begin to decrease again.

- Socioeconomic status: Poorer people and those from lower socioeconomic classes tend to report less satisfaction with the police than those who are wealthier. For instance, Benson[15] found that the respondents from lower social classes were less satisfied with the police. Similarly, Brown and Philip[16] found that income and education both had a positive effect on the satisfaction of people with treatment they received by the police (a variable that can be viewed as both, an indicator of the general image of the police and as an indicator of the image associated specifically with the police process). However, both Hindelang and Jesilow and Meyer and Namazzi[17] report that education had no effect on attitudes toward the police. Decker notes an important concern about the role of socioeconomic status (SES). However, it is not clear whether it is the individual's socioeconomic status that influences attitudes toward the police, whether it is the status of the neighborhood, or whether these two variables interact.
- Gender: The relationship between gender and satisfaction with the police is unclear. At least two studies have found that males

---

[14] Brown, K. and B.C. Philip. 1983. "Subjective and Objective Measures of Police Service Delivery," *Public Administration Review*, 43: 50–58, January–February; Huang, W.S., W. Wilson, and S.V. Michael. 1996. "Support and Confidence: Public Attitudes Toward the Police," in T.J. Flanagan and D.R. Longmire (eds), *American View of Crime and Justice: A National Opinion Survey*, pp. 31–45. Thousand Oaks, CA: SAGE; Jesilow, P., J. Meyer and N. Namazzi. 1995. "Public Attitudes Toward the Police," *American Journal of Police*, 14(2): 67–88; Smith, P.E. and O.H. Richard. 1973. "Victimization, Types of Citizen-police Contacts, and Attitudes Toward the Police," *Law and Society Review*, 8(1): 135–52.

[15] Benson, P. 1981. "Political Alienation and Public Satisfaction with Police Service," *Pacific Sociological Review*, 24(1): 45–64.

[16] Brown, K. and B.C. Philip. 1983. "Subjective and Objective Measures of Police Service Delivery," *Public Administration Review*, 43: 50–58, January–February.

[17] Hindelang, M.J. 1974. "Public Opinion Regarding Crime, Criminal Justice and Related Topics," *Journal of Research in Crime and Delinquency*, 11(2): 101–16; Jesilow, P., J. Meyer and N. Namazzi. 1995. "Public Attitudes Toward the Police," *American Journal of Police*, 14: 67–88.

hold more positive views than females.[18] Other studies have found that females hold more positive views than males.[19] Still another study has found that gender has no effect.[20] In the Indian cultural context, it is generally observed that women normally would detest going to police stations. Given a choice, they would prefer meeting female police officers than male. In the absence of such arrangement, the victim more often has to face embarrassment and humiliation.

- Caste, religion, and race: One of the most persistent findings in public opinion polls, abroad, about the police is that whites are more satisfied with the police than blacks. This finding has been consistent over the past four decades, emerging from dozens of studies and polls, both in the United States and abroad.[21] Generally, Asians and Hispanics are dissatisfied with the police in the USA and European countries. Study done on community policing in Chicago by Wesley and Hartnett[22] revealed this interesting fact. The same community policing efforts had a different impact on different communities. Some groups who had a low opinion about the quality of policing registered improvement in their perception after participating but the Hispanics did not participate and there was no improvement in their opinion. When officers were interviewed, the black and Hispanic officers

[18] Thomas, C.W. and J.M. Hyman. 1977. "Perception of Crime: Fear of Victimization and Public Perception of Police Performance," *Journal of Police Science and Administration*, 5(3): 305–17, September; Brown, K. and B.C. Philip. 1983. "Subjective and Objective Measures of Police Service Delivery," *Public Administration Review*, 43: 50–58, January–February.
[19] Huang, W.S., Wilson, and S.V. Michael. 1996. "Support and Confidence: Public Attitudes Toward the Police," in T.J. Flanagan and D.R. Longmire (eds), *American View of Crime and Justice: A National Opinion Survey*, pp. 31–45. Thousand Oaks, CA: SAGE.
[20] Hurst, Y.G. and F. James. 2000. "How Kids View Cops: The Nature of Juvenile Attitudes Toward the Police," *Journal of Criminal Justice*, 28(3), 189–202.
[21] Bayley, D.H. and H. Mendelsohn. 1969. *Minorities and the Police*. New York: Free Press; Bradley, R. 1998. "Public Expectations and Perceptions of Policing," Police Research Series Paper 96. London: Home Office; Cao, L., James F. and T.C. Race Francis. 1996. "Community Context, and Confidence in the Police," *American Journal of Police*, 15 (1): 3–22; Huang, W.S., Wilson, and S.V. Michael. 1996. "Support and Confidence: Public Attitudes Toward the Police," in T.J. Flanagan and D.R. Longmire (eds), *American View of Crime and Justice: A National Opinion Survey*, pp. 31–45. Thousand Oaks, CA: SAGE.
[22] Skogan, Wesley G. and Susan M. Hartnett. 1997. *Community Policing: The Chicago Style*. New York: Oxford University Press.

were more optimistic about community policing than white officers. The cleavages within the community got mirrored in police department.

In India, the caste factor has an important role to play. At some places, people of certain religions do not trust the police, particularly during communal tension (e.g., Gujarat). In northeastern states of India, and lately in Maharashtra, Hindi-speaking people were asked to leave the state and there were violent attacks on them. In these states the role of the police was questioned.

- Other influences: There are research findings, which have found that people living in the suburbs have better attitudes toward the police than people living in urban areas.[23] Another study confirms, what might be viewed as common sense, that juveniles with a commitment to delinquent norms are less satisfied with the police.[24]

[23] Hindelang, M.J. 1974. "Public Opinion Regarding Crime, Criminal Justice and Related Topics," *Journal of Research in Crime and Delinquency*, 11(2), 101–16; Hurst, Y.G. and F. James. 2000. "How Kids View Cops: The Nature of Juvenile Attitudes Toward the Police," *Journal of Criminal Justice*, 28, 189–202; Thomas, C.W. and J.M. Hyman. 1977. "Perception of Crime: Fear of Victimization and Public Perception of Police Performance," *Journal of Police Science and Administration*, 5, 305.

[24] Leiber, M.J., M.K. Nalla, and M. Farnworth. 1998. "Explaining Juveniles' Attitudes Toward the Police," *Justice Quarterly*, 15(1): 151–73.

9

Benefits of Participation

Participative Policing (PP): A Necessity

Has the community been participating in policing work prior to the concept of community policing or participative policing (PP) was thought about? The answer is yes. The community has been participating in all activities of traditional policing. Traditional policing, which involves receiving complaint/registration of cases/investigation/ apprehending the culprits/putting the case for prosecution, involves the members of the community right from its onset; every step involves the community members. However, the saddest part is that community is oblivious of their participation; hence, their participation is not active. Second, the persons who matter participate. It is a coercive participation of the community rather than a willing participation.

Can PP, which invites "conscious" partnership and collaboration with the community, be a successful method of crime control? I am starting this deliberation with a question. It is not my cynicism; instead, it is the doubt in the minds of parties to be involved that has forced me to start on a questionable note. I am an optimist, and what has led me to be so positive on its effectiveness is what I have already reiterated in the preceding chapters explaining its utility and inevitability. In this chapter, we will further try to weigh up and cement our firm belief.

The bottom line of this chapter is that PP is an indispensable approach now. Neither can the police think of success without the community's assistance nor can the community imagine safety and security without collaborating with the police. They will have to work in tandem, understand the need of each other, synergize their efforts, complement each others' strength, and cover each others' weaknesses. Having that perspective by both will give short-term returns as well as help reap long-term benefits. The misdirected perspective due to the above mentioned causes has not only harmed them but the society and the nation immensely. A clear perspective based on honesty and understanding gives insight into the problems and helps find a solution collectively and constructively. The right perspective will make the real difference and fortify the spirit of collaboration. There is a hidden potential of the masses to assist in policing duties to ensure that proper law and order is maintained, even in an intense terror-threat environment. Every child, adult, or aged person must be prepared to act as a policeman wherever he/she is and whatever he/she is doing.[1] The issues we are dealing with here are crime, its control, and how effective PP is going to be in controlling the crime.

Crime has shown a steep increase in numbers everywhere. Many factors attribute to this hike. Population explosion, struggle for survival, and survival of the fittest in the limited available resources, materialistic wisdom, erosion of values, rise in demand, and greed overtaking need in the basic attitude, are a few causes to be mentioned. With technological advancement and evolution of better brains over the years, the method adopted for committing crime has also progressed. With more exposure to starkness of vices, the heinousness of the crime has also enhanced by a glaring proportion. Sensitivity, which is jewel of mankind, is gradually taking a back seat. Even the white-collar crime, which was normally committed without bloodshed, is now soaked in blood. Life and property have become items to grab at will.

In such a situation where the scenario is not healthy, crime control becomes a challenging effort. In this modernization era, the police everywhere in the country are being trained and equipped to combat the rising crime effectively. Latest gadgets and training modules are pushed in to prepare the force to give a befitting answer to the perpetrators. But the question is that even after considering all this preparation, has the police in isolation been able to control crime to the extent it is required? Have we, in the recent past, seen any decline, or factually have witnessed proliferation? I do not think it is necessary to answer this question. The answer is known to everyone. Why are

---

[1] Khara, M.S. 2009. "Community Participation in Security against Terrorism," *The Indian Police Journal*, LVI(2): 12–15, April–June.

the police, despite making all efforts to run in pace with the criminals, failing to curb crime? Does it imply that the saying "criminals are one step ahead of law enforcers" hold water? The easiest way out of any discussion is to start a blame game. Hurling accusations like lack of professionalism, being hand in glove, apathetic attitude, corruption the cause of connivance, ill-trained force, and so on, are methods adopted to find a solution to lack of crime control. Let us not outrightly reject these accusations. But are they the only reason for the failure?

Community policing is a fact and need of the police. PP is a synonym to this concept. No matter in what state of affairs the policing is, eventually, they will have to go through the phases and consequently open up to the community at large. The prerequisites of community policing are consequential for their effectiveness and efficiency. They will have to trust their client and realize that it is a win–win situation. With time, the role of the police has multiplied and the responsibility increased. Unless they tune up to the practices in vogue, success will elude them, which they cannot dare to afford.

Proactive problem-solving approaches in concert with the community members and relevant city agencies can lead to a reduction in the incidence of specific crimes.[2] A collaborative approach to problem solving involves the police, residents, and representatives of various city agencies who can curtail neighborhood social and physical disorder.[3] PP is a method, which has a solution embedded in its womb to fight against the menace of crime escalation. PP can help reduce the existing chaos of management. PP is involving the community in policing.

This clearly implies that the community involvement is a part and parcel of the police job and without the community's support and assistance, their existence will be at stake. Police cannot work in isolation. Community policing calls for increase in trust and faith between the two. Over the years, the gap that has developed amidst them needs to be bridged. Through the interactive process, new ideas are created and the police job becomes easier and smoother resulting in better performance than possible by individual effort. Community partnerships require collaborative partnerships between the law enforcement agency and the individuals and organizations they serve

---

[2] Eck, John E. and Spelman William. 1987. "Problem Solving: Police Oriented Policing," *Newport News*. Washington DC: Police Executive Research Forum.
[3] Toch, Hans and D. James. 1991. *Grant, Police as Problem Solvers*. New York: Plenum.

to develop solutions to problems and increase trust in the police. The partners are like other government agencies, community members/ groups, nonprofits/service providers, private businesses, and media.[4] The Delhi Police's "Eyes and Ears" scheme wherein small traders, vendors, porters, and autorickshaw drivers have been roped in to provide inputs is an example of collaborative method of crime control.

Community Policing Scenario in India

If the importance of PP is so evident, then obviously there are initiatives to ensure community participation in various parts of the country. Here, I have mentioned a few, and tried to analyze briefly the plausible dimensions of its limitations. These initiatives are more or less the same but were started with different names, by different officers, in different states. Some programs got institutionalized, having been adopted by the state police, and some have remained local initiatives, personalized in the name of the initiator.

The main essence of all such initiatives has been to provide opportunities to ordinary citizens to effectively contribute to the prevention and detection of crime. They are proactive concepts lending a psychological approach to policing. The idea aims at bringing the police and the public closer, boosting the image of the police in the minds of the public, encouraging information sharing, helping the police understand the public sentiments on various issues, and instilling a sense of belonging and responsibility amongst the community members. Almost all the initiatives calling for community participation invite members of the public, male or female, not involved in any civil or criminal case, to be made a member of a committee coordinated by the police.

Mentioned below are a few initiatives taken up in different parts of the country in the name of democratic policing inviting community participation:

---

[4] Community Oriented Policing Services (the COPS Office) is the component of the US Department of Justice. http://www.cops.usdoj.gov/default.asp?item=36 as visited on January 30, 2010.

- Friends of Police (FOP) of Tamil Nadu.
- People's Policing Committee in Himachal Pradesh.
- Nagar/Gram Raksha Samities of Madhya Pradesh (Urban/Rural Defense Committees) and Chhattisgarh.
- Salwa Judum of Chhattisgarh.
- Community Groups of Punjab.
- Mohalla Committees of Mumbai.
- Maithri in Andhra Pradesh.
- Aashwas and Prahari of Assam.
- Sensitive Police-empowered Society and Community Surveillance Group of Haryana.
- Trichy Community Policing Initiatives of Kerala.
- Neighbourhood Watch Scheme of Delhi.
- Samarth Yojna of Coimbatore.
- Aasra in Andhra Pradesh.

There are many more individual and state-level initiatives with different names but with same objective and goal: PP and community involvement. The idea is to establish constructive communication between the police and the community to decrease the trust deficit and set up a democratic police. As can be seen, at different places, the initiatives have started under different compulsions. Some have taken shape to quell communal tension, some for anti-dacoity operations, some to stop trafficking, naxal menace, and some to contain crime and establish peace and tranquility in rural areas. More or less, the objective and methodology have been similar but the causes have been different.

The success of community policing lies in the faith, trust, and confidence that the public have in the police. Howsoever good projects the police may come up with, their success lies in the response and participation they are able to garner from the community at large.

Personally, I do not think any of these initiatives have failed. All of them have their own saga of success to recite. Nevertheless, honestly, have they achieved what was desired of such initiatives? If yes, have they been able to maintain the same momentum and fervor as was during the start? I doubt it. Not many will accept it but being a part of the law enforcement organization and being part of few initiatives myself, which are hailed as great initiatives, I think we fail to review and reconstruct them. All the initiatives mentioned above are still running, and many have expanded their geographical areas and replicated in other parts of the state of origin. However, there are some inbuilt weaknesses in these initiatives.

- These initiatives, though having the best of intentions, have been implemented without proper orientation of the implementers. There is a wide gap between the conceptualizers and implementers. The implementers are the police personnel at lower rung of the hierarchy. Quite obviously, it is directed by seniors and hence fizzes out the moment the brainchild moves out of influencing position. The approach is a piecemeal approach.
- Approaches remain Person Steered Initiatives (PSIs) and they become a victim of Predecessor and Successor Syndrome (PSS). PSIs mean that the efforts made remain associated with the person initializing it. No effort is made to institutionalize those PP endeavors. The problem with the police organization is that participative initiatives do not have any policy support. Due to absence of that, there is normally no budgetary provision to support the initiatives. The success and perpetuation of the projects depend solely on the implementing agencies' concurrence and acceptance. Due to rigid hierarchical setup, it is the senior officers who decide upon what has to be taken up and what has to be dropped. The acceptance and rejection of a proposal is the prerogative of the seniors, going up from SP onwards. After a project is initiated by an officer, its continuity after his/her transfer is totally the choice of the successor. Occasionally, as the initiatives get popular because of a special interest and involvement of a senior officer, the projects tends to get identified personally by his/her name, which is despised by the successor. Smitten by the successor syndrome, the initiated projects find an unceremonious end at the hands of the newcomer. It is the organizational and systemic benefits, which should be the guiding principle rather than personal popularity chart.
- Most of the police officers do not understand how PP works; hence, they keep working for participation fruitlessly. Conceptualizing on a strategy without understanding the intricacies of the concept will be a half-hearted effort. Working with conviction and understanding, dreaming of its necessity and utility would confer a different approach. Rather than pressurizing on the implementation of projects conceived elsewhere, an orientation for attitudinal change toward the initiatives will be the hallmark of the approach.
- The participation of the community is governed by the police. They decide upon who will partner and to what extent. Their

discretion is influenced by convenience. Police personnel prefer to have non-confrontationist partners; thus, the endeavor, over the time, drifts away from reality.

- Due to lack of proper orientation, having no conviction on the utility of initiatives by the successors, the spirit of the partners gets diluted. As the projects are force-driven, the community looks upon the police for continuity. Many initiatives still exist on field, or rather keep growing on papers, but the effectiveness diminishes drastically. They have shifted far from the original agenda and the priorities have now become totally different. Intermittently, to compensate for the loss, some motivated senior comes and tries to rejuvenate them, leaving again to wilt after a change of captaincy. This has been the fate of many initiatives in the country, which have been boasted of being very successful at the onset but now the organizations just decorate the reports submitted on community policing initiatives.

- As no effort is made toward bringing a change in the image of the police, prior to starting on some project, the community is not motivated to partner. Even after commencement of a project, due to attitudinal problem of the police personnel and lack of sensitivity and non-professionalism in approach, the common man tries to keep a distance from the projects.

- Self-efficacy (also known as "social cognitive theory" or "social learning theory") refers to an individual's belief that he/she is capable of performing a task.[5] The higher your self-efficacy, the more confidence you have in your ability to succeed in a task. So, in difficult situations, we find that people with low self-efficacy are more likely to lessen their effort or give up altogether, while those with high self-efficacy will try harder to master the challenge.[6] In addition, individuals high in self-efficacy seem to respond to negative feedback with increased effort and motivation, while those low in self-efficacy are likely to lessen their effort when given negative feedback.[7] Police, for decades being

[5] Bandura, A. 1997. *Self-Efficacy: The Exercise of Control*. New York: Freeman.

[6] Stajkovic, A.D. and F. Luthans. 1998. "Self-Efficacy and Work-Related Performance: A Meta-Analysis," *Psychological Bulletin*, 124(2): 240–61, September; and Bandura, A. 2000. "Cultivate Self-Efficacy for Personal and Organisational Effectiveness," in Locke (ed.), *Handbook of Principles of Organizational Behavior*, pp. 120–36. Malden, MA: Blackwell.

[7] Bandura, A. and D. Cervone. 1986. "Differential Engagement in Self-Reactive Influences in Cognitively-based Motivation," *Organizational Behavior and Human Decision Processes*,

at the receiving end, are low in self-efficacy and hence the very approach toward PP is defensive and with apprehension.

Here are some methods by which community-policing initiatives can achieve the desired results, at the time of conception.

REBUILDING PARTNERSHIPS

Image Dating (ID) is necessary to comprehend on priority basis that image of the police needs a facelift. This is possible only by going down the memory lane of image building, identifying the reasons for development of the chasm, and putting in place a mechanism to minimize the gap. It is easier said than done.

The method adopted to draw a map of image building is called ID or Image Mapping (IM). This involves going through bylanes of history and locating the crossroads where the gap between the community and the police widened. It is interesting to spot those areas, which led in perpetuating the fissure even after independence. Police reforms have been talked about since independence and various committees have been instituted to guide and give recommendations to make policing community-friendly. There have been many initiatives taken over the years, by successive regimes to bring the community and the police closer. Why have they failed to understand the needs?

Police is an organization which has been doing the least to refurbish its image. Police will have to take measures to salvage its image. It will have to commence interaction with the community, work with transparency, share a common platform unconditionally, become more accessible, broaden the base of partnership with a larger community rather than handpicking the partners to interact with, oppose to the image-blotting efforts of the media and other agencies like movies, plays, and so on, and organize interactive sessions with the community and let them peep into their affairs and realize the limitations of the police. They will have to set realistic goals and try to achieve them with honesty. Accepting fallacies and project achievements is necessary for a positive image building.

August (1986): 92–113; Robbins, Stephen P. and Timothy A. Judge. 2007. *Organizational Behavior*, Twelfth Edition. New Delhi: Prentice-Hall of India Private Limited.

TRACKING PARTICIPATION FOOTPRINT

As mentioned earlier, the police have visualized and started many projects seeking community partnership. Had all such projects been successful, the scenario would have been different. It is not that all have failed. But due to PSI and lack of institutionalization or becoming a victim of PSS, the initiatives have met unnatural death.

Hence, it becomes necessary for the organization to track the participation footprint. TPF means that over a period of time, as decided, can be a year or more, all the initiatives undertaken for PP are analyzed and evaluated. The pros and cons of the initiatives are assessed. On the basis of External Objective Evaluation (EOE), the best, successful, and popular initiatives are carried forward and the rest, after consulting the partners, are dropped. This will help in evaluating, analyzing, and revamping the structure. Quite practically, only those initiatives will pass the auditors' test which have been accepted and implemented by the community. Tracking Participation Footprint (TPF) will ascertain the fallibility of redundant activities and benefits of the participative ones. For the success of community policing projects, there should be inbuilt mechanisms for periodic evaluations of the program.[8]

A very interesting aspect of the community is that in the police organizational system, it acts as input as well as the outcome. Its participation is indispensable. Now, the moot point is how to solicit willing participation so that the desired output is achieved. If the participation is active and with knowledge, then obviously the *input* will affect the process in the system and output feedback will provide an opportunity to objectively ascertain the flaws in the system. Objective auditing will help in focusing on the lacunae in the organizational management principles and rectify them.

PARTICIPATION WOULD LEAD TO PRECISION POLICING TECHNIQUE

Precision Policing Technique (PPT) calls for having a Need Analysis Based (NAB) policing approach. Every area needs a different

---

[8] Sen, Sankar. 2008. "Assessment and Evaluation of Community Policing," *The Indian Police Journal*, LV(4): 9–15, October–December.

approach of policing. Parochial and localized approach, depending on needs of the community, is necessary to ensure that optimum output is achieved. Any slum, rural area, shopping place, residential place, or industrial area, need a different approach in policing. The demand of policing is distinct in a slum area than in a posh, residential area. A rural area would need different policing approach than urban. Participation of the community will ensure that policing efforts comply with the local needs. As the management saying goes "it is the customer need which should decide your product." NAB will certainly help in maximizing customer satisfaction.

With PP, the missing two-way communication of the police and the community and within the organization will be established. It will bring the required change in attitude of the police personnel. From a dominant platform, they will step down on the same plane and discuss the issues more explicitly and honestly. PP will help in conflict resolution and problem solving in the community.

The mechanism of checks and balances will automatically be put into force. If the participation is not lopsided and guided, then surely the accountability and responsibility of the police toward the community will increase. Bygone will be the days when the police will get away for any omission of right duty or commission of wrong duty with impunity. The community will closely monitor the action of the police and the output of the system will certainly improve.

A feedback system will be a natural sequel of participation. Feedback, other than all other benefits cited above, will help in self assessment.

Performance Appraisal System (PAS) in the police is one way. It is the internal PAS system which decides if the work of any person is satisfactory or not. PP will open up the PAS system and the community at large will start having a say in their appraisal. The performance appraisal will be more objective and will not be just the discretion of officers in charge. As of now, it is the immediate boss who has to be kept in good humor to confirm a good appraisal. This is the inside evaluation. It is not always useful because some inside evaluators may be tempted or pressurized to misrepresent their findings.[9] Very often, an evaluation is not value-free as evaluators become advocates of their

---

[9] Johnson, William C. 1992. *Public Administration: Policy, Politics and Practice*. Guilford, CT: Dushkin Publishing Group.

own cause and very often their results may be the justification for the status quo rather than useful and objective appraisals.[10]

Corollary to PAS system is the EOE. The basic difference between the two is that PAS is normally that of an individual and second, done by a person or an agency knowing the person appraised. In EOE, it is an unconnected agency, having nothing to do with the police organization as such, which would be assigned to evaluate objectively the performance of the organization. The evaluation is done by that external agency based on the perception of the customer/community, performance of the service provider/police, and by marking the process method utilized. It is not just end results but also the means adopted which are evaluated. With PP, the civil society groups will obviously become active and the police organization will be opened for EOE. In the present highly competitive scenario, EOE is a must as it provides actual measurement of the performance of the organization, in totality. Outside evaluations by independent evaluators are in a better position to use accepted scientific methods to gather data and then report their findings objectively.[11]

In the USA, the evaluation of New York City Community Patrol Officer Program (CPOP) is a good example of EOE. It was done in six police precincts where community policing programs were carried out. Community policing officers were first interviewed at the start of program and later after six months. The researchers graded the officers and the same officers were asked to be graded by their supervisors, and a comparison of the grading was done. Even the community leaders of the precincts were interviewed about the success of community policing effort.[12]

A similar study of community policing was done in Chicago by Wesley and others.[13] This study was very interesting from the fact

[10] Petersilia, J. 1987. "The Influence of Criminal Justice Research," monograph prepared for the National Institute of Justice, US Department of Justice, The Rand Corporation, Santa Monica, p. 102.

[11] Sen, Sankar. 2008. "Assessment and Evaluation of Community Policing," *The Indian Police Journal*, LV(4), October–December.

[12] McElory, E., Colleen A. Cosgrove, and Susan Sadd. 1993. *Community Policing: The CPOP in New York*. New York, London, New Delhi: SAGE.

[13] Skogan, Wesley G. and Susan M. Hartnett. 1997. *Community Policing: The Chicago Style*. New York: Oxford University Press.

that the same community policing efforts had different impact on different communities. Some groups who held a low opinion about the quality of policing registered improvement in their perception after participating but the Hispanics did not participate and there was no improvement in their opinion. When officers were interviewed, the black and Hispanic officers were more optimistic about community policing than white officers. The cleavages within the community got mirrored in the police department. Hence, the EOE system gave an insight on important community issues more objectively, which otherwise could have fallen prey to the internal perceptual differences within the police originating from the community cleavage.

Direct Benefits of Participative Policing

- PP will assist in normal policing, information gathering, and there will be fast dissemination of information which will assist both the community and police.
- Everybody's contribution is appreciated and valued.
- The concept of team work is encouraged.
- An individual's potential is recognized.
- Even the marginalized will be mainstreamed and will get an opportunity to participate and partner with the police.
- PP will support in integration of cultural diversity.
- The problems emanating due to fragmentation of the society on the basis of religion, caste, class, and so on, will be solved.
- It will help in weaving a constructive social fabric.

PP is a holistic approach, which ensures community partnership and ultimately helps in enhancing efficiency and effectiveness of the police. It is a proactive approach. Free access and open interaction is the key to the success of participation. It has to be an inclusive approach. Participation should be at all levels—individual, collective as councils and committees, and with civil society groups. Basically, as policing is concerned with the security of one and all, more active and widespread participation is required. According to the Bureau of Justice Assistance, "PP is a process of successfully studying crime and disorder in small, geographical defined areas so that appropriate resources can be applied to reduce crime and disorder."[14]

It is not at all surprising to find that the police has a blotted image. On research, it has been found that the image is being handed over as any tradition through generations. It is being perceived more from *secondary* and *tertiary sources* than by the *primary source*.[15] Image-building process has never been on the priority list of the police organization, though much of the hatred toward the organization can be attributed to this image. Any organization, before launching a product, extensively gets involved in image building of that product. For the same, a sizeable amount of the project cost is earmarked for advertisement and image building. Surprisingly, the police, whose customer is every citizen of this country, irrespective of any post, class, caste, religion, and political affiliation, hardly spend anything—time, manpower, material, or money—to build their image. PP is the cheapest and easiest method of building their image. The image building will be through the primary source, direct interaction, and hence, objective and reality based. With all the other benefits of PP, there are still some lacunae that need to be fixed and rectified.

An Exemplary Culture: Case Studies

THE TATA GESTURE

The Tata Gesture toward the staff of Taj Hotel, Mumbai, after the 26/11 terrorist attack will give one an insight into how an organization can take care of its employees, customers, and do a lot more.[16] This information is based on what was narrated by H.N. Srinivas, Senior Executive Vice-president, Taj Group of Hotels, dated October 10, 2009, in Goa. He narrated the November 26, 2008, terror attack

---

[14] Bureau of Justice Assistance. 1994. "Understanding Community Policing, A Framework for Action," U.S. Department of Justice. http://www.ncjrs.gov/pdffiles/commp.pdf as visited on June 5, 2011.

[15] Mishra, V. 2004. "Changing Image of Police: An Empirical Study," PhD thesis, Barkatullah University, Bhopal.

[16] This information was received through email. Even if it is paid news, still it gives an idea as to what should be done, and if reality, then Tata deserves accolades.

on Taj Mumbai. There were some important points that manifest the exemplary spirit that an organization should have. In a function, Ratan Tata broke down in public and sobbed saying: "the company belongs to these people." This is what recognition and appreciation is.

All categories of employees, including those who had completed even a day as casuals, were treated on duty during the time the hotel was closed for repairs. Relief and assistance were provided to all those who were injured or killed. During the time the hotel was closed, the salaries were sent by money order to employees who were advised to proceed to their villages. A psychiatric cell was established in collaboration with the Tata Institute of Social Sciences (TISS) to counsel those who needed such kind of help. The thoughts and anxieties going on in the minds of the employees and people were constantly tracked and wherever needed, psychological help was provided. Employee outreach centers were opened where all help, food, water, sanitation, first aid, and counseling was provided. All 1,600 employees were covered under this facility. Every employee was assigned one mentor from the other Tata group companies and it was that person's responsibility to act as a "single window" clearance for any help that the person required.

Ratan Tata personally visited the families of all the 80 employees who were in some manner—either through an injury or getting killed—affected. The dependents of the killed/wounded employees were flown/transported by the fastest means from outside Mumbai to Mumbai and taken care of in terms of ensuring mental assurance and peace. They were all accommodated in President Hotel for three weeks. Ratan Tata himself asked the families and dependents as to what they wanted him to do. In a record time of 20 days, a new trust was created by the Tatas for the purpose of relief for the employees. This was the most trying period in the life of the organization. Senior managers including Ratan Tata were visiting funerals for more than three days, which were most melancholy. The settlement for every deceased member, including who had one day service, ranged from ₹36 to 85 lakh, in addition to the following benefits: (a) full last salary for life for the family and dependents; (b) complete responsibility of education of children/other dependents—anywhere in the world; (c) full medical facility for the whole family and other dependents for the rest of their life; (d) all loans and advances were waived off—irrespective of the amount; (e) counselor services for life for each person. When the Human Resource (HR) function hesitatingly made a very rich proposal to Ratan Tata, he said, do you think we are doing enough? The whole approach was that the organization would spend several hundred crores in rebuilding the property; why not spend equally on the employees who gave their life?

Is it not high time when the police organization should take cue from the above highly inspiring example of the Tata culture and try making necessary amendments. Or, they would find an escape route for themselves on the pretext of the public and private organizational dichotomy. PP, which holds a lot of answers to hidden flaws of the police organization, can only succeed if the police personnel, particularly of the cutting edge level, are taken care of, well motivated, and are convinced with its benefits.

TRUST DEFICIT

One of the worst terrorist attacks, 26/11, Mumbai, could have been averted if the community would have participated as desired. Fisherman Chandrakant Tare had spotted a young man killing a sailor on board on Wednesday, 24/11. He even witnessed them toss the body into the engine room. Assuming he had stumbled upon pirates, he sped away; fisherman Ajay Mestry saw the landing of a trash-strewn fishing harbor near the southern tip of the Mumbai peninsula at around 8:30 am. Also, he saw half a dozen young men, mostly in their early to mid-20s, wearing dark clothes and hauling heavy bags and backpacks. The group that he saw split up and raced toward the shimmering city. Similarly, Anita Rajendra Udayaar, the keeper of a roadside stall full of recycled plastic bottles saw one young man with a bulging bag jogged up from the beach. When she asked where he was heading. "Mind your own business!" he shouted back, she recalls.[17]

SUCCESS OF PARTICIPATIVE POLICING

Narsinghgadh is a subdivision in Rajgadh District, state Madhya Pradesh, having a long history of communal tension (details given in

---

[17] Trofimov, Yaroslav, Geeta Anand, Peter Wonacott, and Matthew Rosenberg. 2008. "India Security Faulted as Survivors Tell of Terror," *The Wall Street Journal*, December 1, 2008. http://online.wsj.com/article/SB122809281744967855.html as visited on November 16, 2009.

following chapter of case study) was a challenge to the police. A natural consequence of riots-communication chasm between communities and of communities with administration makes it difficult for any action to be executed in right perspective. Community policing came handy in this crisis situation.

Through continuous application of PP methods, inviting the community directly into managing their own security affairs by discussion and deliberation in a democratic way, giving them the leadership of navigating the religious processions, policing being just a helping hand available on one beck, and call when needed, being accessible in all matters, did wonders.

Narsinghgarh experiment demonstrated that with a change in attitude, by ensuring participation, and establishing a strong two-way communication, the cooperation between the community and the police multiplied manifold, eventually leading to the expansion of zone of acceptance. Communal tension was at an all-time low and the confidence boosted. Communal dispute, a social crime leading to worst crimes under IPC like murder, arson, loot, rape, and so on, can be controlled by a collaborative approach (this case study has been discussed in detail later).

Here, we are limiting ourselves to discussing only two cases. Both highlight issues which have far-reaching ramifications and put a threat to the national security at large. Rest of the crimes of the society, naturally, can be dealt easily through collaborative PP method. If crimes like terrorism and communal disharmony find a solution in PP, then rest assured, all other crimes can be controlled in collaboration.

BABRI MASJID/RAM JANAMBHOOMI VERDICT DAYS—AN EXEMPLARY MANIFESTATION OF COMMUNITY POLICING

Allahabad High Court was to give verdict on September 24, 2010, which was later deferred and given on September 30, 2010. The country witnessed an unprecedented security beef up and the nation was kept on high alert. The alert was against two, internal radicalisms and externally sponsored subversive act. It was a great experience of community policing in full swing. Honestly, very few would accept it as deliberate community policing activity, but it fitted to my definition very appropriately corroborating my stand in this book. Here, I will try to explain how the effort of the police was fine tuned within the framework of community policing.

To simplify, I will take Bhopal zone of Madhya Pradesh as an example to explain. Madhya Pradesh was highlighted by the Union Government as one of the most sensitive states, high-risk zone of the country, along with a few more, including Uttar Pradesh. In the recent past, Madhya Pradesh had witnessed communal tensions, off and on in various parts. All the four districts under Bhopal Zone—Bhopal, Raisen, Vidisha, and Rajgarh—were highly sensitive districts, having witnessed communal tension within the past couple of years.

After gearing up the local police, few strategies were adopted by the law enforcement:

1. Maximum physical presence displayed:

   • A combined force of Rapid Action Force (RAF: a wing of Central Reserve Police Force), State Special Armed Force (SAF), and the local police were taken for a flag march. Flag march was a show of their strength, preparedness, vigility, presence, and display of no-nonsense business attitude. Besides, the flag march was a strong method of building confidence in the community by giving them a feeling of "we are there at your service to protect you when you need us."
   • Foot patrolling and vehicle patrolling was intensified.
   • Fixed picket were set up.
   • Patrol cars were stationed at strategic points for immediate redress.

2. An intensive campaign of interaction with the community taken up:

   • Meetings with the community members were organized at all levels.
   • Senior officers, even IG and Commissioner, went in most of the sensitive police station areas of each district to meet people of both communities. In *shanti samities* (Peace Committees), they had meetings with both communities together and met individual community members and leaders separately.

- The police station officers and even the DSPs conducted meetings at many places in each of the police stations under their area of operation.
- The community assistance groups (Nagar Raksha Samiti [Urban Defense Committees] and Gram Raksha Samiti [Rural Defense Committees]) were mobilized.
- At beat levels, the police personnel were instructed to meet as many people as possible and develop a rapport.

3. Preventive measures taken:

- All probable mischief mongers and antisocial people with a past record were booked under preventive sections of law.
- A strict punitive measure was declared to be taken against rumor spreaders.
- A very rigorous campaign of dissemination of information was carried out. Information sharing was at all levels: through press, community leaders, and individual level.
- Immediate action against the perpetrator was ensured.

The salient features of this strategy were:

- The action of the police was totally impartial and transparent. Both the communities were taken into confidence and equally informed of the dire consequences in case of breach of peace.
- There was a feeling of inclusiveness and ownership on the part of the community due to continuous meetings for almost 10 days and involving them in action.
- While taking preventive actions, the police picked all the right persons and there was no bargain or compromise during the action (otherwise seldom seen). Due to their sincerity and honesty, there was hardly any case of retribution from the community.
- For the first time, the community and officers/personnel of all ranks came in contact to this extent. The intensity of contact was so high that the trust deficit was totally filled. Normally, in tense situations, for the fear of high-handedness of the police, the trust deficit increases but may be for the first time in history, the gap instead of widening, waned. I remember one of my officers telling me that all those days during duty, he was unable to eat the

packed food distributed by the district administration. He was hosted sumptuous meals by the community members, voluntarily. The community felt involved in due course and the presence of police was welcomed.

- On the day of the verdict, there was almost an undeclared curfew in most of the places, but still there was not a single case of criticism for the police even after the verdict day. In media, and at the community level, the police action was hailed and congratulated. This portrays the success story of police action.

Now if we analyze how the police acted, we will see that the police did what normally they are expected to do, even in calm situations. Perform their duties diligently, honestly, impartially, transparently, and within the framework of law, taking the community into confidence. It was all traditional policing work done with all those qualities expected from the police by the community. The attitude of the police was positive toward the community, understanding well the importance and strength of community partnership. So, undoubtedly, without any argument, the way the police acted fitted completely into my definition of community policing—normal policing with an attitudinal change. More or less what was taken up as campaigns should be a daily routine of police personnel—interact and act.

10

Curative Suggestions to Bring Attitudinal Change in Police

It has been discussed in the preceding chapters that the police's attitude and behavior are major deterrent factors in establishing the police–public (community) partnership. This attitudinal problem can be attributed to the police syndrome and police culture. Some curative suggestions, which would help in improving the police's attitude and behavior, eventually smoothening the partnership-building mechanism between the police and the community, are discussed in this chapter.

Democratization of Police

Democratization of police would mean involving all stakeholders in decision-making process, giving them enough space to express themselves, and have sufficient access to gather knowledge about the work of the police and the police culture. It would mean convergence of ideas for unison in decision-making, thereby leading to value addition and enrichment in the quality of work. A democratic police force responds to the needs of individuals and private groups as well as the needs of the government. It is accountable to multiple audiences and multiple mechanisms. Strengthening of these mechanisms will strengthen the quality of democratic policing.[1] The police, according to S. Venugopal Rao,

---

[1] Devarajan, M.K. 2000. "Attitudinal Changes for Better Policing," *SVP National Police Academy Journal*, 52: 50–56, January–June.

134 *Community Policing*

as constituted today, do not have an inbuilt mechanism for self analysis and introspection resulting in a tendency to develop extreme attitudes of oversensitivity or total insensitivity. Both attitudes are invalid in a democratic society.[2]

The Maharashtra Police Commission (1964) recorded that one important factor which causes resentment against the police is that quite often they have to undertake additional duties related to social legislation, which are outside the sphere of what people usually consider criminal law enforcement. A sizeable number of the complaints received by the police are non-cognizable offences where the police are helpless and are legally restricted to act upon. A common man is oblivious of this limitation. They start accepting that the police are disinterested and indifferent. This feeling of dejection and frustration can be taken care of by democratizing the police work. A natural consequence of stakeholders' involvement through democratization would be free flow of information, which would lead to better understanding and increased awareness.

The expert-based, hierarchical–instrumental policy-making encounters insurmountable obstacles in modern liberal democracies. One of the root causes of this erosion of output legitimacy is the complexity of social systems. Complexity is defined as the density and dynamism of the interactions between the elements of a system. Complexity makes system outcomes unpredictable and hard to control and, for this reason, defies such well-known policy strategies as coordination from the center, model building, and reduction of the problem to a limited number of controllable variables. It is argued that the participatory and deliberative models of governance are more effective in harnessing complexity because they increase interaction within systems; hence, the system diversity and creativity.[3]

---

[2] Mathur, K.M. 1985. "State of Police-community Relations in India Today: How to Improve It?," *Essays on Police-Community Relations*, pp. 114–126. Hyderabad: SVP National Police Academy.

[3] Wagenaar, Hendrik. 2007. "Complexities of Neighborhood Decline of Issues Around the Limits and Possibilities of the Democratic Governance of Advanced Liberal Democracies," *The American Review of Public Administration*, the online version of this article can be found at: http://arp.sagepub.com/cgi/content/abstract/37/1/17 as visited on February 10, 2010.

Conceptual Literacy

Having Conceptual Literacy (CL) of work the police is entrusted with is mandatory. CL indicates that the knowledge of the concept of the task to be taken up should precede action. CL increases adaptability to changes. With more situational change on a daily basis, technological changes knocking on the doorstep, more opportunities and challenges being thrown open, only CL comes to the rescue. It prepares to adapt to changes.

Police, accustomed to the traditional model, have relied on the precepts of control: confront, command, and coerce. Establishing and maintaining a presence and an overwhelming authority are central to the traditional police mindset and training. The new problem- and community-oriented models neither eliminate nor downplay the importance of control in certain situations, but they insert officers into situations where control is at best irrelevant and at worst counterproductive.[4] Community policing and the Scanning, Analysis, Response, and Assessment (SARA) problem-solving model places the police in the very different world of partnership, which requires them to participate, promote, and persuade. In a control model, the police officer is the central figure in the event; in a partnership model, the police are but one of the many interested stakeholders.[5]

Stepping into a new mode without CL is fraught with danger. It may boomerang, finally alienating the community instead of drawing them closer. "Can-do attitude" of problem solving runs the risk of discovering new pitfalls. The problem-oriented policing, with its emphasis on developing new and better sources of information about problems, is particularly vulnerable to backlash as the difficulties may result from faulty analysis if officers pursue intuitively logical solutions to problems they erroneously or incompletely understand. Law-enforcement solutions may backfire when applied to problems that are essentially social in nature and vice versa. When working in ethnically

---

[4] Goldstein, H. 1990. *Policing a Free Society*. Cambridge, MA: Ballinger Publishing; Goldstein, H. 1977. *Problem-oriented Policing*. Philadelphia: Temple University Press.

[5] Buerger, Michael E., Anthony J. Petrosino, and Carolyn Petrosino. 1999. "Extending the Police Role: Implications of Police Mediation as a Problem-Solving Tool," *Police Quarterly*, 2(2), June, the online version of this article can be found at: http://pqx.sagepub.com/cgi/content/abstract/2/2/125 as visited on February 10, 2010.

diverse communities, the need to do something about a particular problem may outstrip the natural learning curve about cultural frameworks; thus, well-intentioned efforts either miss the mark or cause inadvertent offense. Officers may be deceived by the climate of community support and engage in activities that offend community sensibilities. A corollary danger is that community support will embolden officers to pursue unlawful tactics in pursuit of a desirable goal.[6]

The problems mostly occur at the level of the individual officer(s) involved, but have ramifications on the entire organization. Police expand their role in a haphazard fashion in an effort to contribute, with little fore thought given, to the system of evaluation of the consequences. The existing method of evaluating the effectiveness of problem-solving efforts is almost exclusively anecdotal in nature, based largely on short-term results. Neither the elements that identify situations amenable to successful intervention nor the elements of adequate and inadequate performance for officers have yet been determined (both in terms of attempts and outcomes). Police have not yet determined how to distinguish no-win situations or develop ways to successfully disengage from them. The opportunities for meaningful interventions are not equally distributed, nor are the difficulties of identified problems. Both can affect the nature of performance evaluations. All of these elements still need to be developed, lest overreaching may lead to the failure of unrealistic expectations and the abandonment of a promising new tool for policing. Training in problem-oriented policing tends to revolve around the dissemination of anecdotes and case studies, assuming (or hoping) that the lessons gleaned are both certain and generalizable.[7]

CL will also help in strategizing the energy investment. EIS is a method to optimize the outcome from investment of energy. Energy here includes the efforts put in for planning, development, implementation, collaboration, evaluation, process correction, and refurbishing.

---

[6] Klockars, C.B. and S.D. Mastrofski (eds). 1991. *Thinking About Police: Contemporary Readings*, 2nd edition. New York: McGraw-Hill; Sutton, L.P. 1991. "Getting Around the Fourth Amendment," in C.B. Klockars and S.D. Mastrofski (eds), *Thinking about Police: Contemporary Readings*, 2nd edition, pp. 433–446. New York: McGraw-Hill.

[7] Buerger, Michael E., Anthony J. Petrosino, and Carolyn Petrosino. 1999. "Extending the Police Roie: Implications of Police Mediation as a Problem-Solving Tool," *Police Quarterly*, 2(2), June, the online version of this article can be found at: http://pqx.sagepub.com/cgi/content/abstract/2/2/125 as accessed on February 10, 2010.

CL and EIS are complementary to each other. EIS would involve all the strategic management techniques and governance.

Strategic Management and Governance

It is necessary that the organization follows management principles, has a strategic vision, sets objectives realistically, crafts a strategy to achieve the desired outcomes, implements effectively and efficiently the chosen strategy, and sets up a mechanism for evaluating performance, and initiates corrective adjustments.

Strategic vision portrays the organization's future scope.[8] It helps in direction-setting and is valuable in strategy-making. It prepares the organization to look beyond the present and think about the forthcoming challenges. The demand and need can be calculated and achievable objectives can be set in light of the organization's situation and prospects.

Police do not have the culture of adopting and adapting to organizational behavior. The raw deal is attributed to the unprofessional approach toward organizational management. Strategic management would help in planning the course of action, organizing the resources, personnel management, coordinating and collaborating with other parts of the larger environment, strengthening the feedback system, facilitating reverse planning, and adopting corrective measures.

Proper governance would mean maximizing the value legally, ethically, and on a sustainable basis, while ensuring fairness to every stakeholder—employees, individual customers, government, other partners, and the community.[9] The governance is the reflection of the service provider's culture, policies, how it deals with its stakeholders, and its commitment to values. It also ensures conformity with the interests of employees, goal-setters, and the society by creating fairness, transparency, and accountability in activities among the employees and the management.

---

[8] Thompson, J.R., A. Arthur, and A.J. Strickland III. 2003. *Strategic Management Concepts and Cases*, Thirteenth Edition. New Delhi: Tata McGraw-Hill Publishing Company Limited.
[9] Narayana, Murty N.R. 2009. *A Better India A Better World*. New Delhi: Allen Lane by Penguin Books India.

Focus on the Third Tier of the System

Constabulary and senior constables (Cs) (along with head constables) constitute a major chunk of personnel in the police organization. Their recruitment, training (basic), orientation, and in-service needs require a lot of attention. The Tamil Nadu Police Commission had recorded that one of the most important defects in the present police organization in India is the fact that the constabulary, which forms the bulk of the police force, are recruited on certain obsolete principles enunciated by the Police Commission of 1860. Although more than a century and a half has passed and large-scale changes have overtaken the country politically, socially, and economically, the constabulary continues to be recruited from the lowest social levels and is called upon to undertake tasks for which it is not fully qualified. The advancement in education, the growth of political consciousness, and economic progress has contributed to the evolution of a new society, which is far more enlightened than it was a quarter of century ago.

The morale of the cutting edge level personnel has to be kept high, their skills have to be enhanced, their capacity built, attitudinal change brought through basic training and orientation programs, and their approach toward the job has to be made more customer (community/public) friendly. Other human resource development schemes should be scientifically incorporated so as to acknowledge their presence in totality, taking into full consideration their limitations—personal and organizational.

Gender Sensitization

Women constitute almost half of the population and play a crucial role in the society. Police have always been blamed of being gender insensitive. Their style of functioning, more often than not, poses a threat to the fair sex than providing a comfort zone. If the police could provide safety to women and create a sense of security among them, it would go a long way in improving the police–community relation. The Tirkha Committee, therefore, recommended that the representation of women in the state police should be gradually increased and this increase should be quicker in branches dealing with investigation of offences against women and protection of civil rights. Simultaneously, the police should make special efforts to obtain the help of women social workers in social security programs and for active help to Mahila Police Stations.[10]

Changing Outlook

Police has a more threatening presence rather than a confidence enhancing one. There is a dire need to bring change in its outlook so that the public/community appreciate their presence. Police should not only be responders and reactive to the complaints, but also should be pacifiers, have a soothing interaction with the victims and complainants, and specialize in *consulting hearing* and *empathetic response techniques*. Expecting the police to change overnight into the "May I help you" mode is too much to ask for. Nevertheless, in this changing environment of active, educated, and aware community, giving a friendly picture can always entice more participation, collaboration, and partnership.

Changing the method of investigation, using more scientific methods, and so on, can bring a more humane approach to working. Use of hypnotism for detection of cases rather than resorting to torture, which has been one of the main reasons for the blotted image of the police, has been in vogue in many countries. In Southern Brazil, one specialist has claimed to have solved around 600 police cases with the help of hypnotism.

The Montgomery County sheriff's office has dedicated a room for crime scene reconstruction with movable walls, piles of cardboard, and rolls of white paper; investigators can recreate a murder, robbery, or any other crime scene to help them solve and answer nagging questions or to give jurors a clearer look at what may or may not have happened during a crime.[11]

---

[10] Tirkha, M.C., N.K. Singh, and Ashok Patel. *Committee Report on Police*, Tirkha Committee, Madhya Pradesh, pp. 476–78.
[11] *Pioneer*. 2010. "Room with a Re-view," Crime Buster, *Pioneer*, Sunday, Foray, Bhopal, February 21.

There is also a need for the police to properly project itself. Effective public relations are a proper method for that. Public relations are not propaganda or spin advertising. Advertising is a great image-building medium but public relations are a great credibility-building medium. The job of public relations does not mean playing around with facts; it is lending meaningful perspective. It is essentially the ability to communicate effectively to the target audience.

Application of Psychological Principles

There is a need for application of psychological principles to keep the spirits of the police personnel high. Lack of spirit is manifested in their attitude and behavior toward the public. Weird unwanted behavior, which is the cause of negative police image, can be rectified by application of psychological principles. At the outset, the police should be sensitized about the role, importance, and use of psychological approach while dealing with management of public order. Adequate efforts need to be made by the police leaders in order to develop the spirit, temperament, and attitude among their personnel so as to apply psychological principles while handling situations. In order to enable the policemen, especially at the cutting edge level, to understand the problem in question, they should be encouraged to foster qualities like inquisitiveness, empathy, sympathy, holistic judgment, quick grasping of the problem, patience and cool temperament, mutual introduction/dialogue with the crowd, and analytical ability in dialectical terms, which will enable them to take decisions promptly and in a better manner. Root cause and genesis of law and order problem should be understood. Genuine problems must be addressed without any loss of time. The police officers should shed their personal ego and prejudices while effecting negotiations. Humane approach is always welcome.

Despite the situations being tense, while tackling law-and-order problems, the police should not appear to be alarmed. They should act with patience and without any fear or anger. They must cultivate values like charity, compassion, friendliness, cooperation, and so on, vis-à-vis general public. It makes the public take a humane view of the men in uniform. A police officer should integrate himself in the community like other professionals, i.e., academicians, lawyers, doctors, engineers, and so on. Police profession is target-oriented. Performance appraisal is based on the statistics of cases solved and cases resulting in conviction or acquittal. The officers, most of the time, believe in driving the subordinates so that the goals and targets are achieved. They hardly understand that policemen, like other human beings, have families, problems, and needs. If these are ignored, policemen become frustrated and develop negative attitudes. This negative attitude influences the work they turn out. It is required that the officers of today are welfare-oriented and liberal in their thinking, and create an atmosphere in work situation which is conducive for tension-free working.

Keeping Morale and Motivation of the Police High

Motivation and morale have a direct bearing on discipline. Each has its own importance and a definite role, which has to be understood in the right spirit. Discipline should be cultivated and nurtured rather than enforced, and it should not be taken as an end in itself. Discipline implies obedience and if motivation, morale, and welfare are missing, there can be no discipline. However, symptoms of indiscipline should be understood and judged properly and should be tackled and treated with a humane touch. Morale of the force has suffered serious erosion due to the antiquated law, uncooperative public, an alert and activist but complaining press, constantly interfering politicians, multiplicity of command, unattractive working conditions, self-centered leadership, and a variety of other factors.[12]

Diversification can be one method of keeping the freshness of the job. A lease of fresh air comes into the life of officers and the creativity gets a better chance to blossom. In Madhya Pradesh, sports have been put under the leadership of the police officers. Similarly, earlier few of the Chief Executive Officers (CEOs) of Zila panchayat were police officers and they all proved in their respective fields as dynamic and innovative officers.

---

[12] Rao, U.N.B. 2000. "Proactive Techniques for Improving Performance of Police," *SVP National Police Academy Journal*, 52(1): 85–99, July–December.

People work more effectively on a job that they want to do and that they feel is theirs than a job, they feel, someone else wants them to do. Just as people invest themselves more intensely in jobs they like, they also prefer to work in an area where they feel competent. A lack of involvement results in a psychological withdrawal from the job. Intellectually, the superiors see delegation as lack of control. But he/she is badly mistaken on this point. Some superiors feel that praising their subordinates will cause them to relax their performance, but the opposite is usually true. People react best when they receive recognition for their good work. Commendations given in public are most effective because the entire organization knows that good work is being recognized. On the other side of the coin is condemnation or the rebuke, which should be administered in private. The prestige and status of an officer in his/her peer group will be lowered if he/she is reprimanded in public, and he/she might go into a shell or work against the organization. Thus, the credit for good work must be shared and responsibility for mistakes or inferior work must not be divided.

Managing Stress in Police Personnel

The stressful nature of the police work shatteringly affects the health and family lives of many officers, and encourages alcoholism among them. Thus, it is necessary to impart some sort of training to our officers to familiarize them with problems of job-related stress and techniques of stress management. The stressful nature of the job can be made out by the fact that an incident of a policeman committing suicide or losing his sanity and going haywire firing indiscriminately on superiors or in public is not a rarity now. There are endless stories of policemen succumbing under pressure and becoming a victim of stress and strain of the job and the cumulative environmental pressure.

There are a number of causes of stress witnessed by a policeman everyday during his normal policing in India. Consequently, the stress level is very high. Most of the ills of the police behavior can be ascribed to the unmanageable work and spilled over social stress. However, it is a pity that hardly any serious initiative is taken to manage their stress. The efforts that are made are more or less paperwork and a formality. Thus, the need is to take the issue more seriously and sincerely.

Professionalism in Police

Issues of professionalism among the police personnel and their organization in India emerge in the democratic governance and the process of social development. Democratic governance and social change generate certain dilemmas and a conflict within the police organization and among their leadership, exposing them to several and severe stresses and strains. Professional ethos provides a way out of the dilemmas and conflicts before the police and helps them perform their role effectively and efficiently. Professionalism merely does not represent modernization; rather, three sets of attributes constitute professionalism, i.e., specialized knowledge, skills to apply such knowledge in real life situations, a set of socially acceptable value (premises), and an ethical framework.

The expectations and demands of the society from the police are rising even in the face of erosion of its image and decline in credibility. Due to the predominance of the negative image of the police, though there are some indications of change in it, the positive perceptions such as integrity, impartiality, anonymity, and ability to manage crisis are clouded. Since professionalism is a multidimensional process, it has to be a constant process if the police have to keep pace with the dynamic process of change in the society. The equations between the community and the police have to be built on the firm foundations of social accountability and mutual support.[13]

The citizens look up to the police to provide an ambience of security and orderliness so that the day-to-day life can carry on with an *even tempo*. A policeman, for that, requires multitude of skills and also one that demands a certain set of attitudinal dispositions and values. No policeman can be born with these values. Indeed the most professionally competent policeman will still need to upgrade his skills and adapt to the ever-changing demands of the job. Being professional is not just sticking to the core values and duty briefs as originally envisaged, it is also to continually adapt and change with the ever-dynamic situations and conditional ties that emerge in the work environment.

Constant and bold efforts should continue to shape the police department and it should be made acceptable to the society for its professionalism. On the other hand, community education should not be

---

[13] Rao, U.N.B. 2000. "Proactive Techniques for Improving Performance of Police," *SVP National Police Academy Journal*, 52(1): 85–99, January–June.

left to mere change. Various sorts of community institutions should be carefully created to orient the community in such a manner that it may accept the police and respond to their calls in a positive and realistic manner. A well-designed and scientifically evolved scheme of functional decentralization of the police organization can be an effective method of injecting competence in the police system.

Attitudinal Change: Client-oriented Policing

Participative policing advocates attitudinal change in the police personnel when interacting with the community in any capacity, at any time, and at any place. Both work in tandem as partners. The relation between the community and the police should be egalitarian and not hierarchical. Police personnel need to have certain qualities, which will help them in being accepted. Open-minded, sensitive, concerned about people's problems, proactive, analytical in thinking and unbiased, impartial, and a prejudice-free attitude is desirable. If officers do not agree with a complainant's viewpoint, they should try to listen and understand the problem, display empathy and compassion with sincerity, not in a rehearsed way. Skill in planning, problem solving, organizational know-how, interpersonal communications, and perhaps most importantly, critical thinking and patience are the basic qualities of CPOs. It calls for organizational transformation requiring the alignment of organizational management, structure, personnel, and information systems to support community partnerships and proactive problem solving.[14] Getting involved in social service programs may help the people in believing that the police are not an agency of coercion but their friends during periods of need and emergency.[15]

---

[14] Community Oriented Policing Services (the COPS Office) is the component of the US Department of Justice. http://www.cops.usdoj.gov/default.asp?item=36 as visited on February 4, 2010.

[15] Sarolia, S. 1985. "State of Police-community Relations in India Today: How to Improve It?," *Essays on Police-community Relations*, pp. 83–97. Hyderabad: SVP National Police Academy.

ZONE OF ACCEPTANCE

Over the years, particularly in the developing countries, because of high-handed image of the police, the community has drifted away from them. A sense of distrust has prevailed leading to perceptible communication gap between them. Community has stopped accepting the basic tenet of community policing that the police are a part of the community. One of the major reasons for this is that the police are becoming more and more inaccessible. To reinstate an environment of trust, it becomes necessary to increase the zone of acceptance of the police in the community. For that, the police have to become more accessible, transparent to the permissible limit, restore inevitable participatory ambience, and plug the communication gap.

The major reason for detesting community policing has been the fear of losing power. Police is recognized for its power and the policemen think that power sharing would dilute the cause of their very existence. It is necessary to understand that empowering the community does not make the police powerless. It is not a win–lose situation for anyone but a win–win situation where the community and the police are both going to gain by giving better results. The cooperation has synergistic effect and it helps in covering up the limitations of resources and the like. The tactics and strategies to be employed to meet any particular situation require the assistance of an expert. Day-by-day the police job has also become a specialist job and hence the external expert input becomes desirable. There is labyrinth of relationships existing in police work. Police job is not complete without multidisciplined assistance in its function. The appreciation of this maze of relationships by the police rather than sticking to unrealistic boasting as an individual practitioner encourages the police to work collectively with others and the zone of acceptance also increases.

CLIENT SYSTEM

Police will have to accept that they are the service providers and the community is their client. Customer service and their satisfaction should be the police's prime motive. Like any other organization, they too will have to be accountable and responsible for its omission and commission of any action. Efficiency and effectiveness of their existence will have to be proved, every now and then. As any entrepreneur or service provider, the police should do a need-analysis study, understand the requirements of its client, and strategize its action accordingly.

The concepts of synergy and win–win power orientation logically lead to the value of empowering the client system in the decision-making process. In terms of the system—this would mean that whatever is possible—the client system would also become a part of the action system, i.e., participants in the change process. When a consensus or a collaborative approach is appropriate, the target system would also be a part of the action system. In other terminology, participation by those to be affected by the change effort—the "output constituency"—also become a part of the "input constituency," i.e., the decision-makers. Being part of the decision-making does not imply transgressing one's professional domain. It is synergizing the potential of the service provider and the client for the benefit of both. Striking a better understanding will expand the zone of acceptance.

Police Accountability

Accountability means answerability for the proper performance of the assigned job. Accountability means more than the mere responsibility to discharge the duties involved in a job, and includes the responsibility of doing so to the satisfaction of the party for whose benefit the responsibilities are being discharged. In a democratic society, the police remain ultimately accountable for its performance to the people. Protection of the basic rights of the people and compliance with law are the twin pillars of good policing in a liberal democratic society. The mandate of the police to use force to curb greater violence and disorder raises the key issue that the police themselves should not indulge in abuse or misuse of force. The exercise of police powers must be subject to checks and balances. However, checks and balances on the police power, if they are to serve the intended purposes, must be reliable as well as effective in their nature and operation.

The National Human Rights Commission pointed out in its submission before the Apex Court that altogether the rule of law in modern India, the frame upon which justice hangs, has been undermined by the rule of politics. Supervision in the name of democracy has eroded the foundations on which impartiality depends in the criminal justice system. For better accountability of the police, the commission suggested the formation of District Complaints Authority to examine complaints from the public regarding police excesses.[16] If the police in India are to be accountable to the people, responsive to their aspirations, and sensitive to their frustrations, it will call for a wholly new perception of their functions by the leaders, both inside as well as outside the police. It will call for a change in its rigid philosophy of rule of law and accountability to law alone.

Unlike accountability to the law, the concept of accountability to the people is a dynamic and modern concept, which will make the police an active participant in social change instead of being a passive observer and will inject in them a sense of involvement in the process. Unless the people feel confident that the police would not threaten individuals' liberty provided by the law, the police will not likely enjoy popular support.

Use of Proactive Techniques

The traditional way of policing is acting in reaction to a report. The reactionary approach cannot be the only modus operandi to meet he demand of the society. Adoption of proactive techniques, which would include the participation of the community, is a solution to the growing requirement of policing activities. The additional hands, eyes and ears, thoughts and actions, in the form of community partnership are what are required.

Conflict management and restorative justice is a process of resolving conflict in the form of an out of court settlement in criminological literature.[17] Restorative justice is a way of dealing with offenders and victims by focusing on the settlement of conflicts arising from crime and resolving the underlying problems which cause it. It is a rational way of solving problem. The focus of the restorative justice system is

---

[16] Sen, Sankar. 2000. "Police Accountability and Civilian Oversight," *SVP National Police Academy Journal*, 52(2): 70–76, July–December.

[17] Bajpai, G.S. 1997. *Victim in the Criminal Justice Process: Perspectives on Police and Judiciary*. New Delhi: Uppal Publishing House.

148 *Community Policing*

recognition of the community rather than criminal justice agencies as the focal point of crime control. The idea is gaining ground throughout the world as alternatives to the present justice process.[18] The family-counseling centers in Madhya Pradesh, Special Cells of Maharashtra, Haryana, Orissa, and Delhi are examples of restorative justice method used in resolving conflicts arising due to domestic violence. Samajik Nyaya and Shashaktikaran Kendras in Adim Jati, Janjati Kalyan (AJK) police stations (especially set up to deal in cases of atrocities against SC/ST) in Madhya Pradesh are also toeing in line to this philosophy.

---

[18] Bazemore, G. and L. Walgrave. 1997. *Restoring Juvenile Justice Monsey*. New York: New York Criminal Justice Press.

CASE STUDIES

11

Communal Violence in Narsinghgarh, Madhya Pradesh, and the Aftermath

Challenges in the Riot-hit Area

Narsinghgarh is a subdivision in Rajgadh District, in the state of Madhya Pradesh. This *tehsil* has a history of communal tension. On April 2, 2007, communal riots broke out during the *Hanuman Jayanti* procession. When the procession was passing through a Muslim-dominated area, few provoking slogans by the Hindu community participants had incited violent reaction from Muslims. The riots had resulted in three people's death and loss of property worth crores. Police resorted to strict action, which had ultimately alienated both the communities. The incident had serious ramifications in the relations between both the communities and the communities' relation with police. An air of mistrust and suspicion was rooted between the Muslims and the Hindus, and at the same time, the police were looked upon as unfriendly by both the communities. Hence, three clusters had taken shape due to this riot. They registered around 90 cases against each other, and both the communities dragged names of innocent people in these cases; and because of this, the rift widened. It was believed that minimum one year would be consumed in bringing things back to normal. I was shifted from Assistant Nodal Officer, Community Policing Branch, Police Headquarters, to Subdivision Officer Police (SDOP) Narsinghgarh, as my predecessor was forced to quit after riots. I took over the charge on April 13, 2007, evening.

Life after riots is not normal. There is air of distrust, hatred, anguish, dissatisfaction, despair, fear, and what not. A common man who becomes a victim for no reason or no fault of his is most affected. The antisocial elements of the society, who are the direct beneficiaries, work full time to prolong that sense of insecurity and environment of hatred. This puts the administration on their defensive best. Their energy is totally exhausted in building back the damaged environment and reestablishing communication with the community, which for all obvious reasons gets stalled with the incident. The atmosphere is so heated that there is a clear-cut fracture in the society and the blame game is at its best. An unwanted solidarity is displayed by each community and they vouch for the innocence of the perpetrators of their community. They want to believe, without logic, that it was the other community which incited and provoked violence. It is made into a religious conflict—Hindu versus Muslim—and is not simply mob violence and arson, which can be dealt merely by applying the sections of IPC and other laws.

It is a common feature for the administration to be indifferent with the victims and citizens at large after the riots. At the most, one would see a gesture of sympathy with the victims, that too perforce. The riots, anyways, are not incidents which would attract sympathy from the administrators. Riots are normally followed by hacking and sacking of the hapless police personnel, sometimes the axe falling on revenue officers too, on the allegation of being lackadaisical. With the sword of Damocles, hanging over head, the question of being sympathetic toward the citizens becomes a rarity. It is more an attempt to save one's own skin than anointing the bruised skin of others; simple human psyche, I would say.

We, the policemen, always ask, are we not the same as others? We too would have the same feelings of hatred and prejudice as other citizens. This is the attitude, which basically causes the problem of police partiality, high-handedness, and insensitivity in dealing with such sensitive cases. There is hardly any riot incident where the police personnel are not accused of siding with a group. "Even the policemen who had arrested secretly told us that they were on our side" is what one of the activists revealed after one of the most serious Hindu–Muslim conflict in Bijnor, 1990.[1] This is not an exceptional case. There

[1] Basu, Amrita. 2008. "When Local Riots are not Merely Local," in Steven I. Wilkonson (ed.), *Religious Politics and Communal Violence*, pp. 342–76. New Delhi: Oxford University Press, 349.

are a numbers of cases alleging police partiality and such allegations pile up with every communal disturbance.

One exceptional situation I found was the plight of the police station. The Inspector in charge of the police station had proceeded on leave before the riot broke. It was alleged that he had an inkling about the undercurrent; instead of trying to check and find the cause, he escaped by taking a long medical leave. There were two SIs in the police station. One was at his fag end of the career. He was an officer from rank and file, promoted from constabulary. I hope the adversaries of the job had made him too compromising, defensive, and totally indecisive. The other SI, a lady officer, was too brash, who had proclivity to invite controversies, unfazed by the fragility of situation. In such a situation, it is but natural that the motivational level was abysmally low.

To add to the confusion, there were four INSPs from the Criminal Investigation Department (CID) unit of the police headquarters to assist in the investigation of cases registered immediately after the riot. They had their families in Bhopal, hence always wanted to take French leave. They had nothing at stake and just the call of duty was not enough to keep alive the spirit beyond a week; and unfortunately, I had joined just after a week of riots, when their interest had wearied and motivation dried up. Their attitude slackened and they complained to the subordinates that it was the duty of the police station officers to deal with cases. There was a makeshift *thana* in charge, attached from police lines. He had no stakes as he knew that his life in the place was short.

It was a wrong perception of man management. Solution to a problem was sought by pushing too many leaders in a spot. Four INSPs with no defined role and responsibility, no hierarchical work distribution, and no supervisory head to give them clear directions created more problems than finding a solution to the prevailing situation. "Too many cooks spoil the broth." The current deployment went against the management principles; no proper chain of command—against the theory of unity of command—lack of leadership, no responsibility fixation, too much noise in communication, lack of motivation, and lack of goal/target.

In the recent past, the figure theory has become the order of the day in the police organization. A norm, which is followed to strengthen claims on paper, saves one's skin than having to do with effectiveness. Figure theory states that the paper work should be appropriately done; even fudging with statistics is welcome in that endeavor. Officers sitting in places far away rely totally on the figures that reach them on paper. A mastermind in paper work has always the benefit of tilting the side to his favor by manipulating the figures.

It is not that the officers available when I had joined were incompetent; but they had no one to guide them, none on whom they could bank upon in tough situations, and an aura of uncertainty prevailed. Tough action against a few had already landed my predecessor SDOP in soup and his suspension had sent a wrong signal through rank and file. The assessment of his job (my predecessor) had been scathing and he had become a victim of politics. Now this lot of attached officers was in no mood to unruffle the feathers of anyone else.

There has been much written about the police apathy, inaction, or prejudice during communal riots. They have even been blamed of indulging in riots.

> The police and para-military forces are invested with all necessary legal powers to prevent riots from taking place through pre-emptive action, and when riots start, to bring them swiftly to an end. If despite this there are frequent and sustained communal riots, it is because the police, at the behest of the political leadership in the states concerned, have either remained silent spectators or even participated in the riots. In every major riot since 1978 the police have exhibited partisan behavior against Muslims.[2]

It is always a rule to put the action and reaction of the police under a scanner after riots. And there have been instances where the police action has come under a cloud of suspicion. But, is being so judgmental not derogatory?

> The role of the police with regard to communal disturbances is mostly misunderstood. Treating it to be a police problem without analyzing issues involved in the creation of inter-group conflicts, vested interests, and religious, economic and political dimensions is doing injustice to the police. The role of the police is to maintain public order by dealing with situations which emerge as a threat to breech of peace.[3]

As mentioned earlier, post-riot management needs a thoroughly different approach from gun-shooting and cane-wielding tactics adopted during riots. The first step was to test the waters and then decide from where to start. There was a need to break away from the family

[2] Vanaik, Achin. 2009. "India's Paradigmatic Communal Violence," *Socialist Register 2009 Violence Today*, Edited by Leo Panitch and Colin Leys; Socialist Register.
[3] Singh, V.V. 1993. *Communal Violence*. Jaipur: Rawat Publications, p. 163.

of stereotypes, spring some surprises on the community, and identify our allies in our venture and rally them for the cause. We wanted, as a broker and mediator, to establish a dialog between the communities and make them aware of the fact that their peace, life, bread and butter, and harmony were at stake. It was in their benefit to restore normalcy and the police had not much to lose. We wanted to tell them that we, as members of the police organization, would always get our pay on time, get eatables even when a curfew is clamped, get medical aid even at worst conditions, and roam on deserted roads at will, which would all be a far cry for them. The biggest challenge was to have all ears and eyes toward us, to get an audience, attentive and active. For that, we were pressed to prove our sincerity first and make them believe that we were not just rhetoric but meant business.

At the other end, one fact which I was fully aware of was that the police could work in isolation. Howsoever armed we are, with fire-power and manpower, words and real work have no substitute. Striking a communication with communities is inevitable if sustainable peace is the goal to be achieved. Now, in such situations where the police are already a party,—for their high-handedness and allegations of partiality, partisan—to make communities listen to them with trust was no cakewalk.

Except for a few exceptions, I too had inherited the same situation as any officer across the country would have. With the team, we became aware of the fact that the success of any effort, small or big, depends solely on the acceptance and appreciation by the community. The best of endeavors may go to dogs if it finds opposition by the clientele. We decided to take police as any other service sector organization with the community as our clientele. For us, what was required was a "need analysis study" of the community whom we were assigned to serve and then strategize the plan accordingly so that the probability of success went up. PPT needed to be implemented. The administration was pushed to the wall because of non-participatory approach of both the communities.

Reaching Out

After tiring deliberations, with force and other tactics, we realized that there was no other substitute than going to the community and speaking to them, man to man, in person, listening to their woes, complains, and expectations. Giving them a chance to vent out their feelings and being all ears to them, giving them a patient hearing, we decided to embark on our mission of interaction. "Go to their doorstep, with words not guns" became our motto. Guns have always been at our side, hooked to the belt. What we were lacking was word of assurance. With one of the CID inspectors, who had already served in this police station some years back and knew the place well, we started going to each *mohalla* (neighborhood) and to talk to the people, reconstitute the *Nagar Raksha Samiti*s, and instill confidence.

As a preparatory effort, our team had spent many hours combing through the available record, verbal and documentary, to identify people who mattered. We wanted a team of citizens who would stand fast against the odds. Our aim was to galvanize them as our supporters and mouthpiece. Direct police involvement is always perceived as a threat and official interference. The community's own involvement in their affairs gives credence. Howsoever good the intentions of the police are, due to past experience and the age-old image, their efforts are always dragged into the domain of suspicion. We knew that it would take some time before our credibility would be honored. In meetings, the attendance was abysmally low and communication was more of a complaining nature than solution-based. It was high time when community policing was to be put to action, effectively.

In the first eight days, we visited 12 wards out of 14 and conducted a meeting inviting the locals. We sat in their houses, public places, and tried to give a patient hearing. At the same time, we called a meeting of business community, bus operators, and other such collective groups. We had shortlisted the active and prospective troublemakers, inactive influentials, community leaders, and other active members of the community. It was then categorized according to their influence, *mohalla*-wise and for full town. Very much to our expectation, the list of troublemakers was not very big. They were a handful of them who were capable of creating a ruckus in the whole town. So, the target was to tame them. Identifying and having a list of the target group made our job very simple.

The first *mohalla* we visited was Balbatpura Chauraha. We chose to sit in a Muslim's house. The police here too had been accused of being prejudiced to a particular community.

Our second stop was at Champi Chauraha. There was a Hanuman temple undergoing massive renovation. We chose the stairs of the temple as our meeting place.

The process of reaching out to the community had started in full swing. No room or hall was booked for those meetings. Shade under the tree, any inviting house, school premises; all provided the much needed space to us. Charpoys, stools, chairs, *dari* on the floor, and even staircases became our sitting place. This left a much-needed impression on the minds. It gave access to that section of the community which dared not approach the police on their own. A dialogue was immediately established with the man in the street. The strategically designed approach to strike a chord with the masses started showing success.

The immediate complaints put forward which needed to be redressed were:

- The bus operators had lain off all the other community employees due to community pressure.
- The shopkeepers had removed their employees hailing from the other community.
- Innocent persons' names got involved in cases to settle personal scores.
- Many shops had been ransacked and burnt but the revenue officers had failed to evaluate the loss; and even the cases had not been registered, which helped them get compensation or claim insurance.
- There was a sense of insecurity prevailing and freedom of movement curtailed.

There were innumerable other issues but did not directly involve the police. The meetings with bus operators and the business community helped solve the first two problems and immediate relief helped in restoring trust to some extent. Going to their house to hear them and solving problems instantly sent a signal that the police meant business, and a positive one. Regarding the concoction in cases, they were openly invited to produce enough evidence, their alibi, and so on, that would prove their innocence. It was assured to them that the police would seriously take note of their call and do the needful. After testing in a few cases the word spread and persons who had run away from Narsinghgarh started returning. As for ransacked or burnt shops and houses, the police team visited them and wherever necessary, registered cases and forwarded the claim case to revenue officers.

Addressing Practical Societal Problems

Restoring the sense of security and freedom of movement was then the most dicey issue. Rumors in such situations make the maximum damage. At the high point of riots, the content of the rumors is most threatening and the speed at which they get circulated is unimaginable. It is at this particular time when three of the four conditions for generation and transmission of rumors—personal anxiety, general uncertainty, and topical importance—are at their highest level. The credulity is no longer in operation since at high levels of anxiety, disbelief in rumor is suspended, i.e., rumors will be believed regardless of how farfetched they are.[4] The rumors, once afloat, become difficult to control as they get further magnified and each one adds some more emotions or material contents. These additions and distortions are done to make them more penetrating.[5] Even here, the rumors were rife. In a couple of incidents, the shutters were pulled down in a panicky response to rumors. Rushing police to the spot in no time and meeting continuously the community members spelled that the police meant serious business and this menace died within a couple of weeks. We shared our mobile numbers with all in the community and messages used to flow freely, which helped getting information quickly. Couple of times the *sadar* (sociopolitical chief) of the Muslim community complained about persons stalking their men during wee hours of the day and prompt police action instilled loss of confidence in them. Within one month, the *tehsil* had bounced back to normalcy, superficially, though they held strong animosity toward each other.

One very important aspect that came to light during discussions with members of different associations and persons of repute, who had been and were still active in social sectors, was that everybody wanted to distance themselves from hooligans, particularly during a law-and-order problem. The rogues had their field day whenever tension mounted. The so-called vocal influentials retreated into their dens and left the ground open for the antisocial to plough at their will. This indifferent attitude toward own wellbeing despite having an impressive

---

[4] Rosnow, Ralph L. 1988. "Rumor as Communication: A Contextualist Approach," *Journal of Communication*, 38(1): 12–28.

[5] Lindzey, G. and E. Aronson. 1985. *The Handbook of Social Psychology*, Vol. IV. New York: Random House.

following was a surprise for me. I think this attitude has plagued our country, everywhere. It took us a lot of effort to break the ice and get them to spill out their reservations. The following is what they had to say:

We do not want to put at stake our self esteem and pride. These rogues have no stand in the society. Their prestige gets whipped up once they are publicly manhandled by police or taken into custody. If we slap them it would make no difference to them but in contrary even their abusive language would disgrace us in the society. We will become a mocking stock and our reputation will get a beating. Hence, it is better to stay away from such people and save our face.

Whether that was a face-saving attempt or an "escapist attitude" was difficult to discern. Showing one's back to the fire does not extinguish it. Instead, it requires some firefighting attempt. Without picking a fire hose, one cannot douse the fire. It was for us to decide from where to make a start. The society was divided; the opinions to combat the menace were not uniform. The administration in place to put things in order were clueless, the man in the street was bitten by the bug of insecurity and deluged by the waves of rumors, and the political leaders assigned to establish harmony were deliberately and continuously making politically wrong statements, furthering the chasm. I think, such a situation is prevalent in every riot-hit area and this was no exception.

The avoidance attitude came to fore when, after the riot, for the first time, a religious procession was to be taken out on July 16, 2007 from Jagdish Mandir. Though it was not supposed to cross any sensitive area, but locals of both the communities were scared of anymore processions. Even the administration refused to give permission. But the politicians and interested parties stuck to the logic of letting the traditions carry on. A short procession attended by very few people was carried on with crossed fingers. Despite knowing that a tense situation prevailed, the persons who mattered in the society, like representatives of various committees and other such individuals, approached the administration to stop the procession from being given the permission but did not have the courage to stand in public and object.

The season of festivals was in offing and it was realized that to ensure a smooth cruising of things, maximum involvement of the community was imminent. The youth group of Nagar Raksha Samiti, which was inoperational, was rejuvenated. In the first meeting, only six young boys came but later on it swelled up to 70 members with around

15 girls pledging to work day in, day out to ensure peace and tranquility. The real testing time came when month of Ramadan and 10 days of Ganesh Sthapana collided. Then, in one month, there were four big Hindu religious processions to be taken and in between Eid was to be celebrated. All the four were to pass through the sensitive Muslim areas and two during Ramadan time.

Processions become a significant vehicle of violence when local power politics is at stake. Over the years, a specific pattern of procession-based riots has emerged, for ideological and electoral reasons. The growing importance of elections in a democratic framework and the increasingly tense relations between the Hindus and Muslims, 1970s onward, largely explain this development. Political leaders have used processions and riots to mobilize supporters more and more frequently, especially at the time of elections, when it was particularly useful for them to polarize the electorate along religious lines.[6]

One realization I had with my earlier posting was that having a very good relation with other departments serves as a boon. Normally the differences erupt because of ego clashes and nothing more. "I am bigger than you," "struggle for identity," and "not my domain" attitude are the basic reasons for uncalled-for differences and lack of coordination. All the departments working in an area are interrelated. So, having a good relation serves all. With this in background, we had focused to build positive relations with all the departments. Relation with SDM and the judiciary was exceptional. The understanding with SDM, first with Mr Lakra and later with Mr Verma, was so good that we were together in all processions and law and order situations. This gave an impression to the community that administration was together and solutions to minor problems were solved on the spot.

It had become a norm that in *shanti samiti* meetings, the listed members would appear, participate in full volume, but practically vanish in thin air when it came to managing affairs in the field. They had stopped participating in any processions, functions, and gatherings where this small group of crude, brash young blood, whom they deplored, showed up.

This was one important aspect, which we felt needed immediate attention. There was a need to workout on a strategy where both could

---

[6] Jaffrelot, Christophe. 2008. "The Politics of Processions and Hindu-Muslim Riots," in Steven I. Wilkonson (ed.), *Religious Politics and Communal Violence*, pp. 280–81. New Delhi: Oxford University Press.

stay together without any heartburning and detest. Defining the roles of each group in the community was necessary. The community was composed of neither that bunch of raw blood nor those persons who considered themselves men of prestige. They both were constituents and, as citizens, they were equally responsible for establishing peace and tranquility in the area. It was practically impossible to force them to see eye to eye. The very tenor of their language was distinct. The style of discussing on an issue was different, poles apart; the elderly group giving suggestions and the rough group throwing their wishes. Handling both and utilizing the capability of both, to the maximum, was needed to be worked out.

The process of confidence building is a continuous process. It requires a lot of energy and skill. Running from pillar to post, asking everybody to believe you, trust you, bank on you, come forward to share with you, and take your efforts seriously does not serve the purpose. One has to prove first, set a trend, and fall within their spectrum of expectations on a consistent basis. The expectations become endless and are varied. Practically, fulfilling all is neither feasible nor advisable. To surf and remain on the board even in worst of tidal waves is what the community wants to see in you.

Managing Religious Processions through Participative Policing

First, the acid test came during the procession of Dhol Gyaras, (September 23, 2007) which was to take the same route taken by the *Hanuman Jayanti* procession leading to riots on April 2, 2007. We organized two meetings with the organizing committee and they assured that they will not stop at the *chowk*, next to Ramkund mosque, where the riots had taken place. Responsible persons in the procession were identified; they played a sensible role, passing the sensitive area smoothly.

During the initial phase of planning, SDM and we, the police officers, visited the Jamaat Mandir couple of times to become informal with the organizers. The procession was to start from the mandir and was to be led by the Guru ji of the temple, who was revered by the entire Hindu community. We participated in the *aarti* and discussed about the procession in detail. In our second visit, he was totally convinced that our suggestions were for the benefit of the community at large. Some of the youngsters who were very active later became our frontrunners in all processions to follow. They became the permanent representatives of the young Hindu community.

This Dhol Gyaras procession was soon to be followed by Anant Chaturdashi procession (September 25, 2007). This latter procession passed through the main lane of the Muslim community, where the mosque was located, in Ramkund area. This was one interesting feature of Narsinghgarh. The Muslim-dominated area was called as Ramkund and the most influential Hindu temple was Jamaat mandir.

It was proposed by the administration in the (Anant Chaturdashi) procession that the route of the procession should be changed so that the sensitive area may be exempted. During the *shanti samiti* meeting, called in lieu of preparation for Anant Chaturdashi procession, administration proposed to change the route and exempt sensitive areas. The members present accepted unanimously but later after meeting it was thwarted by politicians who thought their interest is not going to suffice. We identified the hidden people who avoided coming in the *Shanti Samiti* meetings but were very influential in the society. We agreed to the old route but handed over the responsibility of providing a safe passage of procession to that section which opposed our idea. They were the office bearers of Rashtriya Swayamsevak Sangh (RSS) organization. I personally invited them home for a cup of tea and discussed the need of their help. They were overwhelmed by this courteous meeting and agreed upon doing the needful. This procession marked a history. Over the years, the procession used to reach the Ramkund Masjid (Mosque) with ear-piercing music playing during the *namaz* time, early morning, around 5 am. However, this time, they respected our desire and crossed this area by 4 am, saving all the chance of tension. It had special significance because it was the special Ramadan *namaz* and one slogan had all the prospects of vitiating the atmosphere in seconds.

We had worked very hard in the preceding days, visiting all the *jhankis* where the Ganesh idol had been installed. Everyday, we participated in *aartis*, met the organizing committees, had informal talks for some time, and started calling them by their respective names. A rapport was established between us and the organizing committee. When the procession started, half the crowd, which was in charge of the idols, was known to us. They were already burdened under the obligation of having us as participants in the functions preceding the procession. There was that confident, acquainted eye contact with them, which played the magic in the procession.

During the briefing to the police force, it was made clear that they will not pass any instructions to the procession. Earlier, a similar message had been shared with the members of the organizing committee and the idol installation committee that the police will be playing a virtually standby role and it was their duty to ensure that the holy idols are immersed in the lake peacefully and with grace. The police personnel were told very sternly to be ready to deal with any untoward incident with an iron hand. No compromises were to be made on the basis of religion or community. Asking the deployed force to keep at bay from procession-goers was deliberate. We did not want to deal with the mob as such. Tackling a mob and dealing with individuals is totally different.

Crowd behavior is very different from an individual's behavior. There is a fusion of personalities in the crowd and it is a group behavior. Identity in a crowd only gets refocused.[7] Individual as such loses his/her identity and the whole group shares a common viewpoint. The passions rise high and wisdom is taken over by the common demand. An attack on an individual in the crowd is perceived as a threat to the whole group. It is a common voice, guided by a decided agenda or any issue, which takes shape in the course of movement of a gathering. It is not necessary that what is decided before is put to action in the same manner. One loud voice supported by few becomes the voice of the crowd. When the group has a propensity to become violent, then it becomes an unruly mob. The mentality of the mob becomes aggressive and more than reaching to a solution, the desire is to cause maximum damage to make their presence felt. The cause for their gathering takes a rear seat and the wish to be identified as a force, power to reckon, takes over.

The crowd amplifies all emotions, heightening a feeling of well-being into exaltation, fear into panic. The loss of personal identity in a crowd, however, makes individuals act in terms of the crowd's identity; for instance, according to the behavior "expected" of an anti-Hindu or

[7] Reicher, Stephen. 1982. "The Determination of Collective Behavior," in H. Tajfel (ed.), *Social Identity and Intergroup Relations*, pp. 40–82. New York: Cambridge University Press.

an anti-Muslim mob. The individual is not operating at some deeply regressed, primitive level of the psyche but according to the norms of the particular group.[8]

Our strategy was to focus merely on the leaders and give them the unuttered instructions just through lively eye contact. It worked miraculously. They fully respected our intentions and did that incredible job. This was a history as never ever the procession had crossed at that hour. A big issue due to proper planning and community cooperation had become a cakewalk.

Now it was time for Eid (October 14, 2007). After the *namaz*, when everyone was returning, we went to the tent erected by the Nagar Palika (municipality) and greeted all the Muslims moving out by embracing them. This further strengthened the bond between the police and the Muslims.

The next important procession was that of Dussehra. During Dussehra (October 21, 2007), the locals discussed the earlier proposal of a change in route of the procession. Agreeing to the logic behind it, they voluntarily decided to cut it short to half the passage through the sensitive Muslim area. Taking the cue, I went to the Muslims and floated the idea of welcoming the procession with flowers and providing water to the participants. This had to be done at the personal level; because reading the politics, it was etched in mind that the local politicians would never appreciate this move as that signified the shift of credit. The Muslims and Hindus who did not like the communities coming closer so quickly certainly played spoilsport.

Perhaps, in the recent past, the police's initiative to strike a chord with the masses and voluntary reception during the Eid Milan had struck a communication between us and they happily accepted the idea. The welcome tent erected with many banners, flowers, and serving *sharbat* was a big surprise to all Hindus. Later on, we came to know that this welcome had never happened in the annals of Narsinghgarh's history. A history was again made. This was the big impact of the police in the minds of the people of Narsinghgarh. The SP later on told us that even the Chief Minister of the State had congratulated him for this gesture. The message had floated beyond the district borders and reached the nearby capital Bhopal.

---

[8] Kakar, Sudhir. 1995. *The Colours of Violence*. New Delhi: Viking by Penguin Books India Pvt Ltd.

It was high time for us to express our gratitude to the Muslim community. Coming Friday, on October 26, 2007, I went to the main mosque after the afternoon *namaz* to thank them for being so supportive. The gathering was spellbound and the seniors, with welled eyes, said that all through their life, most of them being more than 60 years in age, had not witnessed any policeman coming forward to express gratitude. This gesture was taken by the whole community in the right spirit; after that, never ever during my stint did the Muslim community oppose to any of our moves.

Next day was Durga Visarjan (October 27, 2007). Again, this procession was to pass through one sensitive crossing. En route we discussed making small changes in the route for everyone's convenience and were readily accepted without any hassles. It was an incredible acceptance even for us. Both the communities and their active leaders had accepted that the police had all bona fide intentions and they played their role impartially. The situation turned topsy-turvy, the time immediately after riots and now.

In Malwa area of Madhya Pradesh, more than Holi, the festival of colors, the fifth day after Holi, Rangpanchami is celebrated with frenzy. Narsinghgarh subdivision has all that Malwa culture. There was a big procession on that day. And the worst part was that it constituted only the youngsters, and most of them were inebriated. Even the route was through Ramkund, the Muslim-dominated area, passing close to the mosque. We were very confident and already had talked to the main persons in the procession. Luckily, the few most influential boys were teetotalers. The procession started with a lot of fanfare but before it had reached the Muslim area, the message reached us that in two subdivisions of the district (Rajgadh), Biaora and Sahranpur, communal tension had started due to color being thrown on the mosques. In Sahranpur, it had turned into a full-fledged communal violence whereas in Biaora, the police had to resort to using force to disperse the procession. Amidst this information and with all sorts of rumors flowing, we had to take the procession through the Muslim area.

To our surprise, when we reached Ramkund well before the procession to take stock of the mood, the *sadar* (political leader of Muslims) came forward and proposed to station a couple of policemen on the rooftop of their houses and even on the mosque to ensure that no Muslim person pelts stones, as had happened during the riots. Then, he gathered Muslim *parshad*s (corporators) and other influential Muslim leaders and promised us to lead the procession themselves.

When the procession reached Ramkund, they hugged the front-row people in the procession and painted with color by the revelers took the procession through the area. This was an unseen incident. The full credit to the success of our efforts naturally shifted to the community members who had by now decided to take the lead and ensure peace in the society.

The Hindu community reciprocated with the same fervor during the Muharram procession (I was confirmed by the *sadar* that despite Muharram being an occasion of grief, they will not mind the procession being welcomed). They installed three big tents at different places welcoming the procession, and with same zeal and enthusiasm showered flowers on the participants and offered them *sharbat* and water as per demand. The *maulvi* (religious leader of the Muslims) came forward after the end of the procession and addressed the gathering declaring that it was for the first time that the Hindu community had come out of way to extend their warmth. Now it is his duty to ensure that the Muslims keep the spirit going. He was emotionally so charged that he went to the extent of saying that he would sacrifice his life to ward off any disturbance. He had all praise for the police for helping restore this brotherhood atmosphere.

Renewed activity within the community and the feeling of brotherhood which prevailed in Narsingarh demonstrated the effectiveness of community policing efforts, particularly in areas where citizens were afraid to leave their homes. Two major shifts must occur within the police organization if community policing is to work efficiently. Strong partnerships and collaborative efforts must first be established with the community. The command structure of the police organization must then be decentralized so that problem solving, decision-making, and accountability are spread to all levels of the organization. Such decentralization challenges the personnel to be more creative and more effective because the decisions they make are more timely and influenced by firsthand knowledge of the facts. Decentralization also gives higher level managers/police more time to formulate strategies that will improve the organization's performance. In a decentralized policing organization, lower level officers are responsible for the daily policing needs of the community, with guidance and backing from supervisors. Their long-term daily interactions with people and neighborhood patrolling gives them the opportunity to form stronger bonds with the community and are thus are able elicit community participation more efficiently and successfully. This satisfaction of ownership motivates both parties to solve the problems that affect the peace and safety measures of the locality.

Riot Anniversary—*Hanuman Jayanti* Procession

One last incident, in particular, needs to be mentioned to cement the success story of participative policing. It ultimately reaffirmed the importance of community participation and partnership in policing activities.

Hanuman Jayanti procession, the anniversary of the riot, was on April 10, 2008. I had been out in Bhopal for 10 days, during the preparatory stage of the procession, interrogating the Students Islamic Movement of India (SIMI) accused arrested in Indore. As was informed later, during the Shanti Samiti meeting, the Muslim community expressed on their own the desire to welcome the participants of the procession, as a goodwill gesture, to bury the hatchet of hatred for once and for all. The Hindu community hailed their initiative but later on backed off when one section pressurized to deny the proposal. When the same was communicated to the Muslims, the small disgruntled group, occupying a rear seat for a while now, immediately took charge of the situation blaming the liberals for giving too much leverage by compromising their position in the past. They started accusing the liberals for bringing a bad name to the community. Refusal by the Hindu community meant a slap on their face. The tension started mounting. It was rumored that a riot was imminent the next day.

The day before, I had to travel from Bhopal to Indore via Narsinghgarh, taking the SIMI accused, to put them back in Indore jail, under strong security cordon. After a very long day, having worked from five in the morning to seven in the night, decided to return back to Narsinghgarh rather than staying the night in Indore.

On my way back, at around 10 in the night, I received one forwarded message on my mobile, which said that "from the cemetery close to Ramkund, many caskets were being removed full of weapons and those were meant to be used on the procession next day." Soon one more message flashed saying that "we cannot appreciate the welcome gesture of the community who had hurled shoes on the pious flag of lord Hanuman, during last year's procession." Immediately followed a telephone call from an established political leader who said that the situation had worsened and any moment, things may get out of control.

After reaching Narsinghgarh, I telephoned my Inspector and took the stock of the situation. He briefed me about the happenings. I rang up the procession organizers during midnight and asked them to come and meet me at that moment. It took them 20 minutes to gather in my residence. When asked, they said that the administration had slacked a bit and there was no one mediating between the two communities. Some people did not like the idea of being welcomed by the Muslim community and wanted to keep a distance from that community. The reason quoted was a repetition of what was written in the message that I had received. I had to sternly reason out the pros and cons of their attitude. With little deliberation, they agreed.

Early morning, at 6 am, I met the leaders of the Muslim community. They were totally out of humor. They vehemently reiterated the disgrace they had been subjected to. They alleged that the unceremonious rejection by the Hindus was a cause of dejection amongst the Muslim community. The fallout had been a strong reaction within the community. The bold, outgoing, peace-loving, and the well-wishing group, which had thrown the proposal of welcoming the procession on behalf of their community, were now the plumb target of the youth, who lay dormant in this phase of constructive activism and were steamrolled for pessimism in an atmosphere of hope. This, of late, left-out group was now finding their voices echoed. The constructive group was now facing the wrath of the majority in the community and the denial was being construed as a slap on the face, indignity, and a clear message that all was not well. No words were being mixed while articulating their anguish for being indignant. When there is community fusion on any issue, it becomes very difficult to change the course. The takers are few and hidden. The voices of those few are lost in the din of resonance. "We have been dishonored and disgraced," is what they reiterated.

I was told that the administration had become complacent. They had not followed up with the aspirations of both the communities. The tension had not been built in one day. It had shaped in a couple of days and despite administration being brought to notice by the concerned community members, the issue was avoided from being brought to fore. After this, apathy for some time by the administration, the same old group, famous for vitiating the atmosphere, had laid siege of the situation and started dictating terms. This fortified one aspect that working with the community was a continuous effort. The faith and trust in the administration has eroded to such a great extent that despite all effort to institutionalize the work, it gets personalized. Unless the idea is supported by successive regimes persistently, the community starts banking on the few heads.

It was vividly written on the wall—communal affront is inevitable. What a test of time again, after having worked on all plans success-fully for more than a year now. While discussing with my SDM, I told him that this is the end of a cycle. The communal riots had taken place during the procession of *Hanuman Jayanti* and today the wounds have reopened, people have started jogging through their memories, the loss-and-gain mathematics is calculated, and the communities have started reliving the past. The happening is not a symbol of our fiasco but the finals, to be played to prove that the methodology adopted was the best, as it was their own effort. They have now to overcome that sense of indifference, to win over the fear psychology, and to reaffirm the faith that change can be brought only if they wished and no other way; administration, as ever, would be a mere facilitator and mediator. I told him that we will have to pull up our socks again and work on the assigned roles of mediator and facilitator. I wanted to reconfirm to them that it was not the presence of one or other officer, which should motivate them to take charge of situation. We had to reestablish that the reins were in their hand and not ours.

I had to remind the *maulvi* of the promise that he had made in public during Muharram. He had to be convinced that it was not the entire Hindu community but a few who, to get their vested interest met, were spearheading the team of troublemakers. After a very peaceful and exceptional past year, was it worth letting everything go down the drain? The better sense prevailed in them. The leaders retracted from their obstinate position and decided to stick to their old stand of wel-coming the procession. By the time the procession started at 9 am, two tents were erected, *sharbat* and flowers brought, and the procession was welcomed at two places. Even the elders of the Muslim community joined the procession and led it while crossing the sensitive *chowk*. We had succeeded again in our strife to prove to them that peace and tran-quility was dependent on their action and inaction. The police and the administration were mere facilitators.

After this procession, we took special care to reach out again to the community and tell them what they had invited. The whole market had gone on an uncalled bandh, doubting an imminent riot. Many families had shifted out of Narsinghgarh in the darkness of the night. We again went to thank both the communities for respecting our words and accepting our proposal that too put at very odd hours, just prior to the procession.

Throughout, the role of the community members who had taken the decision to help us and the role of young members of Nagar and Gram Raksha Samiti was commendable. They were visible everywhere and all the necessary directions were executed through them. This was not taken ill by any community's members as it was coming from someone not in uniform. Later, people started complementing us that this was our visible police as they were present in numbers in every program. This complement was a proof of policing with the community, for the community, and by the community.

Cooperation of the Press

We were certainly the beneficiaries of positive press coverage. I wonder if we rightly deserved it. It is unlikely and very unusual to find all press, all the time, for one-and-a-half years, being in favor and printing only good words about you. We were those lucky officers to others envy. The relation was so cordial that some taunted us of dictating terms to the press. The understanding built was without bribing them with tea parties or flattering them by visiting any press office. Narsinghgarh being a small place, no journalist had any office and they operated from home. Most of them were stingers, who were agents of a particular newspaper, and at the same time made some money by sending news. It was told, though it proved contrary, that this breed of journalists were the most dreaded as they thrive oñ yellow journalism. They keep news at ransom. Our group was lucky to be spared from their flak, caustic whipping remarks, and taken as hostage. Full support was delivered and they were eager to print every word we wished, though we restrained and kept totally aloof and gave them full space to judge and report.

"Opinion journalism," which has the potential to break and make a person in public domain, which builds the image of a person in public, and gives meaning to every word uttered, even in person, never posed any threat to us. It can be construed as one-and-a-half years' lucky, honeymoon period we had with them. It will not be a wrong assumption to make that to a great extent, this opinion journalism contributed in bridging the gap between me, in person, and the community. With every bit of news published, which projected us as action oriented, was followed by a number of calls from places around asking for help and support. So, print media had a great impact even in small places like this. Normally, it is a routine and habit for people to stand on *chowks* and discuss the newspapers early morning over a cup of tea or a simple chat. This prevents a lot of people from buying newspapers and the *pan* and tea kiosks provide free material. So, your news does not go unnoticed.

Down the road, encouraging "opinion journalism" paid high dividends for us. We were heard above the din with the support of the press and our expectations floated easily to everyone in print and through discussions that followed. Numbers in our activities began to surge and the participation solidified giving us an edge over the anti-social destructive team. Even they started approaching us, to buy our confidence. Media never went into the campaign of trumpeting our mistakes, distorting our words, questioning our motives, and fiddling with the facts made available. We were given that rare privilege of being taken at face value. They never casted any doubts on what we had up our sleeve.

If I have to explain the reason for this long peaceful marriage with the press, it would be difficult to explain. I think our strategy was to involve everyone, cutting across caste, religion, class, and institution in our activities, where the press people too were involved as citizens and given responsibility as any responsible Narsinghagarhi, which gave them the strong feeling of participation. We tried to involve them as citizens in all deliberation and their participation was sought right from the formative stage to the conclusion. We were honest enough to accept our failures, candidly objected to unacceptable things, appreciate loudly any good work done by anyone, and were in high accessible mode throughout. This provided them to get clarifications at any hour they needed and got my viewpoint on everything. The confidence was so high, with all, that they would call and ask me what to write and what to drop, while writing a story on any of our actions. Their internal press wrangles never infected our relations and I shared with all of them the same trustful relation.

Sometimes, I found it very awkward when some story of the police station's inaction was reported and my favorable version in block letters was printed without actually talking to me. They expressed their confidence saying, "What we have written is what you are going to do after reading this report." Was I so readable, transparent, and predictable? Was not that transgression into my opinion? But, trust is give and take. They would not report anything beyond saying, "I would look into the matter personally and act fairly according to facts." I do not know how appreciable it is for a government servant, but for me it did miracles. A strange fabric of a relationship we had weaved, which we pretty comfortably lay on, all this period. I am aware of the fact that such a sweet relationship is exceptional and cannot even be thought of in big cities where different factors come into play. The local press played a critical role in exacerbating tensions between the Hindu and Muslim communities.[9]

Idea of Participative Policing

Narsinghgarh's experiment demonstrated that with change in attitude, by ensuring participation, with the police getting more and more accessible, a strong two-way communication was established and the cooperation between the two multiplied manifold, eventually leading to growth of zone of acceptance. This even proved that client system of collaborative approach applies to all actions.

Nowadays, the man in the street is smart enough to scrutinize the subject, dissect it in every manner, interpret in a desired way, and look for all possible potential error of omission or commission. After calibrating their analysis, they decide upon whether the proposal made has to be accepted, with ensuring participation and promising for support, or just nod affirmative for the fact that it is a wish of administration, which they believe has no teeth to leave a bite mark. Nowadays,

---

[9] Basu, Amrita. 2008. "When Local Riots are not Merely Local," in Steven I. Wilkonson (ed.), *Religious Politics and Communal Violence*, p. 362. New Delhi: Oxford University Press.

even the poor and illiterate can follow the sound and infer with what conviction it is created.

I remember some valuable tips given to me by some seniors before I left to join as SDOP, Narsinghgarh, from Police Headquarters: "You will have to be very strict and don't give any leverages whatsoever to anyone. Show them that you mean business. Your image should be of a very strong officer, send specially to curb with iron hand any disturbance." To this extent, the advice was perfect to be accepted and practiced, but the other part of the advise, "Mind it, don't leave an impression of being soft. There is no need to deliberate or discuss as after such carnage there is no scope left for any discussions. We are not politicians. Not our words but our *danda* should speak," was difficult to comprehend.

Even when the cattle goes on a rampage and runs haywire in the fields, the cowboy tries to talk to them, runs behind them giving instructions, and at the same time wields his cane whenever necessary. Human beings are neither wild nor domesticated animals. We are not supposed to tame them but to reason with them. It sounds very utopian and impractical, but personally I feel it is not so. Concerted, serious, and honest efforts bear fruits. None of these changes can happen of their own accord. Each would require change in attitude among those in power, powerless, and powerbroker alike.

The success story does not end here. The best part came around six months later, after my posting back to Bhopal. I received a call from both community members from Narsinghgarh after the successful completion of a religious procession and was told that they still continued the culture of welcoming each other. They had realized the benefit of participative policing. The trend was set.

12

Timor-Leste
Partners in Policing Model (PIP Model)

Here we would like to discuss the community policing in a new country, Timor-Leste (East Timor). This is considered to be the youngest democracy of the world. Let us try to understand the history, the role of the UN, and other factors, which would influence community policing in the country. A model has been envisaged after study of the community and the politics. This proposed model is called the Partners in Policing model (PIP model). PIP model was forwarded to Asia Foundation, which was working in partnership with the UN and local government on the subject of community policing.

Introduction

Timor, with a total area of 15,007 sq. km, is less than 400 km north of Australia, separated from that continent by the Timor Sea. To the northwest lie the Indonesian islands separated by as little as 50 km by the Savu Sea, while in the northeast the Indonesian islands are separated by Wetar Strait, only 18 km away from Atauro, one of the islands of Timor-Leste. Timor is a part of the Australian continental shelf.

East Timor or Timor-Leste is a new country with a tumultuous past. As any newborn country would have, Timor-Leste is also facing the challenges of transition into freedom. It has a short history of seven years of independence, nurturing under the umbrella of the

UN, which has been existing since 1999 in one or the other form. The UNMIT mission still continues.

History

Timor had been a source of sandalwood, honey, and wax for Chinese traders since, at least, the 1300s. The first Portuguese traders reached Timor around 1509 and gradually expanded their influence and made it a full-fledged colony. The process of decolonization of Timor began in 1974, in the wake of Portugal's "Carnation Revolution." East Timorese were given freedom to form their own political parties. The two most prominent parties were Timorese Democratic Union (UDT) and the pro-independence Revolutionary Front for an Independent East Timor (FRETILIN). The former supported gradual independence as well as association with Portugal, and the latter called for full independence. Portugal sought to establish a provisional government and a popular assembly that would determine the status of Timor-Leste, but civil war broke out between the two main political parties and FRETILIN was left with control of Timor-Leste. A unilateral declaration of independence followed on November 28, 1975. Before the declaration could be internationally recognized, however, Indonesian forces invaded and annexed the newly born Republica Democratica de Timor-Leste (RDTL) by making it the 27th Indonesian province. Some 60,000 people are believed to have died during the initial period of the invasion.

The UN never recognized this integration, and both the Security Council and the General Assembly called for Indonesia's withdrawal. Timor-Leste's official international status remained that of a "non-selfgoverning territory under Portuguese administration." Forças Armadas para a Liberação Nacional do Timor-Leste (FALINTIL), the military arm of FRETILIN, began its guerrilla campaign against the Indonesian forces.

Indonesian rule in Timor-Leste was violent and dictatorial, though unlike the Portuguese, favored strong, direct rule, which was not accepted by the Timorese who were determined to preserve their culture and national identity. Death tolls between 1975 and the early 1980s, due to a combination of attacks on the civilian population, disease and famine went up to 2 lakh. In an effort to obtain greater control over its descendants in the new province, Indonesia invested considerable financial resources in Timor-Leste, leading to economic growth averaging 6 percent per year over the period 1983–1997.

On May 5, 1999, UN brokered agreement with Portugal to hold a referendum or "popular consultation" on the options of autonomy within Indonesia or full independence. Despite a sustained intimidation campaign launched by the Indonesian military using "militia" as proxy, on August 30, 1999, the Timorese population voted overwhelmingly for independence (78.5 percent). The Indonesian armed forces and their militia responded with extraordinary brutality. The entire territory was laid waste-some, 80 percent of the buildings were looted and burned, all government records were lost, and most of the physical structure was destroyed. One-third of the population was forcibly displaced to West Timor and other neighboring islands. The rest of the population sought refuge in the mountains. Independence came, officially, on May 20, 2002 with the inauguration of a President and Prime Minister.

UN's Presence

UN, since the agreement was signed on May 5, 1999 in New York, has remained in Timor-Leste in different forms. On June 11, 1999, United Nations Mission in East Timor (UNMIET) came into existence to conduct "Popular Consultation," a referendum to choose between independence and autonomy under Indonesia. After that, on October 25, the Security Council established the United Nations Transitional Administration in East Timor (UNTAET) as an integrated, multidimensional peacekeeping operation fully responsible for the administration of Timor-Leste during its transition to independence. When Timor-Leste's independence was restored on May 20, 2002, UNTAET was succeeded by the United Nations Mission of Support in East Timor (UNMISET) established on May 17, 2002, to provide assistance to core administrative structures critical to the viability and political stability of the country and other mandates for postindependence support.

The mandate of UNMISET completed in May 2005 and a successor political mission, the United Nations Office in Timor-Leste (UNOTIL), came into force on May 20, 2005, to support the development of critical State institutions. UNOTIL was scheduled to end its mandate in 2006. However, due to fresh violence and disturbance including assassination bids on the President and Prime Minister, on August 25, 2006, the UN decided to establish the UNMIT to maintain law and order until the National Police of East Timor (PNTL) could undergo reorganization and restructuring. If the hearsay is to be believed then UNMIT is planning to wind up its mission by 2012.

Implementation of PIP Model in Timor-Leste

Before delving with the methodology of implementation of the PIP model, it will be pertinent to understand the scope and chance of its implementation and the status of community policing in Timor-Leste.

SCOPE OF PIP IN TIMOR-LESTE

Before evaluating the scope of the PIP model, it is better to understand the scope of traditional policing in Timor-Leste. As per the studies, surveys, and facts, traditional policing is not what the community is relying on to solve their cases in this country.

The survey of The Asia Foundation has found that 75 percent of the general public in Timor-Leste primarily relies on traditional justice mechanisms (i.e., elders, *suco* chiefs, and community leaders in general) for maintaining security (Figure 12.1).[1] Three-quarters of citizens point to one of the three types of community leaders—the *suco* chief, elders (both elected *suco* council elders and informal elders), and community leaders in general—as being primarily responsible for

---

[1] Chinn, Liam and Silas Everett. 2009. *A Survey of Community Police Perceptions: Timor Leste (TL) in 2008*. Dili, Timor-Leste (East Timor): The Asia Foundation.

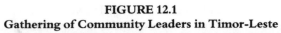

FIGURE 12.1
Gathering of Community Leaders in Timor-Leste

maintaining security; and this opinion is valid even in Dili, the capital city. Even the community leaders themselves feel that they have this responsibility. Only 15 percent of the citizens and 21 percent community leaders believe that the PNTL has primary responsibility for maintaining security in their locality. But, there is absence of a clear consensus on primary responsibility for maintaining security, which suggests that specific social patterns unique to each locality determine the factors responsible in maintaining security. This establishes the fact that the role of traditional policing is limited. Even the local police accept the fact, which is manifested through their action. They contact the community leaders three times more than they contact the community. Perhaps, the 21 percent of community leader's trust on PNTL has been developed by this regular and frequent contact between them. For PNTL, this 15 percent of community reliance is too small a number to be effective and successful.

When the United Nations Police (UNPOL) with PNTL have contacted community leaders, they have raised their concern over the action of the police coming into the community and arresting suspects, particularly in domestic violence cases and not informing *aldeia/ suco* chiefs. They have claimed that the police's intervention had been unwanted and unsolicited, and they have registered their unhappiness by stating that the police intervened despite knowing that many times the matter could have been solved by them in a traditional way. They complained that many times the suspect is released by the police the following day and the accused returns back to the community and creates more problems (CPU's report).

Howsoever, these self-policing systems are strong; its operational practicality in the coming days will always be at risk. The societies are no more homogeneous. The essence of modern society lies in its multiethnicity, multiculturalism, multiracial (multicaste in India). The influence of external environment, economic pressures, lingual variance, urbanizational demands, broader legal bindings, and the like, dilutes the play of self-policing structures. The community's dynamism has changed. The importance of modern policing cannot be totally neglected and the self-policing systems presence can only be perpetuated once it collaborates with modern policing structure.

The situation in Timor-Leste is very conducive for community policing. PNTL, the local police, is being raised with sizeable numbers of them being those who had no prior policing experience, and those who have it had been all together different, in disturbed situation. To be precise, by the end of the day, June 9, 2,847 PNTL officers were finally certified out of 3,103 registered PNTL officers. It translates to 92 percent of the eligible PNTL officers.

The resumption process is still underway and except for few, majority of the police stations in Timor-Leste are still being manned by UNPOL, with PNTL getting field training by associating with UNPOL. The police organization in Timor-Leste, i.e., PNTL, is in a fledgling stage and hence there is enough scope for instilling in them the spirit of community policing. The situation in Timor-Leste is unique in its own way and if properly and strategically implemented, community policing can become a standard way of policing.

Two major issues posing a security threat are "socioeconomic and religious conflicts," and martial art groups/gangs are what citizens presume in Timor-Leste. Even the community leaders have a similar opinion. Both security issues are community-based and involve a group and the community more than the individual. In Dili as well as in districts, it is believed that people coming from outside the community are more a threat than people within the community. It clearly underlines that individually committed crimes are not considered to be a security concern. In both cases, the community solidarity is emphasized and certain level of fraternity exists in homogenous community.

According to the 2009 *East Timor Law Journal*, martial arts groups and youth gangs have around 20,000 members across the country.[2] If the second part of the above statement is understood and believed, these gangs and groups pose more threat to other gangs/groups/communities than within their own group. This journal also supports it and states that *bairo* (village) based youth gangs do not resort to violence. As the name suggests, these youth gangs/martial arts groups are a herd of agile, enthusiastic, and active youth. The concern escalates once we understand the socioeconomic dynamics of the society. There is wide spread unemployment, education standard and level is in shambles, opportunities for self-employment and finding a job are meager, their energy level is high but are disoriented, with influx of external materialistic world environment the desire and demand is bound to increase but have no means to meet them. With such a situation, it is difficult to tame them and chances of the society falling prey to vices and eventually into crime is quite logical. It is in this perspective that it becomes necessary for regrouping them in a constructive way and channelizing their energy in a positive way.

In dealing with crimes related to violence, physical abuse, and threatening, citizens and community leaders both preferred the police to act upon than any other agency. PNTL said that their interaction with the community leaders was three times more than their interaction with a common man. To combat crime and maintain security, PNTL claimed to rely 94 percent on *suco* chiefs, 87 percent on elders (elected or informal), 81 percent on religious associations, 40 percent on martial arts group, and 57 percent on Non-governmental Organizations (NGOs). Their reliance can pave a way in deciding the members of PIP Council. Even the public had a similar perception about the association of the police with the abovementioned groups and persons. In the same order, the community opined that these groups can play an active role in facilitating dialog and cooperation between the community and the police.

Though 66 percent of PNTL accepted that they hardly received any community policing training, 93 percent claimed to be implementing community-policing principles in the locality where they serve.

---

[2] Wright, Warren L. 2009. "The Regulation of Martial Arts in East Timor: An Overview of Law No 10 of 2008 on the Practice of Marital Arts," *East Timor Law Journal*, 1. http://www.eastimorlawjournal.org/ARTICLES/2009/Regulation_of_Martial_Arts_in_East_Timor.html as visited on February 3, 2010.

According to them most important community policing principles were sharing of information on security, law, protecting children's rights, combating crimes, drugs and illegal weapons, implementing RDTL laws, and the police regulation and awareness programs.

An estimated 150,000 people, constituting approximately 15 percent of the population of Timor-Leste, were displaced from their homes in 2006. Still, a sizeable number of the Internally Displaced Persons (IDPs) are living in 51 camps in Dili and Bacau districts and rest are living in host families in Dili and other districts. The smooth, peaceful return and reintegration of IDPs to their fractured communities and their homes, which were occupied by squatters, is a big security concern. Though the return process claimed to be peaceful, it always results in scaling up of social tension and occasionally ends up in conflict.

Police, in their response, claimed that their maximum interaction with the community, 81 percent, was when they were organizing awareness programs of some sort with the community. Though, the national public in survey gave a contradictory data stating that only 1 percent of them attended police organized awareness programs in the past year.

The major limitation of PNTL as per community leaders and PNTL themselves is manpower and equipment. PNTL claim that they are short of vehicles, communications equipment, and investigative equipment.[3] These shortages will always remain as it does in all parts of the world. The only way to plug these shortages is to have additional hands, ears, eyes, and nose; and that can be found nowhere but in the community whom they are meant to serve.

Ninety-eight percent of PNTL, 92 percent of community leaders, and 76 percent of citizens felt that the police and the community can collaborate to improve the security. The encouraging part of this data was that this opinion was being held by all public respondents, cutting across age group and sex (male and female).

The successful implementation of the PIP Model in Timor-Leste holds better chance as explained above. Some situational benefits are:

1. The PNTL is a new police organization. They have not yet tasted the unbridled power of an established police force, as elsewhere in the so-called developed societies; hence, the opposition to the concept of PIP is less.

---

[3] This data and situation were what existed in August 2009, when I was in East Timor studying.

2. PNTL, having come from a traditional society, knows the importance of community leaders and community choice; as has already been revealed in Asia Foundation study.

3. There is already a community policing system in place, which has been interacting with the community intermittently and implementing many projects. Required now is proper application of the PIP approach, which would encourage the police to invite the community to participate as partners.

4. Timor-Leste is still a traditional society with little influence of the materialistic external world. The traditional power centers still hold sway over the communities' action. PIP in such traditional societies becomes a natural approach of the police for its success.

STATUS OF COMMUNITY POLICING IN TIMOR-LESTE

There have been community policing efforts going on in Timor-Leste. The UNPOL has established a National Community Policing and Humanitarian Unit (NCPHU) to monitor the community policing activities in the 13 districts.[4] There are projects which are being implemented by the UNPOL CPU team and by the PNTL in police stations. Many pilot projects are undertaken by the CPU team (Figure 12.2). They reach the community for executing the projects. Some projects undertaken by them are like cleaning the locality, market management, multi-antigen immunization campaign initiated by United Nations Children's Fund (UNICEF), promoting the "Plant for the Planet: Billion Tree Campaign" started by the United Nations Environment Program, "snail trail" program for children on how to cross roads, traffic awareness campaign, Unexploded Ordinance (UXO) awareness program, Domestic Violence Awareness program, use of Timor-Leste Television (TLTV) to disseminate information, crocodile awareness program, pasting posters related to operational issues like elections, and so on.

---

[4] UNMIT. 2009. *National Community Policing and Humanitarian Unit (NCPHU)*. Report submitted to United Nations Integrated Mission in Timor-Leste (UNMIT) Operations Office, Timor-Leste (East Timor).

FIGURE 12.2
United Nations Civilian Police (UN CIVPOL)
in Action in Timor-Leste

As on last week of June, 2009, out of total 1,559 UNPOL officers working in Timor-Leste, 1,004 were deployed as community policing officers.

PIP Council in Timor-Leste

The PIP concept involves participation of the community in the policing activities. It is always a pleasure to have maximum participation from the community. If every member starts participating and realizing their role, then the concept of security and definition of the police function will drastically change. This utopian structure, though being the most desirable situation, is still is a far cry. The practical possibility is the involvement of a selected few who are the representatives of the community. They should be such who understand the needs and expectations of the community at large. The survey vividly depicts the chosen representatives in Timor-Leste. PIP Councils will have to be formed involving these members actively.

PROPOSED MEMBERS OF PIP COUNCILS

The proposed members of PIP councils would be:

- *Suco/aldeia* Council members (most active one or two members);
- *suco* chief/*chefe de aldeia*;
- community leaders/elders;
- members hailing from varied discipline—lawyers, sociologist, psychologists, social workers;
- members from municipality, teachers, doctors, other government services; and
- police personnel (normally beat in charge).

The PIP councils will have to be decentralized. The council will have to be established at district level, *suco* level, and *aldeia* level. This will facilitate two-way communication. First, the communication will be established bottom–up and top to bottom. Second, the problems will be understood locally and at the same time assistance will flow from top.

The PIP Council members will have to take up the membership enrollment campaign. Each willing candidate will have to fill a form clarifying his/her credentials and then the police beat in charge officer, taking the assistance of the *suco* chiefs and other local community leaders to comprehend their utility in the PIP councils, will scrutinize it. The police station in charge officer will accredit the membership and maintain the record. Once made a member, the police station in charge officer will be issuing them an identity card undersigned by him. The police station will have to be cautious regarding the misuse of identity card.

PIP Council member's work will be a conduit to interaction between the police and the community. They will serve as a guide and friend of the police in situations of law and order and also in educating the other ends on the needs and expectations of both. The members will help in disseminating the needful information to the citizens and contain spreading of rumors in cases of sensitive issues.

By now, we have started appreciating the fact that role of the police is getting extended beyond the written duties and responsibilities. Their social role has far outreached than their normal maintenance of law-and-order functions. Their presence is conspicuous in all sectors now. In line with this spirit, the issues discussed in the council meetings will be involving all aspects of life. It is not necessary that only the police-related issues be put on agenda. These PIP councils must become a forum where general community issues along with security issues are discussed. The meeting agenda and issues of concern coming up must be documented and referred to the concerned authorities for redress. Regular follow-up mechanism has to be set up so that indifferent attitude of the designated authority is dealt with concertedly. If the issues need attention of higher authorities, then the highly placed PIP councils must take up the issue at their level. A continuous mechanism of checks and balances would be established, herewith.

ORGANIZING PIP COUNCILS

The area for formation of PIP councils can be divided as beats considering the operational viability. In densely populated areas, it is suggested that smaller groups of 20 members encompassing 3–4 adjacent colonies (*aldeia* or *suco*) depending on homogeneity of requirements should be organized. This has multiple benefits:

- More members in the group will have the sense of responsibility and consequently will be involved actively in the activities.
- There will be more concentration on common problems and it will be brought into notice and addressed properly.
- Dissemination of information will be fast and more appropriate.
- More representation as members from their own people will help in building trust and faith in the group.
- Areas being densely populated will be manageable.
- The locals have clear knowledge of the rather cumbersome topography of the area:
  - In the sensitive areas, there should be proper representation according to the population of the area. It is necessary to have heterogeneous representation with members from all walks of life and all ages. Proper representation cutting across all religions and parties will help in bringing issues of all kinds to the fore for discussion and redress.
  - It is always advisable to have people from different professions and services—private and public—to be made members so that they are helpful in addressing the issues, then and there, or come out with constructive advice.

- Proposed membership strength for all the beats has been given below in the diagrammatic representation of existing and proposed PIP Council beats (Figures 12.3 and 12.4).

Each sub-beat will comprise of 20–25 members and 4–5 colonies.

FIGURE 12.3
PIP Councils for Small Places

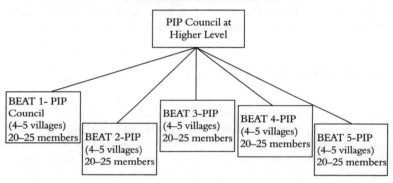

FIGURE 12.4
Proposed PIP Councils for Big Cities

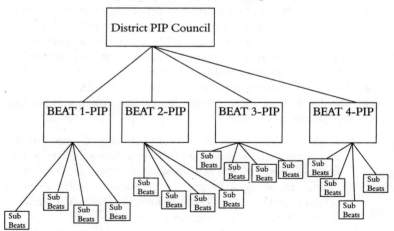

13

Coordinated Response to Combat Violence against Women

A Participative Policing Initiative of Madhya Pradesh Police, India

Violence Against Women (VAW) is the most socially tolerated violation of human rights and it is widespread, cutting across all sections of society. There is a concern over the increasing rate of crime against women and its ramifications in society. This case study attempts to focus on the initiative of the State and police to respond to VAW through implementing Family Counseling Centers (FCCs) within the police system in Madhya Pradesh and special cells in other states.

Women experiencing violence and seeking support are forced to deal with many different departments and civil society groups to meet their different needs. As a result, justice and support become increasingly inaccessible for vulnerable and poor communities thus perpetuating VAW in both public and private realms. This chapter explores the reasons that lead to the need to respond to domestic violence through FCCs, the benefits of the strategic alliance between the police and civil society, the initiation and progress of setting up of the FCCs, objectives and activities of the FCCs, and the process of intervention and efforts to institutionalize it across the state. This case study concludes with a critical analysis of the FCCs and the present issues concerning the FCCs that needs to be addressed.

While looking at domestic violence issues, the police are expected to expand their role beyond primarily criminalizing domestic violence by arresting the offender to encompassing a variety of social service functions through a process of constructive involvement of stakeholders. This approach focuses on the role of the police as problem solvers rather than crime fighters.

Police of the state of Madhya Pradesh in India has taken a few pioneer steps to strategically address the issue of VAW through partnership and support of civil society. The movement of change in the police response to domestic violence arose from an unusual confluence of political and legal pressures from women's rights activists and organizational concerns over the liability of the police's continued past practices of neglecting domestic violence victims.

The Reality of Violence against Women[1]

Violence against Women (VAW) is the most pervasive and least recognized human right violation in the world. According to XI Plan Report of the Government of India, one in every two women in South Asia experience violence in their daily life. Social, cultural, political, economic, and legal factors in the region combine to leave women vulnerable to community sanctioned violence and exclude women from social development processes. Official estimates from the Ministry of Law and Justice suggest that women in over 60 percent urban homes experience domestic violence and only 5 percent of these women land up complaining to the police. National Family Health Survey (NFHS)-III data places the number of ever-married women who have experienced domestic violence by husbands at 37.2 percent for India. Overall, one in three women aged 15–49 years have experienced physical violence, and about 1 in 10 women have experienced sexual violence.

Interestingly, the 2007 NFHS-III report highlights that about 16 percent of women who have never married have experienced physical violence since they were 15 years of age, generally by a parent, sibling, or a teacher. Among never-married women who have been sexually

[1] Ministry of Home Affairs. 2007. "Crime in India." India, New Delhi: National Crime Records Bureau; International Institute for Population Sciences (IIPS) and Macro International. 2007. "National Family Health Survey-3, 2005–2006," Volumes 1 and 2. India, Mumbai: IIPS; International Council for Research on Woman. 2000. "A Multi-site Household Survey on Domestic Violence," Women-International Clinical Epidemiologists Network. Washington D.C.: International Council for Research on Woman.

abused, 27 percent say that the abuser was a relative.[2] In another interesting nationwide study done by the International Center for Research on Women (ICRW), 85 percent of men admitted resorting to violent behavior at least once and 32 percent confessed committing acts of violence against their pregnant wives.[3]

According to the data available with National Crime Records Bureau in total, crime against women has increased by 12.5 percent over 2006 and 31.85 percent over 2003. Cruelty by husband and family (Section 498 A of IPC) constitutes 3.8 percent of total IPC crimes, with a conviction rate of 20.9 percent. In 2005–2006, there was an 8.2 percent increase in the rate of cases filed. Dowry deaths, i.e., Section 304 B of IPC, constitute 0.7 percent of total IPC crimes and from 2006 to 2007, there was a 6.2 percent increase in the rate of cases filed.[4]

Locating and Responding to Domestic Violence in the Structure of the Family

It has been established through research and studies that in a family, women play second fiddle to their male counterparts in an Indian society. This inequality may be attributed to the patriarchal setup and oppressive societal structure. This eventually provides an upper hand to male members in a family who use power and domination to subjugate, especially their wife and other female members.

It has to be understood very clearly that domestic violence does not merely connote violence against one woman or person. It has multiple implications. Battering of a mother in the house has a spillover effect. One slap on the woman is heard by children and others in the family. That one slap accepted by the woman without opposition cements the belief in the girl child that it is an accepted norm and by that she becomes ready to suffer subserviently for her entire life; for boys, the

---

[2] International Institute for Population Sciences (IIPS) and Macro International. 2007. "National Family Health Survey-3, 2005–2006," Volumes 1 and 2. India 9, Mumbai: IIPS.

[3] International Council for Research on Woman. 2000. *A Multi-site Household Survey on Domestic Violence*. Washington, D.C.: ICRW. http://www.icrw.org/docs/DV_India_Report4_52002.pdf as visited on August 12, 2008.

[4] Ministry of Home Affairs. 2007. *Crime in India*. New Delhi : National Crime Records Bureau, Government of India.

slap becomes a symbol of authority and the solution to all household problems involving women folk. Consequently, for all in the family, this hitherto becomes a way of life and a part of their culture.

Family is still the most sanctified and closed setup in the Indian society. It is considered almost a taboo for discussing the issues emanating within the closed four walls in public. This social sanction of secrecy is one of the main causes of women suffering violence for long. Women have been suffering atrocities in their families but they lack proper forums to get their problems addressed. They take the issue to the police or courts only when the situation gets beyond control. The dragging of the issue to courts is a certainty of no comeback and inevitability of a split in the family. Moreover, domestic violence has spillover effect on the children in the family and there is all probability of them getting wayward.

Law, Women, and Police: Section 498 A, IPC

The engagement of Indian women's movement with the law since the 1970s has been primarily on the issue of VAW, rape and dowry law reform campaign, and violence in matrimonial relationships recognized in section 498 A in the IPC (cruelty by husband and his relatives, including mental cruelty). Section 498 A is inherently a progressive legal provision, which made cruelty to women a cognizable and non-bailable crime. By criminalizing domestic violence, the section 498 A had the effect of creating the much needed space for women who were facing physical and mental violence in their matrimonial home. Even though the State responded to the issue of domestic violence by criminalizing it through the Act, yet it only achieved partial success in combating the problem. This happened because of a combination of issues. First, family ideology and predominance of patriarchal attitudes circumscribes the full scope of this law. Second, misinterpretation of the law by perceiving it as a mere dowry-related torture became deterrent on the issues of women suffering physical, emotional, and mental violence; and third, reluctance of the police to arrest due to attitudinal inclination toward male chauvinism.

Normally, the police in a traditional society bogged down by dominant cultural prejudices are reluctant to intervene and use IPC sections against violent husbands as they feel that any legal intervention will jeopardize the family and marriage of the woman. It is also an accepted fact that divorced, deserted, and estranged women do not get the best of treatment by the society. Even though the IPC is to be used by the police to stop VAW in domestic situations but covertly police, women, and society believe that using this provision will mean irreversible and immeasurable harm to the marriage and a permanent break with the marital family. With family still being presumed to be the sanctified institution of society, the police prefer to see a resolution rather than a break.

Police department usually is the initial agency contacted in the midst of a domestic assault. The general public recognizes the police as an agency providing a free service 24 hours a day, seven days a week. Furthermore, in the midst of a crisis, many victims want police intervention because the police are easy to contact, provide a highly visible power and authority figure, and are capable of providing a speedy response. Though all-day access is highly significant, there is a mismatch between what a woman victim of domestic violence needs as emotional support and access to services/options that the police can offer. As more often than not, women survivors of domestic violence are looking for protection and prevention of violence along with mediation and counseling for reconciliation.

Then, what is the appropriate response to domestic violence? This complex question, still without clearly defined answers, is the subject of intense controversy and debate. The continuing controversy remains regarding the appropriate response of society in general and the criminal justice system in particular, to domestic violence.

Many a times, the complainant approach the police station and request not to register a case but to mediate and resolve the crisis. In such situations, the police face multiple tribulations:

- Legally, there is no provision for counseling according to the Acts/Code. They are bound to register a case if there is any cognizable report coming in or in case of non-cognizable offence to officially redirect to court.
- There is no specialized unit of counselors/trained personnel available in police stations to provide the much needed socio-psychological support counseling and there is no structured/institutionalized set up to provide counseling.

- In dealing with VAW, the police image of being mysterious, face-less, unchangeable, and powerful comes in the way of providing socio-psychological support. In addition, the police themselves are not trained in this realm.
- When the police try to intervene with counseling without any legal support (without case registered), invariably the police is accused and cornered for being biased and acting with vested interest.
- Looking at the perceived image of the police and having no community participation, their intervention is more criticized than welcomed.

Connecting with Other Initiatives on Violence against Women in Police Systems

Examining experiences of different states, it was seen that there are different responses to VAW existing within the police system. Some of the police initiatives being Mahila Thanas, Women's Help Desk, Crime against Women Cell, and so on. These efforts were largely managed by the police themselves without forging partnerships with the civil society.

One of the first unique effort of forming a strategic alliance was experimented as the Special Cell for Woman and Children established in 1984 as a collaboration between the Maharashtra police and Tata Institute of Social Sciences, Mumbai, to provide professional support and social services to women and children facing violence through trained social workers.[5] The Government of Maharashtra—the police and the Department of Women and Child department—understood the needs of the violated women, and then made efforts to institution-alize a response to it by making Special Cell a Government-supported/funded program in 2005.

In last 25 years of its work, Special Cell has shown that a strategic alliance with the police can make a significant impact on women's

---

[5] Special Cell for Women and Children. 2005. "Documenting Effective Intervention and Strategic Alliance between Maharashtra Police and Tata Institute of Social Sciences." Mumbai: Special Cell, Tata Institute of Social Science.

search for support and justice. The effectiveness of the Special Cells in Maharashtra police system sparked off the interest of both women's groups and state officials of other states. This led to Special Cell being replicated in several other states viz. Andhra Pradesh, Rajasthan, Delhi, Haryana, and Orissa to combat VAW.

The struggles and efforts of the Special Cell emphasized the importance of a formal systemic response to VAW. The intensive process-oriented work required to support violated women through both informal and formal systems of justice, social service itself being one, have been acknowledged by creation of the role of the protection officer and role of service provider in the Protection of Women from Domestic Violence Act, 2005.

The Special Cell model paved the way and gave the direction as to how the police system can be strengthened, allied with, supported or improved upon through larger Special Cell process.

Family Counseling Center and Significance of Police Setting

Conflict management and restorative justice is a process of resolving conflict in the form of out-of-court settlement in criminological literature. Restorative justice is a way of dealing with offenders and victims by focusing on the settlement of conflicts arising from crime and resolving the underlying problems, which cause it. Madhya Pradesh police, after studying the pattern of crime against women within a family, deduced that there are numerous cases where the issue could have been easily settled if an external agency would have constructively intervened, at an earlier stage. Laced with the above important information, it was decided by the Madhya Pradesh Police in 1995, to set up FCCs like Parivar Paramarsh Kendras to help the women who were victims of violence by creating a platform for bringing together the police and civil society groups. The righteous intention was to provide support to women, to stop/challenge violence, and help families settle their differences amicably, out of court.

However, the most challenging aspect was to encourage the women in distress to approach the FCCs. Police was still carrying the old-age image of being noncooperative and inaccessible. To dislodge this impression, the local community was involved in the process, as a partner, to combat this scourge of domestic violence. Counselors from the same community, hailing from varied discipline such as lawyers, sociologist, psychologists, social workers, and so on, with experience partnered with the police to address the issue of VAW and work with various stakeholders to resolve the problems amicably. To counter the problem of direct police intervention, these FCCs were registered under Societies Registration Act and worked independently. The police and community involved did the documentation of activities jointly.

The FCCs are strategically located within the premises of police stations making maximum use of the available resources. There has been no extra budget involved for running FCCs as the police station in which it is situated is helping out with available resources. The counselors have volunteered to provide services as a part of their social commitments. This has ultimately helped not only the family in dispute but also the police and community people involved by sensitizing them for a relevant cause.

Opening of FCCs in the wake of the increasing growth of registrations of cases of domestic violence in the recent years was unavoidable and a revolutionary and historic beginning by the Madhya Pradesh Police to challenge the menace of domestic violence. Domestic violence is a crime, which has been suppressed for long and is now surfacing due to awareness. By striving for compromise or settlement instead of litigation, it was believed that counseling centers would relieve the immense pressure on the judicial system. It is somewhat a paradoxical scenario, where the police had decided on to take this additional responsibility of "resolving" and securing harmonious relations between women and their violent partners. It has so positively galvanized the police's functioning for the alleviation of women's oppression and sufferings that it has unequivocally been hailed as an impressive humanitarian endeavor of the department.

Institutionalization of FCC: Statistical Inputs of Family Counseling Units

In response to the domestic violence, Madhya Pradesh police started its first FCC at Indore in October, 1995. Eventually, inspired by the success of this experiment, by the order of the then Director General of Police, Police Headquarters, Bhopal, such centers were opened in 12 more districts. Since then, there has been no turning back. Armored with the stupendous success of this scheme, it was expanded and replicated, and on this date, there are in all around 212 FCCs functioning in 48 districts of the state. There are more than 1,000 counselors voluntarily giving their services at these centers.

Since its inception in 1995, a total number of 152,308 complaints were received in 2008 out of which 88,418 cases were amicably settled and only 2,228 First Information Report (FIR) registered on the behest of the complainant. It has been decided by an official order that all police stations having more than 50 cases of VAW registered will open an FCC. The statistics in Table 13.1 are self-explanatory to depict the confidence showed by the community in the FCCs of Madhya Pradesh Police.[6]

Counseling is provided through teams drawn from social workers, lawyers, medical professionals, NGOs, teachers, and volunteers drawn from the same community that can appreciate and understand the situations better.

To monitor the activities of FCCs, in Police Headquarters, independent Community Policing Branch has been constituted with a very senior officer of the rank of ADGP working as Nodal officer. To further strengthen the institution, an official gazette has been promulgated giving it a statutory status.

Objectives and Activities of the FCC

The women who approach FCC in police stations are victims of domestic violence. They have suffered from a range of behavior, which can be conceptualized as domestic violence—some obviously criminal in nature, other more manipulative—which in total are intended to exercise coercive control including physical, sexual, psychological, and verbal behavior such as battering, sexual abuse of children, dowry harassment, elder abuse, and marital rape. In addition, the center

---

[6] Data made available by Community Policing Unit, in January 2010, Police Headquarters, Bhopal, Madhya Pradesh.

TABLE 13.1
Family Counseling Center Data

Year	Total Application	FIR	Disposal/Amicably Settled	Under Counseling
	Year-wise Chart of Family Counseling Center			
1996	2,379	52	2,327	0
1997	3,080	91	2,989	0
1998	2,905	116	2,789	0
1999	3,123	118	3,005	0
2000	3,912	189	3,723	0
2001	7,283	37	6,256	990
2002	13,134	191	8,742	4,201
2003	15,707	227	8,030	7,400
2004	16,430	230	7,134	9,066
2005	15,602	323	7,185	7,667
2006	27,555	196	12,602	14,638
2007	29,348	237	12,290	16,971
2008	25,850	221	11,346	12,350
Total	152,308	2,228	88,418	73,273

Source: Author (collated from data of Community Policing Unit, Police Head-quarters, Bhopal, Madhya Pradesh, January 2010).

received cases of alcoholism, infidelity, non-compatibility, and non-consummation of marriage, where counselor had to intervene as this also caused trauma and emotional violence. All these are some examples of VAW and are used to abuse, violate, and control the woman/wife.

The main objective of setting up of FCCs was to provide an amiable specialized forum to the families facing some resolvable problems and help them to reach an amicable solution. Though it directly targeted the women in distress but had a spread-out effect on the entire family, particularly the children, who were prevented from becoming delinquents. The following objectives were envisaged for FCCs:

- To challenge and protect the woman from oppression and all forms of violence in both public and private spheres.
- To provide social, psychological, and legal support to women victims of violence and their families.
- To provide violated women and their families with counseling support and referral services such as shelter, medical support, and even support from the police wherever required.

- To save the time and money of the complainant who otherwise would be going through cumbersome court procedures.
- To create a congenial environment in the community and to sensitize them with regard to VAW.
- Prevent the children of the affected mother/family from psychological and social harassment, which could lead to delinquency and other harmful consequences.

Processes of Intervention

- Women's complaints are sometimes received directly at the FCCs, some are forwarded by senior police officers and rest redirected from police stations after analyzing the prospects of mediation in resolving the issue.
- On receiving a complaint, oral or written, the first step is to listen patiently to the violated woman. Attempt is made to understand her situation and after consultation, arrive at how she would like to handle her situation of violence. Counselors help her explore her options; in the process, build the woman's self-confidence and empower her to take decisions.
- If the woman is willing, joint sessions are conducted by inviting members of the family to the counseling centers where violence of the partner or by the family is challenged. Negotiations and settlements are so conducted that it strengthens the woman.
- A woman police officer enters the details of each case in a separate register. The jurisdictional police station helps in summoning the parties.
- Counseling is done keeping at the center core values such as:
  - Violence inflicted on a woman is never the woman's fault.
  - Violence of any kind mental, physical, sexual, or financial is non-negotiable.
  - Woman's safety and security are of utmost importance.
  - Understanding the problem and its intensity.
  - Helping women and families to make informed and considered choices and decisions.

- To see a woman experiencing violence as a survivor and not as a victim.

- Special care is taken that the outcome is in favor of empowering the woman and rebuilding the family as a whole, and in the process, even children of the family are taken care of.
- Qualified specialists in various fields like psychology, medicine, teaching, law, and so on, enable the affected woman and her family to undergo meaningful counseling at various stages until a mutually acceptable settlement is arrived at.
- Follow up of cases after intervention is one of the most important aspects for ensuring non-recurrence of violence/discord. In normal situations, every fortnight, a team visits the concerned family to have a feel of the situation. It is ensured that their visit looks informal so that they do not feel that their privacy is impinged.

Critical Analysis of the FCC

This intervention of FCC initiated to counter domestic VAW through its strategic location in the police system is a step ahead taken by the state of Madhya Pradesh.

STRATEGIC LOCATION WITHIN POLICE

The role and effectiveness of FCCs functioning within the boundaries of the police station has generated differing views. Some believe that counseling done in police station invokes fear and by its very nature is unprincipled and counterproductive. Whereas, some others feel that the strategic location in the police is a helpful attribute which acts as a deterrent and compels the recalcitrant man/husband to come to the negotiating table. The legitimate authority inherent in the police enables the FCC to say "No to Violence" at the individual level and the societal level. The synergy resulting from the different strengths and contributions of the police and FCC enables a coordinated, multiagency response to the issue of domestic violence.

INADEQUATE TRAINING AND EXPOSURE

Despite the fact that FCC has an attractive record of accomplishment, the functioning recently has attracted few criticisms. The FCCs are afflicted with a problem of lack of training. Both the police personnel and voluntary counselors working in the center are "do gooders" who may or may not have training in counseling or perspective in VAW. It is critical that the police and volunteers working with women victims require training so that services can respond more sensitively to the fundamental causes and factors responsible for violence.

The working of FCCs requires volunteers who are experts and specialize in the field of counseling, as counseling victims of violence and their families is a very specialized subject. The counselors have to be free from prejudices and biases, recognizing complex social and individual realities of women. The training is crucial as counseling volunteers needs to validate individual histories and experiences and belief. It requires comprehending women's capacity and to facilitate the process to get evolved, considered with informed choices. To cater to such demands, the counselors involved should be either professional counselors or else, they should be exposed to proper orientation and training program. Besides, refresher course by experts from the field should be organized at regular intervals.

REACH INTO THE RURAL AREAS

FCCs were initially opened in cities, then in district headquarters. Distance often deterred the families to approach centers in police stations located in headquarters. To make the services available in far-flung areas, now the FCC has penetrated into *tehsils* and other remote rural places, in accordance with the Gazette Order Permanent (GOP), which mentions opening of centers where there is record of more than 50 cases of atrocities against women registered in one year.

The inherent problem of opening FCCs in such remote places is that the counselors enrolled are not necessarily trained, which more often than not, affects the quality of counseling. And also, sometimes people are unaware of the existence of the center. In many districts, particularly in villages, there is also an implicit taboo for women to step in the premises of police stations. Inadequate publicity and incompetent functioning of the FCC are responsible for the poor response to it and it defeats the very rationale for which it was set up. For any FCC to be effective, it should be seen working in close propinquity with citizens in its vicinity.

THE CULTURE OF RECONCILIATION

The primary accusations against both the police and FCC are their proclivity toward compromises. Police and counselors both come from the same patriarchal understanding and are conditioned by the widespread social norms, which uphold the sacredness of the family as an institution at all cost. Police intervention is seen as being detrimental to the family unit and therefore, under the garb of counseling, the police tend to ward off from registering cases of atrocities against women. FCC should not be used to reconcile the cases of atrocities against women forcefully with bias to preserve family at any cost, thus jeopardizing women's safety.

Moreover, the presence of FCCs in police stations gives it a tag of being pressure centers. FCC has been criticized for using pressure tactics on either side to reconcile. More than counseling, it is the fright of registration of case which prompts the parties to reconcile. Besides, there have been incidents where counselors have overstepped their limits, to the extent of ordering the groom party to bring the dowry items and hand it over to the bride's family. There have been complaints where the counselors have been judgmental, like a judicial authority. It has to be kept in mind that these kinds of forced reconciliations do not last for long. Forced compromises always run the risk of making the woman more vulnerable, putting at stake her safety.

RECRUITMENT, MONITORING, AND SUPERVISION OF FCC

This entire work of FCC is managed on an honorary basis by the concerned police station and there is no remuneration of any kind, whatsoever, to the volunteers for services rendered. Today, there is an increasing concern over the current trend of reducing volunteerism in the field, leading to lack of adequate workforce to effectively implement FCCs. There is a need to set a mechanism in place to identify appropriate and adequate human resources to carry forward the work.

A proper recruitment and training procedure has to be set up. As of now, there is no committee or board in place to select them. They are arbitrarily picked, according to the liking of the police officers, and those who are picked do not necessarily go through any training or orientation. Police personnel deputed in these centers to monitor the activities are untrained in the field of counseling of VAW or domestic violence.

There is no proper monitoring of the centers. Largely, it is dependent on individual direction and commitment of the district SP. One constable or HC is deputed for documentation. Resultantly, in absence of institutionalized practices, no officer regularly monitors and supervises the work going on. Very often, it also depends on priority given by officer in charge to counseling activities. In addition, recruitment is very subjectively done, keeping personal qualities and personal contact as prerequisites.

The success of FCCs can be attributed to the early institutionalized initiative and some real committed officers and counselors. What is required is a fully formalized recruitment procedure and training program to make it fully professional.

ALLOCATION OF RESOURCES

Counseling is a very specialized task and has to be done with high level of integrity and confidentiality. It requires separate space within the police office to do so. Many a times, this is not possible as a police station might have inadequate space and infrastructure.

Issues of Concern

The State often seeks to preserve the family as a social institution at the cost of women's interest. Further, by elevating the family beyond critical inquiry, the lopsided power equation and the position of women's subordination is cloaked. This State program of FCC has only achieved partial success in its endeavor to counter domestic violence. The section 498 A of IPC has been largely ineffective in criminalizing acts of domestic violence to the extent desired and punishing the male abuser. This is primarily the outcome of a combination of factors such as the police being reluctant to register the case under the section and routing of the case to FCCs.

In the FCC, it is often seen that people involved in the cases are invariably made to undergo counseling in an attempt to forge reconciliation. It is only when reconciliation fails that the legal process is initiated. While this may serve to preserve the sanctity of the family, the women's physical and emotional safety is jeopardized thus prolonging her search for justice and relief. Here, it is important to underline for both, the police and FCC, to see violence on women as an abuse of women's human rights since it threatens her safety and security and also her existence.

Police must not fall into the trap of the number game. Sometimes in an attempt to give importance to quantitative figures, the quality of the work is compromised. It is very easy to see domestic violence as a problem of poverty, husband's alcoholism, or decline of traditional family values. Police needs to take the position that the criminal justice system should take action consistently, with recognition that acts of domestic violence are crime and not simply a conflict situation needing certain reconciliation through mediation. Officers should sincerely and regularly monitor the activities of counseling centers. The importance of counseling should not be undermined. It is as important as investigation of cases. Every case should be dealt with professionally. Even follow up mechanism should be diligently pursued as indifference may ultimately lead to disruption in family.

However, FCCs have been one of the best and successful community policing initiatives of Madhya Pradesh Police. The figures in Table 13.1 clearly indicate that a large numbers of cases have approached the FCC at the police office and considerable numbers of them have been amicably resolved keeping women's and children's needs central. The accomplishment suggests that this initiative can be replicated in all parts of the country. Also, this initiative indicates that a combination of state agency and committed experts and volunteers from civil society groups has potential for good practice on the issue of domestic violence. Nevertheless, it should be ensured that the choice of counselors should be proper, conducive ambience created for counseling, parties involved are treated with dignity, and the police closely monitor the working without being a threatening figure. Thus, the collaboration of the police and FCCs is a fine example of participative policing. This follows the principle that sometimes third party, external intervention provides ample opportunity for conflict to settle. This proactive, participative community policing initiative of Madhya Pradesh Police has an explicit objective of empowering women victims of domestic violence.

14

Experiences of Timor-Leste (East Timor)

Domestic Violence Redressal Forum— A Redressal Mechanism in Timor-Leste

The studies mentioned in the previous chapters, case studies conducted earlier,[1] and the PIP model, point out that in Timor-Leste, the mediation by elders, *suco* chiefs, and community leaders is preferred to police intervention. But the choice of mediator is not uniform and depends on local factors. At the same place, it may differ to different families or complainants. Some may directly reach the police. A Domestic Violence Redressal Forum (DVRF) can be formed in which all the above-stated mediators can be made members supported by specialist counselors to mediate. The presence of an already accepted mediator will encourage the women in distress to approach the DVRF and will help combat this scourge of domestic violence.[2]

A DVRF can be formed in districts/villages/*aldiea* and big areas with considerable population after doing a need-based analysis study to provide mediation at an early stage and prevent from dire consequences in the family. Composition of the forum will ensure that the approach for resolving the complaint will take care of the following necessities.

---

[1] Chinn, Liam and Everett Silas. 2009. *A Survey of Community Police Perceptions: Timor Leste (TL) in 2008*. The Asia Foundation: Timor-Leste (East Timor); Wright, Warren L. 2009. "The Regulation of Martial Arts in East Timor: An Overview of Law," *East Timor Law Journal*. http://www.eastimorlawjournal.org/ARTICLES/2009/Regulation_of_Martial_Arts_in_East_Timor.html as visited on February 3, 2010.

[2] This model was submitted to Asia Foundation, East Timor to address domestic violence which constituted a sizeable number of total crime.

Proposed Members of Domestic Violence Redressal Forum

- *Suco/aldeia* council members (most active one or two members)
- *Suco* chief/*chefe de aldeia*
- Community leaders/elders.
- Specialist counselors (hailing from varied discipline—lawyers, sociologist, psychologists, social workers, and so on)
- Police personnel (normally beat in charge)

The proposed members suffice the desire (according to the study) of the victim of domestic violence. They will find a face in DVRF, whom they had been banking on, traditionally, to mediate in the past. The choice of members of DVRF and the mediation mechanism will be sensitive enough to take care that

- the approach adopted is socially compatible;
- it will not threaten the existing sociocultural fabric;
- it will not challenge the local accepted authority; and
- the members, being drawn from the same community, will be in a position to appreciate and understand the situation in a better way and will provide the counseling, backed by following three most desired ingredients:

  - knowledge of law;
  - social pressure; and
  - counseling skills.

In the forum, the choice of specialist counselors is an important factor. A lot depends on their skill. They are the persons who will play as a catalyst in mediation process but to the parties, look friendly with all respect to their traditional ethos and values. There should be proper representation of women in the forum. If the community elders/*suco* council members or *suco* chief is a woman, it would always help in understanding the plight of women within local culture. It would be better to have women counselors and women police officers if possible, but that should not be mandatory. Sensitivity and empathy are the most important qualities required in a police officer than their gender. For that, the counselors must have following qualities:

- properly trained in counseling;
- good listener;
- empathetic;
- versed with local traditions;
- conceivable knowledge of sociocultural milieu;
- do not force own view and perception; non-imposing;
- highlight pros and cons and leave decision on the parties; and
- respect the traditional authority and work within existing framework for maximum acceptance.

Position of Police

Sociologically, in any society with more contact with the external world, there is enculturation or assimilation of external culture. It is normal phenomena that the traditional norms and informal authorities get diluted gradually and formal institutions gain relevance, power, and importance. With the passage of time, this is bound to happen in Timor-Leste as well. The police will have a more important role to play than what they do today. But the question is if the PNTL is equipped enough to fulfill that responsibility. Involving the police in DVRF will provide them with the opportunity to come closer to the community and in the process, get trained and will be community oriented. Eventually, with their participation, the much required trust and faith in the police will also be built.

The Asia Foundation survey report says that only 19 percent of citizens claim that they would first contact the police to assist in a case of domestic violence involving a female friend or relative.[3] It has also been assumed that these cases reach the police only after their traditional mediation setup fails to redress to their satisfaction. PNTL, on

---

[3] The Asia Foudation. 2009. "A Survey of Community Police Perceptions: Timor-Leste (TL) in 2008." Dili, Timor-Leste (East Timor): The Asia Foundation.

the other hand, claims that maximum number of cases they mediate are domestic violence (39 percent) and dowry and other traditional events (36 percent). Dowry being one of the major causes of domestic violence, if we sum it up with domestic violence cases, it amounts to 75 percent of mediated cases of PNTL. Now, in cases where the complainant approaches the police station, many a times they request to mediate and solve the case than registering an offence. In such situations, the police face multiple problems.

- There are no specialized units of counselors available in police stations to provide the needed counseling and there is no structured/institutionalized setup to provide counseling.
- When the police try to mediate, their approach is dictatorial and immediate. Normally, an amicable solution can be found only after mediating for a few sessions. They have a proclivity to pass orders than mediating with sensitivity. For their approach, invariably, the police are accused of being biased and autocratic.
- Looking at the perceived image of the police and having no community participation, their intervention is more criticized than welcomed.

By being a part of DVRF, the police is partnering in mediating the cases with support of specialists and traditionally trusted persons. If DVRF is unable to resolve the problem, then police may act and take it for prosecution and leave for court to decide without wasting any time in police stations by involving in unnecessary mediation.

Some logical reasons for police presence in the DVRF are:

- It is a reasonable presence because when all types of mediations fail, the victim tends to get recourse from formal legal structure, i.e., the police.
- The effort being quasi-legal, the presence of police or legal aid will empower the victim.
- It will ascertain that legal course is always possible and easily accessible.
- It will give the procedure a legal sanctity.
- A different image of the police is reflected, which is not threatening but supportive.

Importance of Community Leaders

The presence of community leaders and *suco* chief/council can be understood by the following facts:

- Police interacted with the community leaders three times more than they interacted with the public (Asia Foundation report), which establishes the fact that even the police accepts the importance of their influence.
- According to the Decree Law No. 5/2004, which outlines the power and responsibilities of a *suco* chief along with consolidation of national unity, they are entrusted for provision of goods and services designed to meet the basic needs of life and development of the community. Perhaps, in a poor country where survival is at stake, the development aspect is vital for the stakeholders, i.e., the community. Besides, the traditional faith existing in the power of *suco* council and chief, their constitutional power to cater to their basic needs is another important factor for the perpetuation of influence.
- Already it is an established fact that people prefer being mediated by CL, *suco* chief/council, and elders than police; hence, their presence will be widely accepted.

Aim and Objectives

The main aim of the DVRF is to empower the women folk without antagonizing the male. With giving due respect to the existing traditional system, bring to fore the cases of domestic violence and develop a fast, effective, and efficient redressal and counseling system.

The objectives behind setting up of DVRF are to provide an amiable specialized forum to the families facing some solvable problems and help them reach an amicable solution. Though it directly targets the women in distress, it has a spread-out effect on the entire family, particularly the children, who are saved from becoming delinquents. The following objectives were envisaged for DVRF:

- to provide a platform to strengthen the family bonds;
- to provide relief to the women from oppression and family-related crime;
- To save the time and money of the complainant by not going through cumbersome court procedures or traveling far distance to police station;
- save families from disintegration and from getting into a retractable stance by going to courts;
- to create a congenial environment in the community;
- save the children of the affected mother/family from psychological and social harassment, which could lead to delinquency and other harmful consequences;
- to bring about the concept of building integrated families;
- to provide legal support to the affected women and children;
- to ensure maximum reporting of domestic violence to either formal agencies or informal traditional setup;
- to redress the cases individually and collectively;
- to raise the issue and find ways of reducing it by social interventions clubbed with specialist inputs;
- to encourage and motivate the local influence;
- to understand and address the issue of domestic violence seriously; and
- act as a referral agency if the problem is amicably not solved.

Methodology

The methodology adopted for accepting complaints and their redressal will require a collaborative and concerted effort of community and the agencies involved in DVRF. For the acceptability of DVRF, its publicity is important. The traditional partners like community elders, *suco* chief, council members, and *aldeia* members will have to propagate the relevance of DVRF. For that, these members need to be properly educated and taken into confidence about the importance of DVRF. In the past, according to convenience, the complainant had been going to either of the members for resolution and they wielded unrestricted power and authority to mediate. In a group, it would certainly get diluted and mediation table shared with others would certainly get diluted with sharing of mediation table with others. A proper egoless understanding between the members becomes necessary for the DVRF to be effective and efficient. DVRF has to be established only after intensive deliberation with the partners and stakeholders to ensure least opposition and maximum acceptance by the community. Once it comes into existence, following procedures will be followed:

- Complaints will be received at the DVRF directly or redirected from the police stations depending on the gravity of the case. If the case requires immediate legal action, the police will register a case and investigate. Cases in which the complainant makes a request for settlement through mediation or if police on receipt of complaint feels that it can be amicably settled through expert mediation, they will be referred to DVRF. The consent of both parties will be mandatory before being referred to DVRF and the police station will keep a record of referred complaints.
- On receiving a complaint, a simple process of inviting members of the family or parties affected to the counseling centers will be taken.
- Counseling is done by:
  - understanding the problem and its intensity;
  - examining likely solutions;
  - qualified specialists in the various fields like psychology, medicine, teaching, law, and so on, make the affected persons undergo meaningful counseling at various stages until a mutually acceptable solution is achieved; and
  - no parties will be threatened whatsoever—solutions will not be imposed on them but suggested with providing an insight into the pros and cons.
- Special care is taken that the result is always loaded in favor of rebuilding the family as a whole, and women and children of the family in particular.

- A systematic process to follow up solved cases is in place to ensure that the problem does not recur and the family lives in harmony. Police also joins this process to ensure that the family rebuilding process continues undeterred.
- Much of the work will be done by counselors and other members of DVRF and the police presence will be more supportive than decisive. They will support the documentation process and keep a copy of the proceeding for records.
- Proper documentation of the cases is done and records properly maintained in the DVRF.

Follow up of cases after disposal is one of the most important aspects for ensuring non-recurrence of discord. In normal situations, every fortnight a team visits the concerned family just to chat and have a feel of the situation. It is ensured that their visit looks informal and encouraging so that they do not feel that their privacy is impinged.

Normally, it is seen that gender biasness of the members of DVRF always mars the impartiality of counseling. This is natural fallout when human beings are involved. This can be weeded out only by consistent review and deliberations between the members and occasional presence of external partners like some specialist who appears in one of the sessions, once in a while, to monitor the progress and train. The presence of women members in DVRF will certainly help in showing the other side of the picture.

Pushing solutions down the throat of the parties is always perilous and should be shunned in all situations. This has all chances of boomeranging. Solutions not accepted in totality will have a short lifespan and in fact the dominant party will retaliate next time with much vigor, stoked by the humiliation and harassment they had gone through by attending counseling sessions earlier. This sometimes endangers not only the family peace but the life of the weaker party.

Support System to DVRF

It is not always possible for the victims or the complainants to reach DVRF center or police stations to report. There are many instances when the neighbors or other family members who are concerned, and not the direct party, may feel that intervention is necessary. To keep themselves anonymous, they would prefer to have a system where they can report without being identified. In such situations, setting up Helpline Call Centers having toll-free telephone number will be helpful. It is going to provide 24-hour service to the needy. It will have to be ensured that an operator is available to man the telephone round the clock, who will direct the complaints to the concerned authorities without delay for redress. If the operator is a trained counselor then she/he, though preferably a female, will do the needful telephonic counseling if immediate intervention is desirable. Documentation of all the calls received and made will be kept properly and the course of action taken mentioned clearly.

Shelter homes will have to be set up which are going to cater services to the women in distress. The category of distress is varied, ranging from domestic violence victims, abandoned women, destitute, and others like victims of Commercial Sexual Exploitation (CSE), rendered homeless due to natural catastrophe, or any other reason. This will provide shelters to women in case no amicable solution is reached in DVRF and the woman does not have any other place to go and staying in the same family means certain abuse, physical or mental. These two support systems—helpline call centers and shelter homes—along with DVRF, ensure more accessibility, sustainability, and rehabilitation security.

15

For a Better Future

Major factors responsible for the growth of community policing and its sweeping effect across the globe are:

- Increasing dissatisfaction of the community over the services provided by the police. There has been a continuous rise in complaints and criticism of their mode of working.
- Over the years, the police's contact with the community has become more selective and regulated, resulting in a trust deficit. There is perceived loss of community respect and esteem for the police resulting in a tarnished image of the police.
- There has been exponential and diversified growth in crime. Both, the community and the police, are suffering due to this enhanced threat, which is beyond neighborhood crime. Numerous laws have been enacted to combat these varied natures of crime but their effectiveness is limited till there is participation. The need is felt by both, the police and the community, for each other's support. As the nature of crime has become more complex, there is a stronger need for association. Police has to increase citizens' awareness on their vulnerability. Community has to be prepared for accepting the police, appreciate, and facilitate change.
- With the loss of the police-intelligence base in the community, a need for stronger networking in the community is felt. There is an increase in external pressure for the police to deliver. The community is more aware, educated, and has started claiming their rights.
- Now, it is hard to see a homogeneous society. A multiethnic, multiracial, and multicaste community is the order of the day. Dissolving the borders and encouraging free movement with

high aspirations for a better life is the basic feature of globalization. There is a growing disparity between the have and have-nots. A natural fallout of this new societal trend is the new nature of crimes making it imperative for the police to shed its traditional approach of isolation, collude with partners, and synergize the expertise and inputs of the community and the police. There is a need to enhance the mutual trust and responsibility to achieve this partnership, which only community policing approach can promise. In a heterogeneous society, community policing helps in educating and sensitizing the police personnel toward the plight of different groups. This prepares them to analyze their policing needs from their perspective.

- With change in the external environment, the police have been hard pressed to match its capability to cater to the demand of work. But to whatever extent they update themselves, technologically and professionally, the gap between the demand and supply keeps increasing. It is better that the community realizes it at the earliest that the increasing gap can be contained only when they start participating actively. Ultimately, it is for their benefit. Police too has to understand that now policing is not limited to normal societal crimes like theft, robbery, or other property and body offences. With terrorism (including all types within country insurgencies) stealing the crime show, now, the definition of secured society has become different. The scenario has become too complex. It is not only the security of the community that is talked about, but the security of the security personnel too is at stake. The casualties suffered by the police personnel have far exceeded in a year than what used to be in decades in the past. International and national terrorism has pushed the police to the walls. Naxalism and other disgruntled groups are the termites, which are eating out the peace in society and giving new dimension to the definition of internal security. The penetration of these threatening agencies is so deep that now onward, no crime can be wished off thinking it to be a normal crime. There have been instances when tying the loose ends has led to unravel dangerous connections and plausibly frightening ramifications.

- With socioeconomic and political changes in the society, the responsibility of the police has increased. The fields of intervention have multiplied, at the same time, witnessing augmentation in workload in the traditional policing areas. Now, new dimensions have added up with boundaryless communication in techno-savvy global village. The concept of neighborhood has become more technical with physical neighborhood concept becoming an age-old definition in some context and having relevance in others.

• All this calls for an urgent need to expand the police base. The immediate call is to decentralize the services at the neighborhood level to meet local demand and internationalize work globally. The requirement of public cooperation, reliance on expertise, and experience of specialists of various disciplines authenticates this shift in the attitude of the police seeking community partnership and participation.

Cursory View of Some Global Community Policing Initiatives

The community policing activities in all parts of the globe started with a similar background and intentions akin. The main goal of community policing is crime control, proactive prevention, establishing peace, and tranquility in the society by forging partnership and eliciting participation of the community. The primary objective is to educate the community about their role and responsibility in controlling crime. Emphasis on community policing should not be viewed as de-emphasis on traditional policing. It is complementary and supplementary.

The involvement of the police in activities that are not usually defined as purely policing, like concern for public health (blood donation camps, de-addiction, trauma centers, and so on), economic matters (as widely prepared in Holland), in the various states of India cannot be termed as community policing in the purest form.[1] These are the activities that bring the police closer to the community, bridging the trust deficit, forging cooperation, but actually the paramount objective of community policing is to control crime and maintain peace and

---

[1] Fitzsimmons, Stephen J. and Warren G. Lavey. 1976. "Social Economic Accounts System: Towards a Comprehensive, Community-Level Assessment Procedure," *Social Indicators Research*, 2(1): 389–452.

order. Community policing can be termed as progressive policing as it calls for policing with, for, and by the community.

In all parts of the world, there has been an assortment of community policing programs, based on issues to be addressed. Largely, they have been framed with need analysis, though how scientifically needs have been assessed is debatable. All these initiatives have been similar in nature, however may vary in structure. They started with the same intention of reducing crime, ensuring security, and providing order in the community. They were proactive methods adopted to achieve the desired intentions. Some are mentioned below.

In Australia, the boy's club in New South Wales was set up to establish better rapport with families in the community. The public relations campaign of New Zealand, where parents are involved through school activities and the like, and high use of television, road signs, and so on, has shown tremendous rapport of police with the community.[2]

Singapore and Japan, both having their economy heavily relying on tourism and business, have adopted exemplary community policing methods. Police and citizens work together and are rewarded for preventing crime. Deployment of neighborhood police posts, specialized in the function of emergency response, assisting in solving small problems that were not necessarily of criminal nature and involving civilians in planning and implementation, help bridge the communication chasm.[3] In Japan, the neighborhood police station and the neighborhood police officers are known as *koban*. The *koban* visits families without displaying intimidating behavior and elicits the cooperation of residents. There is widespread civic association in police activities.

In Denmark, neighborhood police stations have been opened to bring the police closer to the community. France, like many states in India, has juvenile squads working closely with government agencies. In Germany, community policing "contact officers" and "consultancy bureaus" targeted to reach the community. Canada, on the principle of identifiable policing, worked on directed patrol, zone policing (Toronto), foot beats (Edmonton), mini stations-store front operations (Montreal, Victoria), and crime prevention programs. Community

[2] McClellan, Linda S. 1982. "The New Zealand Police: Community Relations and Crime Prevention," *The Police Chief*, 49(4): 47–48.
[3] Bayley, David H. 1989. "A Model of Community Policing: The Singapore Story," *National Institute of Justice*. Washington DC: US Department of Justice.

policing facilitated community involvement in planning and other social services like development of the tumbler ridge in British Columbia.

In England, the unit beat policing (introduced by Home Office), neighborhood-watch schemes, self-help associations, consultative efforts (legislation of police and criminal evidence act of 1984), public relations campaigns, and multiagency cooperation (Kirkholt scheme in Manchester) are various community policing efforts undertaken. In Israel, the initiatives taken up by civil guards, neighborhood beat patrols, "police-in-the-community" project, concept of "section officer" (akin to beat/foot patrol officer) are programs of police to collude with the community.[4]

USA, which has serious research and development team for community policing, worked for some time on the "broken window" theory to look into the extraneous conditions affecting crime in the neighborhood. In Utah, Business Leaders against Organized Crime (BLOC) to promote crime prevention, the Downtown partnership in Atlanta, Differential police response of California, Problem-oriented Policing of New York City, and many others in other parts of the country, all are attempts to improve the police–community interactions and provide community the chance to participate in law enforcement intervention planning.

In Afghanistan, the Police-e-Mardumi is a pilot project using multipronged approach to build service delivery resulting in greater public confidence in the police, higher number of officers reporting incidence and building indigenous processes paving the way for greater stability in area.[5] As a widely accepted phenomenon, the community policing is being implemented in countries like Lebanon, Macedonia, and other small countries as well. Some Indian initiatives have been mentioned in Chapter 8 of this book; hence need no repetition.

Can we make comparisons between a program run in one country and another program run in a different part of the world? Canada's community policing has been largely influenced by the work done in the USA and England. The ills engulfing of civil guards' working method of Israel can be easily compared with the urban defense councils/village defense councils (UDCs/VDCs) of Madhya Pradesh or similar neighborhood assistance programs in other parts of India where there have

[4] Friedmann, Robert R. 1992. *Community Policing-comparitive Perspectives and Prospects.* Harvester Wheatsheaf, Hertfordshire: Hemel Hempstead.

[5] Mukerjee, Doel. 2010. "Police-e-Mardumi: Indegenious District Level Civilian Police in Afghanistan," Paper Presented in Global Community Policing Conclave, Kochi, Kerala.

been complaints of community members volunteering to seek personal benefits. There was a large turnover of volunteers, attrition of volunteers, and negative image of guards and stray cases of complaints against members of UDCs/VDCs.

One important aspect to be accepted is that partnership with the community should be expected only from that portion that respond and are capable of partnering. Their competency, willingness, and response are prime factors of collaboration. There is inherent danger in the process of reading these factors in the community. Due to the past image of the police, the community will not be forthcoming and hence unless properly evaluated, the analysis can be misleading.

Recommendations

There is a big gap in the perceived responsibility of the community in community policing efforts. They fail to identify themselves in the process and keep waiting for the police to guide, direct, push, pull, create space, and shape their role. The lack of perception of the actual benefits accrued from community policing challenges its sustainability and momentum. Anyway, most of the community policing efforts are initiative-based and on the principle of "Now and me," i.e., personalized effort of a single officer based on the interpretation of a situation by them. Every initiative, when initiated, is hailed as "state-of-the-art level" program, which will change the face of the society and the police. It is projected as one and only of its kind, ironically, soon to be replaced by another "state-of-the-art" initiative with another person wearing the creative, out-of-the-box thinker boot.

Community policing calls for long-term commitment; it is not a quick fix. Achieving ongoing partnerships with the community and eradicating the underlying causes of crime will take planning, flexibility, time, and patience. Management can measure progress by their success in meeting intervening goals and must strengthen the concept inside and outside the organization that success is reached through a series of gradual improvements. Police and community have no choice but to join hands and work in tandem. It is now the necessity of both to cooperate. Police will have to change its face and start accepting the organizational principles so that their personnel are motivated, charged, and professionally competent. The relationship between the community and the police has to become more practical and trustworthy. Proper check and balance mechanism have to be instituted.

Community policing is a multiagency, multidisciplinary act, including social service and other utility agencies. It is truly a "collaborative method of operation," where all stakeholders are involved in providing a more secured, peaceful, and progressive society. A natural corollary of community policing is openness, accountability, and improvement of police services. Community policing is a vehicle for achieving more transparency, build trust, help networking, achieve participation of the community, and make policing more effective and efficient.

The implementation of a community policing strategy is a complex and multifaceted/versatile process, which requires planning and managing for change. Community policing cannot be established through a sheer modification of existing policy; that will call for profound changes that occur at every level and in every area of a police agency—from constabulary to DGP. A commitment to the philosophy of community policing must guide every decision and every action of the police department.

A certain amount of opposition to community policing is a natural and obvious appearance, both inside and outside the police system. It is basically opposition to change. With proper anticipation, analysis, and evaluation, the management must create a new, unified organizational outlook and strategies must be developed to deal effectively with obstacles to change. That requires a personal leadership of considerable power and strength of determination. Supervisory leaders must learn new style of management. Teamwork, flexibility, mutual participation in decision-making, and citizen satisfaction are concepts that initially may threaten the supervisor, as they are more at ease with the dictatorial role and routinized policing by the book. Thus, the education of supervisors in new styles of leadership and management must be given a high priority if they are to carry out their responsibility for the success of community policing. Close collaboration between patrolling officers and their supervisors is as critical for successful community policing as the partnership between the officers and the community members.

Performance evaluation is one valuable management tool for facilitating change, and can help communicate agency priorities to employees. The insight, initiative, and creativity shown by the personnel should be considered in the performance appraisal; the motivation behind the action also must be considered. Mistakes made in an honest attempt to solve a problem should not be evaluated in the same manner as mistakes made through carelessness, lack of commitment, or deliberate disregard for policing policies.

Essential element of successful implementation is communication. Communication must be timely, comprehensive, and direct. CL is a direct outcome of effective communication. The behavior of the police leader will set the tone and pattern for the entire organization. The chief must explain the concepts of community policing thoroughly to the entire police organization, the local political leadership, public and private agencies, and the community at large. All participants must understand their role in community policing efforts. A lack of commitment from any of these stakeholders would result in failure. Regular communication will encourage active participation and decrease resistance and opposition. Lines of communication must be maintained both within the police organization and between the police and participants within the community. Successful implementation requires the smooth flow of information.

Training is the key to effective implementation of community policing. Training should communicate and reinforce the changes taking place in the organizational values and policies, and should help build consensus, resolve, and unite both inside and outside the police organization. Community policing skills should be integrated into the training curricula, not treated as a separate component of the training program. All police personnel must become skilled in the techniques of problem solving, motivating, and teambuilding. Training, besides involving the entire police system, should also include civilian personnel who can enlist participation in community meetings, help the police organization sharpen its marketing message, and incorporate sophisticated technology into the organization's service-oriented operations. The purpose of training is to inculcate in the personnel the feeling of "we" rather than "they" when interacting with the community. It should be fully guided to bring the desired attitudinal change in every police personnel, new entrant through basic training, and serving personnel through refresher course, where they agree that policing is null and void without community participation and partnership.

Keeping in spirit of PPT, the implementation plans will have to vary from department to department and from community to community. The most appropriate implementation method will depend on internal and external conditions facing the agency. In some agencies, current

operations procedures and management practices may already con-
form closely to community policing, while in others, extensive changes
may be necessary. This will affect how a chief guides the organization toward the goals of community policing. A thorough assessment
of current programs will help identify what will be required to integrate
community partnership and problem-solving strategies and expanded
crime control and prevention tactics with preexisting policies. Identifying priorities for change will also permit police agencies to establish
interim milestones for monitoring progress.

The implementation of community policing strategy must be a
dynamic and flexible process. Ongoing input, evaluation, and feedback
from both inside and outside the police organization are essential to
making community policing work. Encouraging feedback in all areas
of implementation becomes essential to obtaining organization-wide
support. Management must instill the system with a new spirit of trust
and cooperation that will be carried over into the relationships between
the police system and its community policing partners. All phases of
community policing implementation must be carefully planned and
properly timed to maximize success; even good ideas can fail if they
are poorly executed. Planning must be responsive to changing requirements, circumstances, and priorities. A strong research and planning
capability that is open to suggestion and criticism will allow refine-
ments and revisions to be made during the implementation process.
Such flexibility is crucial to the success of community policing. Usage
and application of learning-curve and experience-curve concepts can
help in understanding the gaps and plugging the loopholes.

Local political leadership may be eager for fast results, but police
leadership must make it clear to the city and district officials that implementing community policing is an incremental and long-term process. Political and community leaders must be regularly informed of
the progress of community policing efforts to keep them interested
and involved. The police organization, from the chief executive down,
must stress that the success of community policing depends on sustained joint efforts of the police, local government, public and private
agencies, and members of the community. This cooperation is indispensable to deterring crime and revitalizing our neighborhoods.

All said and done, all written and discussed, all thought and shared,
all agreed and disagreed, and all criticism and appreciations, I still do
not understand why we are so hell bent to rechristen the word policing

as community policing. Why do not we, after dissecting and diagnosing, accept that normal policing in itself is community policing? Community policing is not a packet of initiatives taken up by a bunch of police personnel. Rather than making it look as a different initiative, we should take curative–corrective measures and bring that much needed attitudinal change so that the community starts identifying police personnel as one of them, as an organization in existence to bring peace and harmony. Let policing be accepted as work "for the people, with the people, and by the people" with the same traditional policing goal of giving public a safe and secured society and better quality of life.

In an informal discussion, a media person taunted to my optimistic theory of partnership. He said I sounded too optimistic with my idea suggesting that a very small step of participation taken by both (the community and the police) would solve most of the problems. Unperturbed, I told him that this optimism itself reflected my pessimism. The two are intertwined. It is true that a small effort would change the whole security system scenario, but this small step has been rejected for too long. Blending the ownership of law enforcement with partnership is required. Even now, unfortunately, neither the police nor the community has realized the importance and inevitability of this partnership in the right spirit. It is high time they start appreciating each other's contribution. The sooner they realize it, the merrier and safer it will be for both.

Index

About the Author

Veerendra Mishra is Assistant Inspector General of Police, Madhya Pradesh, India. He has a PhD in Psychology with his research titled, "Changing Image of Police: An Emperical Study," and has completed Certificate Courses in Human Rights from Human Rights Education Associates (HREA), USA, and the Indira Gandhi National Open University (IGNOU), New Delhi. He has extensively studied the workings of police—both local police bodies and international bodies such as the United Nations Police (UNPOL). He has been instrumental in preparing Community Policing Training Modules for The Asia Foundation, San Francisco, USA. He has also helped develop the National Operation Procedure (NOP) for United Nations PTNL in Integrated Mission in Timor-Leste (UNMIT).

Dr Mishra has been part of United Nations missions in Bosnia-Herzegovina, Kosovo, and was also on a personal visit to UN mission area in Timor-Leste where he successfully initiated community policing initiatives with the objective of reaffirming the security of minorities and rebuilding partnerships between fighting ethnic communities.

He has to his credit various articles in newspapers and journals as well as a short story book based on his experiences during various postings.

The author can be contacted at vmishra2005@gmail.com.